Techniques of Interior Design Rendering and Presentation

Sid DelMar Leach, ASID

Architectural Record Books, New York

The editors for this book were Sue Cymes and Patricia
Barnes Mintz.
The designer was Elaine Golt Gongora.
It was set in Electra by University Graphics, Inc.,
printed by Halliday Lithograph Corporation and
bound by the Book Press.

Published by Architectural Record,
A McGraw-Hill Publication
1221 Avenue of the Americas,
New York, New York 10020

Library of Congress Cataloging in Publication Data
Leach, Sid Delmar.
    Techniques of interior design rendering and
presentation.
    Includes index.
    1.   Communication in design.
    2.   Communication in architectural design.
    I.   Title.
NK1510.L46   658'.91'729   77-13528
ISBN 0-07-036805-8

234567890   HDBP   765432109

Nothing is quite as disheartening to the serious student as seeking knowledge and not being able to find a source from which to learn it.

ACKNOWLEDGMENTS

I would like to acknowledge and thank those
illustrators, designers, architects and decorators
who gladly released their work for use in this
book. A special thank you to Robert M. Morris,
Jr. AIA, who acted as audio visual consultant.

To
S
From
DM

Table of Contents

Bank Interior—Size 18″ × 24″—2H & H pencil on Clearprint® 1000 H tracing paper.

Project: French Bank of California/BNP San Francisco, CA. Architect/Interior Designer: Michel A. Marx, AIA and Assoc.; Illustrations: Sid DelMar Leach/Umberto Baldini

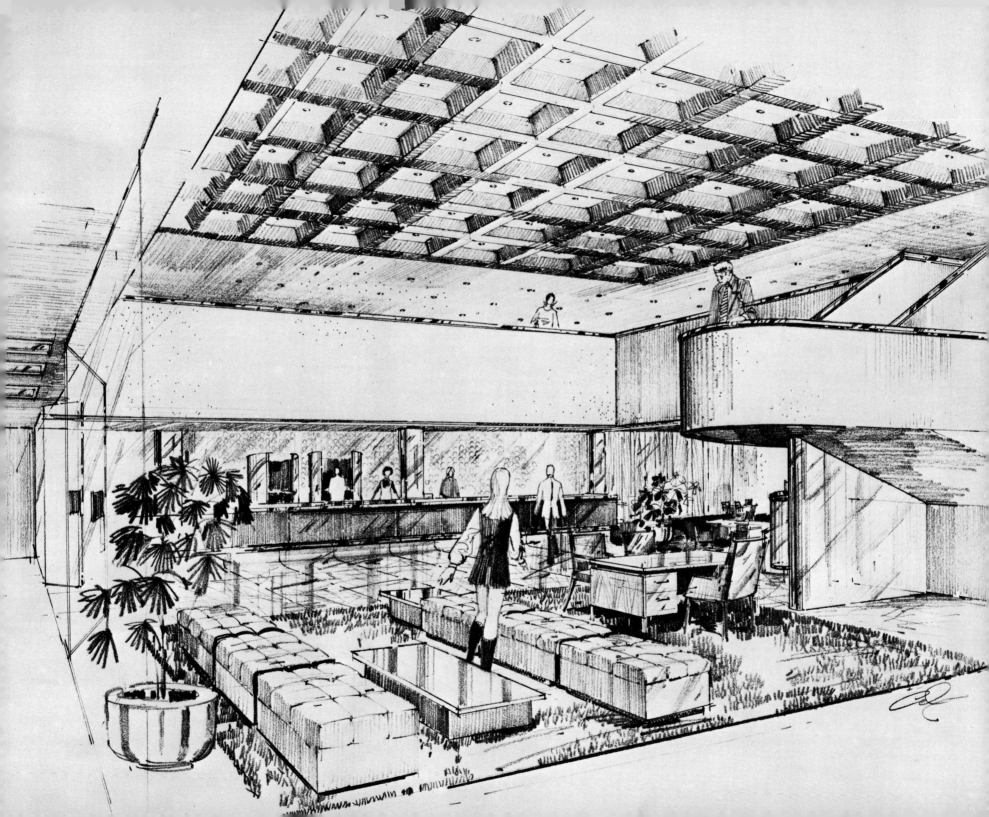

CHAPTER 1

What is Design Presentation

IN ANY FIELD OF DESIGN where presentation may be used, ideas are being transferred—ideas that are not tangible items. In the fields of advertising, art, architecture, interior design, graphic design, fashion design, and industrial design, as well as other related fields, presentation has to do with the transferring of ideas from the designer to the client.

Aesthetic ideas are not truly transferrable without some form of visual aid. Verbal descriptions are usually not adequate to fully explain nontangible items; therefore, before a designer can establish real communication with his client, he must let the client see as well as hear these intangible ideas.

Visual communication together with verbal description can complete that desperately needed connection; the bridging of the gap, so to speak, between the designer's brain and that of the client. Pictures, charts, sketches, slides, motion pictures, models, and material samples are used for this purpose.

A NEED FOR PRESENTATION IN THE DESIGN PROFESSION

The act of conveying an idea from one person to another may take many forms. Quick line drawings in dirt were first used to draw battle plans and maps, in order that confusion among warring factions would be kept to a minimum. Leather or animal-skin maps came into being long after papyrus was used for graphic communication. Stone-chiseled hieroglyphics have lasted many centuries and still communicate some form of story to the beholder. If written description also appeared along with the pictorial art, nothing was left to the imagination of the viewer. So it holds true today; the conveying of ideas from one or more persons to another party or parties is most efficiently accomplished through the combined methods of graphic (visual) and audio (verbal) communication.

Presentation today may be related to almost anything; but, for the purposes of this book, we will assume presentation to be directly concerned with the artistic, architectural and graphic arts, and interior and industrial design fields.

TYPES OF PRESENTATION

Basically, presentation may be divided into two groups—the informal and the formal. *Informal presentation* can be the most basic communication between two people—one designer and one client. Here, anything from a simple sketch to a full-color rendering may be used to transfer ideas.

The *formal presentation*, however, is usually much more structured. It may involve one designer or a design team consisting of persons in related fields. The client in this instance can be any number from two to as many as 20 or more members of a board of directors.

Audio and visual aids used may be simple or as all-encompassing as tape-synchronized slide presentations or motion pictures. The greater the audience size, the larger the graphic aids must be in order to keep interest on a high level. Every one of the clients to whom the presentation is directed must be able to see, hear, and understand clearly what the designer is trying to convey.

DESIGN PRESENTATION AS A SALES TOOL

Why is one in the design business? Most of us must earn a living. In order for a designer to earn a living, he must sell his design ideas. He does not have a product that is necessarily tangible—thoughts cannot become a reality unless acted upon. Theory of design, unlike mathematics and science, cannot necessarily be proven because so much depends on sense of aesthetics and personal tastes. Good taste is directly associated with education. Some feel that good taste is only a direct result of money—lots of money. This is not so. It costs just as much to produce design in bad taste as it does design in good taste. In short, good taste has to do with the appreciation of quality through education.

EDUCATING THE CLIENT

The selling of design may require the designer to educate the client; and most often, this education cannot be completely verbal. A client needs to visualize a product; therefore, graphic communication is essential to show the client what the designer is talking about. Remember, a good design presented poorly with unprofessional graphic aids and an unprepared presentation will not sell. However, an inferior design presented in the most professional manner will have a greater possibility of success.

TOOLS NEEDED TO SELL DESIGN

Visual aids in the form of sketches, renderings, color boards, photographs of specific items, materials samples, and so on, are items required in any design presentation. Job size, monetary value, and client preference all determine how extensive these aids need to be and in what form they should be represented.

SKETCHES

Sketches are line drawings that suggest reality rather than represent it exactly. Sketches are rough, quickly executed representations of ideas and are not meant to be finished art. It is not uncommon for the designer to sketch in the client's presence, as idea transfer is more easily accomplished at that time. No matter how small the job, nor how informal the presentation, there is always that moment when sketching is required to clear up certain points. Further explanation of a subject can usually be accomplished quickly through these on-the-spot drawings. To accomplish this, one must feel comfortable about drawing and sketching in the presence of clients. Clients usually enjoy watching their fantasies appear before their eyes as the designer sketches and draws. Instant pictorial images are both a starting point within a new design project and a source from which required information can be obtained from the client.

RENDERINGS

Renderings are mentioned throughout this book. In the design profession, renderings may be described as black-and-white or full-color representations of a proposed design. Illustrations are sometimes referred to as renderings or delineations, and vice versa. In this book, these terms will be used interchangeably. Renderings may be small or large, loosely or precisely drawn to scale.

Renderings are very much like sketches except that they are finely executed and, therefore, cost much more to produce. A great deal of time can be devoted to a rendering as each portion must effectively represent its real counterpart. Renderings are expensive in that fabrics, furniture, surfaces, lighting, human figure representations, plants, landscaping, and other features must be faithfully reproduced or effectively suggested.

COLOR BOARDS AND SAMPLE BOARDS

Usually in presentation of advertising art, interior design, and other forms of design having to do with physical materials, samples and actual colors to be used must be included. Sometimes in a one-to-one presentation of an interior design, large-scale fabric samples or carpet sections must be shown.

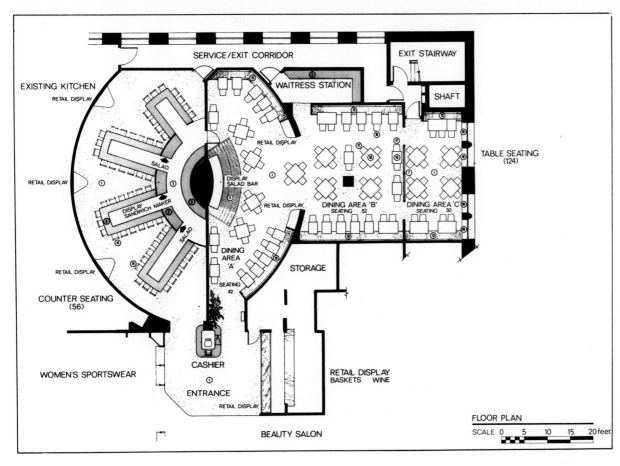

FIGURE 1-1 labels (within plan):

SERVICE/EXIT CORRIDOR

EXIT STAIRWAY

WAITRESS STATION

SHAFT

EXISTING KITCHEN
RETAIL DISPLAY

RETAIL DISPLAY

RETAIL DISPLAY

SALAD

DISPLAY SALAD BAR

DISPLAY SANDWICH MAKER

SALAD

RETAIL DISPLAY

TABLE SEATING
(124)

DINING AREA 'B'
SEATING 52

DINING AREA 'C'
SEATING 30

DINING AREA 'A'
SEATING 42

RETAIL DISPLAY

STORAGE

COUNTER SEATING
(56)

WOMEN'S SPORTSWEAR

CASHIER

ENTRANCE

RETAIL DISPLAY

RETAIL DISPLAY
BASKETS   WINE

BEAUTY SALON

FLOOR PLAN

SCALE   0   5   10   15   20 feet

FIGURE 1-1: Floor-plan drawings used for presentation should be clear and easy to read. *Architect/Designer: Rodger Clark Bush, AIA; Illustrator: The Architect; Project: Preliminary Presentation Floor Plan for a Restaurant within a Department Store.*

More complex commercial projects usually require that small samples of tile, carpet, paint, fabrics, and so on, be secured to a board for ease of both presentation and transportation. A busy executive does not have time to wade through many fabric and carpet samples and would rather see the entire project at a glance. These color boards are very time consuming to produce.

FLOOR PLANS AND ELEVATIONS
In an architectural presentation, plans and elevations are usually provided to be used as communication tools among all parties. They are usually large, unwieldy, and printed on coated paper by the Ozalid® (a dry) process [although blueprinting (a wet process)—white lines on blue background—is returning in some instances].

Presentation of these items in conjunction with renderings and color boards poses several problems. First, size must be unified. Secondly, confusion within plans and elevations must be eliminated through the removal of superfluous notes and dimensions. Thirdly, all pertinent portions of the plans and elevations must be darkened so visual confusion does not result. (See Figure 1-1.)

Size relationship is best handled photographically or photostatically. Photostats are very adequate, providing the finished size requirement is not greater than the capacity of the machine. Of course, the larger jobs can be handled with use of film-positive prints. Many times one wishes to color floor plans for presentation. Water-color mural paper is a great surface to help accomplish this. The techniques in Chapter 14, "Color Rendering—a Simpler Approach," will work very adequately for this task. One must not forget to dry mount all plans and elevation prints before coloring. This will ensure stability during application of color.

One should not make plans too busy. With the directional changes of wall boundary lines becoming the predominate theme within borders, overkill is easy without realizing it. Plans should read as simply and straight-forwardly as possible. Remember, the designer has renderings and color boards to use for further clarification during the presentation.

Matting of plans and elevations should follow the same criteria used to determine the size and color of matting used on color boards and renderings. All boards to be used in one presentation must relate to each other by use of a common mat color and mat-board design, such as title block, borders, and client description.

MODELS
Industrial design, package design, architecture, and furniture design depend heavily upon models in presentation. Interior design offers too many restrictions to represent in model form. Fabrics and furniture in scale are not available in commercial model supply outlets, and the amount of hard work involved in making scale representations of fabrics and furniture would make the total cost of the model prohibitive and not worth the effort. Sketches and renderings are almost as descriptive and the cost is much less.

One of the few usages of models in the interior design profession is in the presentation of store design and planning. Here, most of the scaled-down "fixturing" is square and cubical in nature. This is much more easily scaled to model size than complex shapes and designs of furniture, as would be required in a residence design.

Models may run into the thousands of dollars, based on the complexity of design and the quality of work offered. Many projects do not monetarily justify the financial outlay required for this type of presentation.

COST OF AIDS FROM OUTSIDE SOURCES
Renderings, models, and color boards cost a great deal of money. It is not unusual for a 24-in × 36-in interior rendering of a restaurant in today's market to cost $300 to $400.

Human nature being what it is, clients will usually resist paying for any drawings, renderings, or models outside of a specified design fee. It is,

therefore, not too uncommon for the designer to include a clause in his contract that would require the client to share in these expenses or cover them completely. Design fees should be high enough to cover all necessary graphic aids, but many times fees are the first choice of the client when trying to cut the budget. One must weigh the profit potential of each job and educate the client as much as may be required. Part of the designer's responsibility is to make the client understand the importance of accurate and representative visual aids, and that it is in the client's interest to visualize the project in the planning stages as completely as possible. He must realize that many of his dollars are being put into a project of his choice and while he has the right to change his mind, this is best handled in the early phases of design.

WHERE DOES ONE OBTAIN PRESENTATION AIDS?
Sketches should be handled by the designer personally. Because these aids are quick to execute and inexpensive to reproduce, the designer will find that he probably will rely heavily upon them. When drawn with pencil or pen, these sketches may be copied on any copy machine (if the lines are dark enough) or, if drawn on tracing paper, they may be reproduced by blueprinting or the Ozalid® (ammonia) process.

If one desires to use the Ozalid® process to reproduce sketches for presentation purposes, blue-line prints should not be used. These are the least flattering of prints, as the color of blue line is distracting. Black or sepia should be used for presentation wherever possible. Black- or sepia-line prints are easily colored with colored markers if quick color reference is desired, and this can be done in the designer's own office.

Renderings are available from outside sources by free-lance artists. Usually these artists specialize in certain types of renderings, such as interior, architectural, graphic, or industrial design, and their products are professional in every aspect.

Models are available through free-lance model-building agencies or model supply houses. They are most often more expensive than renderings, but many products require models to aid in client acceptance. The student should have some fun sometime and build a model of one of his own design ideas. It is a tremendous experience in both scale relationship and building methods. Only after one has built his own model can he then appreciate why models cost so much money.

How can one learn all of the skills necessary to perform the tasks required to create design selling aids? In this book, each step will be covered in detail. Through study, drive, energy, practice, and more practice, one will succeed.

CHAPTER 2

Use of Renderings in Design Presentation

ARCHITECTURE, INTERIOR, INDUSTRIAL, AND FURNISHINGS DESIGNS all require renderings of finished products. (See Figures 2-1 through 2-4.)

Illustrations are only visual representations of hypothetical products. Since such products require visualization by a client before he or she accepts it, the artist may be required to conceptualize these products by drafting rough drawings and producing finished art, i.e., renderings. (Renderings are graphic concepts of yet nonexisting items.)

Often in the early design phases all aspects of the product have not been decided upon by the architect or designer, and renderings, if properly executed, can be a proving ground for the related design components. Renderings should be as exact as possible. Color, texture, material presentation, mass, detail, and related surroundings are all elements contained in this type of artistic representation, and each must be as representative as possible.

The initial illustration may contain many details that will be changed in later design phases. It is important that the final renderings be a true representation of what the client wants. For example, if the building represented is not drawn accurately and to scale in an architectural illustration together with the proper landscape, color, materials, etc., both the architect and client will be deceived. This deception could cost a great deal of money if unwarranted changes were instigated on the basis of an inaccurate rendering.

Interior design renderings, on the other hand, tend to be much less representative but are an equally important tool to the designer, as an aid to both presentation and design formulation.

Usually, renderings are a finished art product, unlike a quick sketch. These finished illustrations may take many hours to complete. Because these selling tools must be accurate, much painstaking planning, drawing, and measuring takes place to execute this type of illustration. Sketches, on the other hand, are usually unstructured and quickly executed selling aids.

Finished art, unlike preliminary design sketches, is not usually done "in-

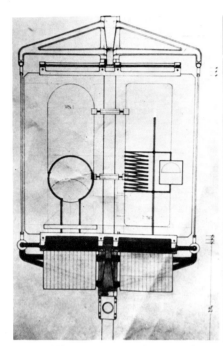

FIGURE 2-1 *Left*: Preliminary drawing of exhibit display unit.
Designer: The Burdick Group—Bruce Burdick, Director; Illustrator: The Burdick Staff;
Project: Energy Exhibit Design, Department of Exhibit Modules, Electricity Exhibit,
California Museum of Science and Industry, San Francisco, CA.
FIGURE 2-1a *Right*: Completed exhibit display unit.
Designer: The Burdick Group—Bruce Burdick, Director; Photograph: Courtesy of the Burdick

Group; Project: Energy Exhibit Design, Department of Exhibit Modules, Electricity
Exhibit, California Museum of Science and Industry, CA.
FIGURE 2-2: Opaque water-color rendering of a design for an extension table.
Note how background suggestion and lighting complement the subject matter
without distracting from it.
Designer/Illustrator: The Author; Project: Custom Furniture Design.
FIGURE 2-3 *Opposite*: Renderings are used both for presentation to a client and
as an aid to the architect during the design phase of a project.
Architect: Garo Dorian, AIA and Associates; Illustrator: Umberto Baldini; Project:
Philippine Trade and Cultural Center, San Francisco, CA.

house" (done by someone on the design staff). When a staff designer or the designer himself is unable to do this type of art work, free-lance sketch artists and renderers may be hired through art agencies, and clients must be aware that they may be required to pay for such services.

CHOOSING A MEDIUM

One must ask the questions: How will renderings benefit the design presentation and what medium will best suit the final "look" required for the project? How much will the drawings cost? How will they be reproduced, or is this a consideration? What is the time required to execute the necessary number of drawings? What size will best suit the situation?

Pencil or ink illustrations are probably the least expensive to execute. The initial cost of either pencil or pen illustrations is far outweighed by the versatility of the finished line drawings.

The finished line drawings may be:

1. Photographically reproduced and dry mounted for color application

2. Blueprinted (wet process, white line on blue ground)

3. Ozalid® (ammonia contact process) printing on paper stock (very inexpensive, usually blue-, black- or sepia-line on white ground)

4. Ozalid® printed on mylar (for color underlay)

5. Ozalid® printed on reproducible stock (sepia)

6. Copied on photocopy machines

Of the above rendering media, pencil is the cheapest to produce. (See Figure 2-5.)

Compared to pencil work, pen is much more expensive to produce

FIGURE 2-4: Executive Conference Room
Architect: Ray Binnicker, AIA; Interior Designer: Noal Betts—Noal Betts Design, Inc.;   *Project: Fidelity Bank N.A.—Fidelity Plaza, Oklahoma City, OK.*

8

FIGURE 2-5 Pencil drawing of preliminary design phase.
Designer/Illustrator: The Author; Design Consultant: Anthony Hail; Project: Main Dining Area - The Big Four Restaurant, San Francisco, CA.

FIGURE 2-6 Pen illustrations offer the best clarity for both blow-up and reduction in size.
Architect: Donald James Clark, AIA; Illustrator: Herbert Lawton; Project: Residential Interior—Hillsborough, CA. Interior Designer: Donald James Clark, AIA.

because of the many lines required to cover the same amount of space. Pen, however, offers the best possible reproduction, reduction, and "blow-up" clarity. Large-scale pen drawings show clear black-and-white characteristic form when blown-up many times or reduced, providing the original drawing was done on a smooth drawing surface and executed carefully. Pen also photographs well for use in audio-visual presentation. (See Figure 2-6.)

COLOR IN RENDERINGS

If audio-visual aids are being used, money is usually available to add color to the pen drawings. This can be done with mylar overlays and mural paper (dry mounted for water-color washes). (See Chapter 14, "Color Rendering—a Simpler Approach.")

Full-color illustrations, those taking many hours of detailed concentra-

tion on the part of the illustrator, are used on jobs that warrant an approach that is as close to photographic as possible. In order to justify the expenditure of money for this quality of art work, the size of job and budget allotted for design must be considerable. Price tags for full-color acrylic or tempera renderings (opaque colors) range from $150 to $3,000 or more.

Colored markers (water-soluble or non-water-soluble color) packaged in metal-top containers, deliver color through a hard felt tip. These tools offer a fast and highly effective result that, when applied properly, give a drawing strong color and definition with very little time expended. Colored marker work is usually combined with a pen under-drawing and is highly effective. (See Figure 2-7.)

Because of the difficulty of execution, *transparent water color* is not the most desirable medium for interior design. Transparent water color is best used for exterior architectural renderings, but if executed properly, water

9

FIGURE 2-7

FIGURE 2-8

FIGURE 2-9

color can create a beautifully soft representation of an interior. (See Figure 2-8.) Water-color renderings are among the most expensive to produce. (See Chapter 13, "Transparent Water Color.")

Opaque color (acrylic, tempera, and poster colors) is a very highly thought-of medium. Illustrations done in these media are expensive to produce, but the end product is one of the best selling tools available for high-budget architectural or interior design projects. With these media, reproduction clarity is unquestionably the best. (See Figure 2-9.) Color intensity, tone, and chroma are vivid, strong, and truly representative. Reduction quality may be compared to that of a good color photograph. (See Chapter 12, "Opaque Color Rendering.")

Pastel renderings, unfortunately, are not very popular. This author has done pastel renderings, using soft pastel and black charcoal pencil on tracing paper. The technique is very effective and a fast way to produce an acceptable color presentation provided the drawing is neither too complicated nor detailed. Much clarity of the drawing is lacking, but the value of having a color rendering for very little money is worth examining. (See Figure 2-10.)

Color renderings done with marker, colored pen, pastel, and colored pencil, that give a looser illusion of reality, may be used when the budget dictates. The use of colored pencils is a fast method of giving sketchy color representation, but lack of clarity, color intensity, and a generally wishy-washy look characterize this medium.

When learning to do drawings and renderings, most students do not see past the "pretty picture" aspect of an illustration. Although they are, hopefully, pretty pictures, they are also more than that. Renderings are accurate, finely executed pictures that tell enough of a story to make the viewer want to relate to the subject matter within.

Remember, illustrations are used to tell a true pictorial story of a design. They cannot be inaccurate or client deception will result. Accuracy in all parts of the illustration is imperative. One must select the size and medium of these selling tools that will most benefit the total selling experience. It is, therefore, important to be aware of what each medium will do for different design project presentations. Each medium has its own strong and weak points and the end result of a particular piece of finished art at the time of the presentation must meet the established requirements. With proper graphic selling aids, designer-client communication can be a rewarding and profitable experience.

FIGURE 2-10: This pastel rendering, done with a combination of soft stick pastel, charcoal pencil, and colored markers on Clearprint® tracing paper, is a good example of how these combined media can be used successfully within a rendering. *Interior Designer: Merline Leaming, ASID—Clark Leaming Co.; Illustrator: Gary Collins; Project: Residential Bedroom Design, Salt Lake City, UT.*

FIGURE 2-7 *Opposite Top Left:* Colored markers may be used in combination with reproduced pen drawings when fast color renderings are desired. (For color plate see page 172.) *Designer: Barry Brukoff—B. Brukoff Interiors, Inc.; Architectural Consultant: Michael Wolfe Siegel; Illustrator: Charles Pigg.*

FIGURE 2-8 *Opposite Bottom Left:* Although difficult to execute, transparent water-color renderings may be used successfully for interior spaces. *Interior Architecture and Design: Bolles Associates; Interior Designer: Michael Bolton; Illustrator: The Author; Project: Sheraton Harbor Island Hotel, San Diego, CA.*

FIGURE 2-9 *Opposite Right:* Opaque color renderings offer excellent reproduction capabilities in both black and white and color. *Interior Designer/Illustrator: Michael Zokas.*

CHAPTER 3

How to See

"BUT, I HAVE BEEN LOOKING all of my life."

Yes, you have been looking all of your life, but have you yet learned to see? Seeing is much more to the designer and artist than just being aware of everyday observations within one's surroundings. As you learn to draw and begin to realize how all objects can be simplified into basic shapes, you will become increasingly more aware of your environment.

Common sense has much to do with learning to see and remembering what one sees. Anyone who can divorce his or her thinking about the appearance of some object from the way in which he or she has been trained to all of his life and can analyze its appearance in a truly objective manner, is a long way toward learning to draw that object. There are those who are surprised that the illustrator or artist must analyze and think about what is put to paper, but the fact remains that realistic or representative illustrations are formed with great logic in mind. Artists are usually deep thinkers with regard to the world around them.

Without going into great detail at this time, let us examine some objects with which we are familiar. Our discussion will include light, shade, shadow, and background. These terms will be covered later in this chapter, and the reasoning behind this discussion will also become clearer.

One must, upon first observation of an object, decide instantly, without any analysis, what about the object is different, memorable, unusual, and so on. Is the shape the most memorable? Is the size most important? Does the detail become primary? The student should not become too involved in detail at first. Objects stripped of confusing detail must depend primarily on size and shape to become memorable to the viewer. Through observation of light, shade, and shadow, you will learn why you see what you see.

What determines what we see? Shape? Color? Texture? All of these and more; except that before shape, color, and texture can be observed, there must be *light*. Light to the artist, designer, and architect is much more than just a means by which to observe one's surroundings.

Light falls on objects on earth in the form of sunlight, which in turn creates reflected and abstracted light. Light casts shadows because an object blocks light rays going from the origin to a given surface. Sunlight is usually of the same strength or brilliance within a given area and it provides light which is then either absorbed or reflected from the surfaces of objects. Color, texture, and temperature can affect the absorption of light, thus directly affecting how we see. In simple terms, dark colors absorb light, light colors reflect light, and textures break up light rays and bounce these rays around in all directions. (See Figure 3-1.)

Textured surfaces do not reflect as much light as smooth surfaces even if the surfaces are equal in color and tone and the amount of light falling on them is equal. Textured surfaces cause light to be bounced and abstracted to such an extent that the reflecting qualities are greatly reduced.

As light is absorbed or reflected, one is able to determine shapes, planes, and textures.

TRAINING ONE'S MIND TO SEE

In order to retain visual objects in the mind, one must form relationships between those objects and very simple shapes. Training one's mind to register color, texture, and shape begins as soon as the eyes are opened. Through environmental understanding, immediate necessities, parental assistance, and experimentation, one's senses become more aware. We train our mind to observe our environment only as much as is necessary.

Learning to sketch and draw from your own surroundings will train your mind to comprehend more fully what you see. (Refer to Chapter 8, "The Importance of Sketching.") You will begin to examine your environment more carefully than you have previously, and mental pictures will stay in your mind longer the more you develop your ability to see.

As one learns to transform three-dimensional objects into two-dimensional illusions, one gains the ability to see, observe, register, and remember.

Aside from rules of perspective, one must *know* the items one observes. Seeing something from one vantage point is very limiting. One should be aware of what all sides of an object are like to get to know the feeling of space occupied by that object. An illustration of any object is made up of both positive space (that volume actually occupied by the object) and negative space (that volume of visual air or white paper around the object). This is a very important point to relate to when designing, rendering, or sketching on any drawing surface. Negative space is as important aesthetically as is positive space. In other words, knowing what to leave out of a drawing is just as important as what to put into it.

One of the greatest aids to remembering the shape of an object is the reduction of its over-all shape into its simplest component forms; i.e., cubes, spheres, cylinders, cones, and pyramids. This process in reverse will

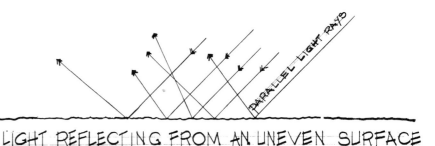

LIGHT REFLECTING FROM AN UNEVEN SURFACE

FIGURE 3-1: Parallel light rays striking an uneven surface are bounced about in an uneven pattern.

also assist the beginner in transferring, through perspective, ideas and designs into finished sketches and renderings. The importance of being able to break down an object into geometrical solids cannot be stressed enough at this stage of a designer's development. When one organizes a volume of space into smaller units, each unit becomes easier to remember and comprehend. (See Figures 3-2 and 3-2a.)

"Remember what you see and you will be able to draw." These were the words of this author's first design instructor. "Looking exercises the eyes, but seeing exercises the mind." Again, words from that same instructor. How often do we hear, "Oh, isn't she talented," or, "He draws so well." It is my belief that one is not necessarily born with the ability to draw. This ability or talent is learned. Ability to draw depends on desire, training, practice, and more practice. However, I do believe that people are born with abilities to retain more knowledge in certain areas than others. The ability to draw is linked very strongly to this retention capability. In the field of design, along with training and a practical and working knowledge of materials and building methods, one must learn to see as part of the training experience.

UNDERSTANDING WHY WE SEE THINGS AS WE DO

By casting a strong light on an object, one illuminates surfaces, casts shadows, creates shade and, to a great extent, determines how that object is viewed. Light from the sun is not always present, so one must illuminate one's surroundings with man-made light. Light falling on objects determines what we see. All things within our visual surroundings are seen by us in three dimensions: height, width, and depth. When one converts a three-dimensional object to that of two dimensions by placing forms on paper, he must rely on the technique of perspective, implied shade and shadow, texture, and line to create proper illusion.

FIGURE 3-2: Objects seen in nature can be broken down into less complex shapes. The building shown in this perspective under-drawing is simply a pyramid on top of a cube.
Illustrator: The Author

FIGURE 3-2a: Compare the above finished pencil drawing with the preliminary perspective shown in Figure 3-2. Pencil texture and variation of line weight in combination with shade and shadow principles are used to convert a cubical solid and a pyramid into a realistic and pleasing drawing.
Illustrator: The Author

Architectural plans and elevations may be measured to determine true height and width. True height, width, and depth in perspective cannot be represented in true measure; therefore, one must rely on illusion created by value.

Value is the lightness or darkness in shades of gray of an observed item. If one considers the absence of a strong shadow-casting light source, he will find that values are still present. Reflected light is the prime source for the creation of values in this case. (Value, value studies, shade and shadow will be graphically explained in Chapter 6, "Value Study of Shade and Shadows.") Value created by light striking and being interrupted by an object determines how the illustrator transfers the illusions of depth to his viewer.

Black-and-white photographs, television, and motion pictures all convert color into value studies. Everything one observes when looking at these pictures is represented in values of gray from white to black.

LINES OR NO LINES

From childhood, one tries to draw or in some way communicate ideas in graphic form. As crude as it may have seemed, we all used a pencil, chalk, pen, or some item and traced an outline on paper to represent some tangible thing. This containing of an object within a boundary line was our first natural attempt at graphic communication. Any three-dimensional object may appear to be bounded by line, but, as the reader will discover, no line actually exists.

For example, if no light falls on an object and it is viewed against a brightly lighted background, that object will appear in the form of a silhouette. (See Figure 3-3.) Regardless of the angle from which the viewer observes this object, it will appear as a silhouette if the same object-to-background light relationship exists. If one were to photograph this silhouette in black and white, the observer would discover that he could trace a

FIGURES 3-3, 3a *Left and Center:* Any unlighted object seen against a lighted background will be seen in silhouette. One could encase the entire image within a continuous line, but in actuality, no line exists. Relation to its background as well as light being reflected from an object determine how we see that object. Refer to Figure 3-3a to observe how the picture changes with the addition of light.

FIGURE 3-4 *Right Top:* With the complete absence of light, this round tennis ball appears as a flat black disc against a lighted background. **FIGURE 3-4a** *Right Bottom:* The image of the tennis ball changes from a flat black disc into a spherical solid when illuminated.

boundary line around the black silhouette and contain that object within a line; but no line exists. In reality, the perimeter of the object you see is determined completely by its relationship to background. If you photograph the same object from different angles, you will find that the perimeter of the silhouette changes with the vantage point taken.

An ordinary tennis ball may also be used to examine these points. Using the ball as an example of a true sphere, let us view it unlighted against a brightly lighted, white background. We will see a round, flat shape. If we now photograph the silhouette we have created, the result will be a black circular shape against a white background. (See Figure 3-4.) No longer does one see a round ball; no longer does one see a three-dimensional item. Graphic deception can be used to describe this illusion. Lack of light falling on the ball is the cause. If we now trace a dark line around the perimeter of the black disc, one may encase the object. This line is, of course, only representative because we know that there is no real line around the object,

only its perimeter as seen in relationship to the background. Background then, not line, determines the perimeter shape.

If, on the other hand, one were to illuminate the ball and leave the background unlighted, the whole picture would change. Shade and shadow would determine that the object is a spherical, three-dimensional solid, instead of a flat black disc. (See Figure 3-4a.) Through examination of the illustrations in this section, one should determine that lines are not necessary to graphically depict things if value is properly represented.

The human body is a prime example of nonangular forms and surfaces. Light striking the body will cast shadows, create shade, and determine form. No lines are actually needed to represent the drawn figure if shade, shadow, and relationship to background are utilized. Values determine what is seen in this instance. Some artists seem compelled by the use of a medium such as pencil or pen to outline all forms and fill in the spaces. Other more aware artists will use light, shade, and shadow to represent the

FIGURE 3-5a *Left:* Notice how the light falling on the many facets of this interlocking group of polygons gives them dimension. No lines actually exist where planes intersect, but light reflection helps our eyes to determine these planes.

FIGURES 3-5b, 3-5c *Center and Right:* The silhouette of this solid changes when viewed from different angles, but no form is apparent without light.

reality much more effectively. If one observes an unlighted person against a brightly lighted background, one may draw the same conclusion as was drawn about the tennis ball previously mentioned.

Softness of pastel, water color, acrylic, or oil colors will, of necessity, relieve one's use of line. The absence of line requires the artist to more fully examine the complex shape of volumes (representations of mass in art or architecture) and solids (three-dimensional geometrical elements). Illustrators use hard edges to define characteristic lines in human beings, and, although these lines really do not exist, the effectiveness of a drawing may sometimes depend on this technique. Lines are important; and as long as the student has the understanding of where, how, and when to use lines, they can be a very effective tool in illustration.

Angular solids in pyramids, cones, and polygons may all be examined in the manner stated previously, with the exception that from this viewpoint planes (not forms) contribute to surface determination. There are no lines

on the surface of a polygon. If one were to illuminate this angular solid, one would see that value determines the break in planes. (See Figure 3-5a.) All the intersecting planes become lost when not illuminated; however, upon lighting this polygon, one immediately determines surface form. If we create a silhouette, as in the case of the polygon, and photograph it from many angles, the perimeter is forever assuming a new shape. Remember, value not lines determines the visual break in planes of an angular geometric solid. (See Figures 3-5b and c.)

When the beginning student becomes more aware of why we see, the previous examples will seem more meaningful, and understanding of complex forms will be easier to recall and will be more interesting. Illusion and reality are only divided because of the mind of the viewer. It is up to the artist, renderer, architectural illustrator, or designer to create reality within the graphic tools he uses to sell design and reality in presentation is a necessary part of the product being sold. Illustrations are nothing but illusions of reality, and illusions cannot be created if the creator is not aware. Remember, looking is not necessarily seeing, and seeing is a function one can cultivate in order to become more aware.

The student may wish to further explore a similar viewpoint on this subject by referring to *Perception and Lighting as Formgivers for Architecture*, Chapter 3 "The Process of Visual Perception," William M. C. Lam, McGraw-Hill, 1977.

CHAPTER 4

Materials

THE MATERIALS REFERRED TO and used for the illustrations in this book are as varied as the chapters themselves. The student will find that in order to learn the techniques for design illustration, some money will have to be spent.

Good art supplies do cost money as does anything of quality, but quality in these items may make the difference between doing a small or a great amount of work to achieve the same end. High-quality materials will last a long time and are a good value for the money invested. This section is not an advertising section for any one manufacturer of art supplies, as numerous companies manufacture items of equal durability and quality. Although the following list may seem long, one should remember that these items may be purchased individually over a period of time.

Many items are those that are preferred by this writer and other illustrators referred to in this book, but each student will probably find his own special "pet" items that will become favorites through constant use.

The student will find that in order to do his best work, a special place at home or studio should be set aside for the purpose of his studies in drawing and painting. Good lighting is essential (preferably north light) for both work done in color and line.

A good tilt-top drawing table is a must. This table should be equipped with square metal edges that will accept a T square, or one should obtain a sliding parallel bar. The T square is best for perspective applications, whereas the parallel bar is best for drafting.

Posture and positioning of materials are very important for both the physical comfort of the artist and his mental attitude. One cannot do good work if he is not comfortable. An adjustable drafting chair is desirable. This chair should swivel, be capable of vertical height adjustments, and be equipped with back-support adjustment mechanisms.

Fluorescent light is the best all-around light for drafting, as line work does not depend on color accuracy. Diffused illumination in the proper foot-candle measurement is important to the draftsperson to avoid eye strain and discomfort, since shadows cast by drawing tools and hands are held to a minimum under this type of light.

Natural or incandescent lighting will give one the best illumination for matching colors. Fluorescent lamps emit light-wave patterns that will change some colors observed under this light. If true color match is desired, natural light is definitely preferred.

MATERIALS NEEDED

TRIANGLES

The following triangles are needed for both drafting and perspective layout:
a. 45° (1 large, 1 small)
b. 30°–60° (1 large, 1 small)
c. Adjustable triangles (large)

PENCILS

A pencil with wood-encased lead is the type most familiar to most people. For the studies in this book, both wood pencils as well as mechanical lead holders with leads of varying hardness are required. The lead in both types of pencils is available in varying degrees of hardness.

The following is a list of types of pencils with lead designated from hardest to softest:
a. Carpenter's pencils—2B, 4B, 6B
b. Graphite stick—2B, 4B
c. Wood-encased sketch pencils—4H, 2H, HB, 2B, 3B, 4B, 6B
d. Mechanical pencil—4H, 3H, 2H, H, F, HB

Lead holders come in many styles, and the serious draftsperson will have one for each hardness of lead being used.

Leads for our purposes come in three types: one for paper; one for mylar drafting film; and the heavy graphite stick which we will use for creating value studies. The lead for use on drafting film tends to be softer than graphite, though designated by the same numbering system, and breaks much more easily; it is sometimes referred to as "washproof."

MISCELLANEOUS ITEMS

Also needed for good table-top organization will be:
a. Drafting brush
b. Masking or drafting tape (in dispenser)
c. Push-pins

d. Erasers—pink, white, ink, art gum, and the kneadable type.
e. Pencil sharpener or lead pointer
f. Erasing shield
g. Utility knife
h. Sanding block
i. Carpet (cleaning surface for pencil lead)
j. Dry cleaning pad to keep the drafting or drawing surface clean. (This pad is filled with powdered eraser.)

DRAFTING, SKETCHING AND WATER-COLOR PAINTING SURFACES

These surfaces come in a wide variety of thicknesses (weights), surface textures, and sizes, and it is difficult for the beginner to know what to buy. For purposes here the student will need:
a. Architectural sketch paper (white)
b. Clearprint® tracing paper
c. Drafting film (this is available with a mat-finish surface [frosted] on either one or both sides)
d. Kid-finish bristol board—2- and 4-ply weight (for ink or pencil)
e. Plate-finish bristol board (for ink)—2- and 4-ply weight.
f. All-purpose sketching-paper pad
g. Cold-pressed, medium-rough-surface water-color board
h. Rough-surface water-color paper (for sketching out-of-doors)

The most important single element that makes a water-color illustration clean, fresh, and alive is the illustration surface used in its production. An excellent-quality water-color board is essential.

Water-color board is basically a medium-weight water-color paper that has been secured to a backing of high-pressure laminated cardboard. An illustration with lots of detail requires an extremely flat working surface. It is not recommended that the student use water-color paper for illustrations. The paper tends to buckle when wet and must be secured to a backing before use.

Long before commercially made water-color board was available, water-colorists used to stretch their own surfaces. This is still done in part today, but it is only important from a fine-art standpoint and will not be covered in detail here.

The student may obtain single-strength water-color board for practice exercise, but he should never settle for anything except double-weight board when the illustration is to be used for a presentation of any kind.

Double-weight, cold-pressed, medium-rough board will have just the right amount of "tooth" to give the best brilliance of color and quality of detail of any surface available to you. If the surface is too rough, brushes will tend to skip across the high points and sharpness will be lost. If the surface is too smooth, it does not have enough tooth to adequately absorb the color and reflect the color brilliance to the viewer.

Illustration board may be used in lieu of water-color board (for opaque colors only) but the color reflection and surface texture leave much to be desired by the professional illustrator.

Note: Rather than have the art supply house cut the 30-in × 40-in board to size, the student should buy large sheets and cut his own. This way, waste is kept to a minimum.

INK, POINTS, AND PEN HOLDERS

Ink, points, and pen holders are in a class by themselves. Many illustrators that favor ink drawing use a technical type of pen. This unit has a built-in reservoir and uses interchangeable points to vary line weight. If, however, the student is serious about pen drawing and sketching, the quill point should be considered. These points, of course, were once the sharpened end of a feather quill, but with the advent of the steel penpoint in the late 1800s, the feather quill became obsolete.

The student favoring ink drawing will need:

a. Waterproof drawing ink (black and brown) in a nontip bottle complete with filling dropper.

b. Three ink points. These should be steel points—medium, fine, and superfine.

c. Pen holders are needed to support the fine steel point. These are usually equipped with a cork barrel that can slide forward over the point to protect it from damage. (See Figure 11-7, p. 115 for reference.)

COLOR

The sections having to do with color require the following:

a. Colored markers. Markers are available in many forms, ranging from short and fat to long and thin. These marking devices have a hard felt tip that will dispense fast-drying ink from a built-in supply. An incredible variety of colors is available; but for purposes here, one should buy one basic color set; one set of architectural wood tones; and one set containing grays, stone colors, and other colors directly related to nature or out-of-doors.

b. Bottled opaque water colors. Bottled poster colors are offered in small two-ounce glass bottles, the larger eight-ounce plastic "flex" bottles, and pint plastic bottles, as well as quart glass bottles. Manufacturers usually refer to this medium as either moist water color, poster color, or tempera. Normal usage will dictate the size of bottles to buy. The smallest is a good size for colors not used very often.

c. Tube colors. The above criteria will also hold true when buying tube colors (transparent water color as well as opaque colors such as gouache, polymer, and casein). The beginner should note that the following sizes of bottles or tubes are recommended in various color ranges. Many factories have pet names for various colors and these colors may be matched by another manufacturer under a different name; therefore, it is best for us to group colors into ranges instead of into actual color names.

Bottled and tube colors are listed below as to their usage and frequency of replacement.

a. Eight-ounce flex bottled opaque water color; large tube (1½ in × 6 in), gauche or casein; or large tube (¾ in × 2½ in) acrylic transparent water color
    1. All earth tones (burnt umber, burnt sienna, yellow ochre, raw sienna, raw umber, etc.)
    2. Black and white (do not buy white poster color as we will use white casein to mix with poster colors for body and permanence)
    3. Olive greens and Hooker's green
    4. Browns not already purchased under earth tones

b. Two-ounce bottled opaque water color; ¾-in × 2-in-size tubes of guache, casein or acrylic; and the ½-in × 3-in-size tubes of transparent water color.
    1. Reds
    2. Oranges
    3. Yellow, except yellow ochre
    4. Blues
    5. Violets and purples

c. Large tube casein (1½ in × 6 in)
    1. White (This color is to be used both for mixing with poster colors and for highlighting. Be certain color is finely ground and no granular separation is apparent. Tube shelf life is determined by the manufacturer, so do not purchase tubes dating beyond shelf life. If casein is old it will not mix with poster colors without separation.)

BRUSHES

No illustrator can turn out top-quality work if he does not use excellent, quality brushes. Sharp detail, fineness of line and edges, and ease of cleanability are some of the many advantages one can expect when using the best-quality brushes. The extra cost of the best brushes will be far outweighed by the lack of frustration you will encounter when rendering. It is recommended that even the student and beginner buy the following top-quality camel hair or sable brushes. If these are kept perfectly clean, they will give years of service.

    a. Flat Ferrule with Flat Tip—½-in, ¾-in, 1-in

    b. Round Ferrule with Flat Tip (lettering brushes)—⅛, ⁵⁄₁₆, ½-in (2 each)

    c. Round Ferrule with Pointed Tip—#0, #1, #3, #5

    d. Flat Ferrule with Flat Tip (one-stroke brushes)—⅛-in, ⁵⁄₁₆-in, ½-in

MIXING CONTAINERS FOR COLOR

    a. Egg Trays. Bottled colors are best mixed in small cups, or more preferably, in a multiple-unit container such as a plastic, flexible, egg tray. These trays have 12 cups per tray, and because they are flexible, cleaning is easily accomplished even if the paint has hardened. Colored trays are not recommended because accurate color matches are not easily obtained with them. The recommended type is either clear or white, whichever is more readily available.

    b. Butcher's Tray. This item is very necessary for obtaining accurate color matches. It is used both as a trial surface on which color can be tested, and as a primary mixing surface when using tube colors of any type. Butcher's trays are available in a number of sizes and are coated with white baked enamel which aids greatly in the clean-up process. It is recommended that the student purchase one small and one medium tray.

WATER CONTAINER

A good, quart-size, flexible, plastic, food-storage container will serve you well as a water container. Keep in mind that flexibility aids in cleaning.

MASKING MEDIA

Masking medium and frisket papers, as stated previously, are suitable for use when working with diluted acrylic colors, designers' colors, and transparent water colors (only when the paint being used is of a light body type). Frisket paper is not recommended for use with heavy-bodied bottled colors or acrylics of high viscosity because of copious edge buildup along the masking line.

Pressure-sensitive masking papers are available from a number of sources. The frisket paper recommended here is that type of paper used by sign painters to mask letters when painting trucks and buses. This paper, which is very similar to masking tape, is available with a removable crinkle back and is somewhat translucent. It does not raise the nap of a good water-color paper and is easily removed. A great advantage to the renderer is in the size offered. The only way the student can buy this medium is in rolls 18 in to 48 in wide. As one begins to work, he will see how much of an advantage this large size can be. A note of caution: do not buy too much at one time. It has about a six-month shelf life and must be kept very dry and cool. If allowed to become warm and damp, the sticky adhesive transfers to the drawing surface, and can be very difficult to remove without leaving a paint-repelling residue. Pressure-sensitive masking paper can usually be purchased in small quantities from sign painters. This material is stocked by them in large rolls, and it is therefore impractical for the illustrator to purchase such a large amount considering the short shelf life of this product.

Liquid masking medium is also available; however, very little use of liquid frisket is made by the interior illustrator because of the difficulty of removal if painted over with acrylic or heavy opaque water-color paints.

STRAIGHTEDGE

You will need a good, straight, brush guide when painting sharp, clean edges. You must obtain a short, 18-in plastic-edged straightedge. The least expensive thing that we have found to give good results is a small T square with the end removed. This guide is an invaluable tool when the technique of using it properly is mastered (refer to Figure 12-11, Chapter 12, p. 134).

CHAPTER 5

Perspective Theory and Practical Office Layout

PERSPECTIVE DRAWING IS ESSENTIAL for anyone who deals with presentation art production. Students of art (whether it be for commercial, industrial, architectural, graphic or interior design presentation) must know how to draw. Perspective is the basis for all drawing. Proper illustration techniques mean nothing in a drawing executed using improper perspective. A drawing will not "read" if basic perspective rules are violated. It is, therefore, imperative that perspective drawing be learned before any other techniques in this book are studied.

A person who is not skilled in all forms of basic drawing may marvel at illustrations executed in precise perspective structure without realizing that knowledge is responsible for the results. It is this knowledge that eliminates any mystery surrounding both the studied forms of illustration and more free-style art forms.

Many very good books on this subject are available, in which both free-hand and technical applications are covered at length. It is not the purpose of this book to teach all forms of perspective; but, a review of some basic office methods of perspective layout and applications to illustration techniques will be covered in detail. It is assumed that the student has some prior training in art.

WHAT IS PERSPECTIVE DRAWING?

Most books pertaining to perspective layout give the reader insight into certain facets of perspective drawing and offer a good basis from which to build understanding of this essential tool. Our study will elaborate on those aspects having to do directly with interior-design perspective development.

The designer faced with putting to paper ideas and thoughts about a particular project or product must do so in a realistic and believable manner. To do this successfully, he must first learn to see and understand the environment around him (see Chapter 3, "How to See"); then he must

FIGURE 5-1 *Below and Opposite:* A review of some basic principles of perspective theory.

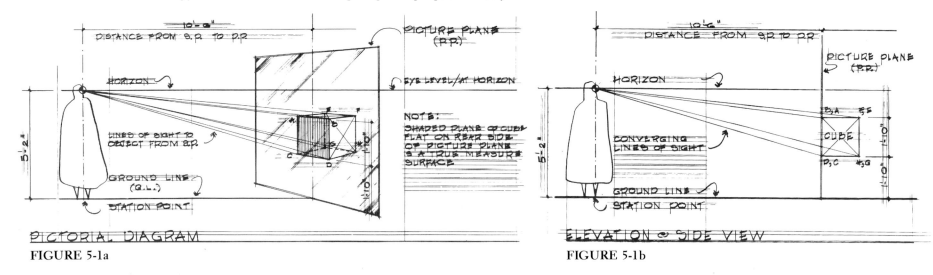

FIGURE 5-1a

FIGURE 5-1b

learn the rules of perspective drawing so he can transfer what he sees onto a two-dimensional surface such as paper or illustration board.

Many very complex methods are used to teach perspective. Mechanical projection, as would be done in an architectural office, is very tedious, complex, and time consuming. Freehand perspective is faster, of course, but less accurate for the person that has not trained his eye to "see into" a drawing. Photographic perspective is excellent when working with vast spaces or large, complicated, building projects, and does not depend as heavily on projection principles as do the mechanical methods.

Whatever the method used to create an image, perspective is used to help establish an illusion of reality and is the basis for all finished drawings. In the area of interior design, renderings of space must be accurately represented because a deceptive representation of space can be costly to both the designer and the client and create bad relations among all parties concerned.

REVIEW OF PERSPECTIVE THEORY AND PRACTICE

For a short review of a few principles of perspective, study the following examples. Notice the location of the picture plane, horizon line, vanishing point (V.P.), ground line (G.L.), and station point (S.P.) in the various diagrams. (Refer to Figure 5-1 a through d and 5-2 a through e.) These elements are related to and dependent on each other.

The beginner should think of a perspective drawing as an outline created by converging lines of sight passing through a sheet of glass (picture plane—P.P.) between the eye of the viewer and the object being viewed. Each point on the object would, as its image passed through the glass sheet to the eye, imprint this image onto the clear flat plane. The resulting connection of imprinted image portions would create a two-dimensional illusion of a three-dimensional object on this picture plane. Figure 5-1a clearly illustrates this.

In order to complete the studies in this book, the study of both one-point and two-point perspective is essential. The student must learn skills

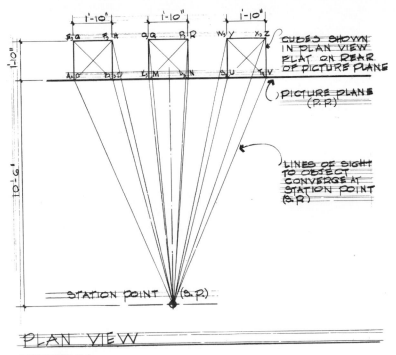

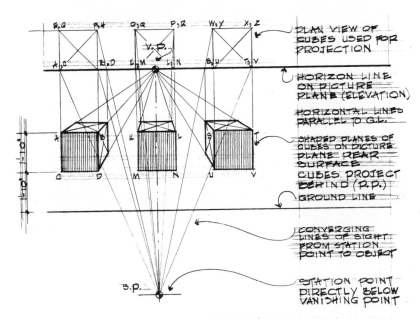

PLAN VIEW

FIGURE 5-1c

PERSPECTIVE USING PROJECTION METHOD

FIGURE 5-1d

in perspective construction techniques so that all situations with regard to field of vision and angle of view can be easily handled.

One- and two-point pespectives related to interior spaces may be laid out in the office with relative ease. Perspective grid charts are available to aid in the preliminary plotting stage of the drawing, but the author's personal opinion is that these charts are more confusing than helpful to the beginner. In lieu of the charts, quick office methods have been developed that aid the draftsperson and renderer in plotting perspective drawings that are closer to the illustrator's intention than a preplanned commercial grid chart would be. The renderer should study the following as clear examples and explanations of both one- and two-point perspectives. Three-point perspective is used mostly on advanced architectural subjects and will not be covered here.

To review basic perspective theory, study the diagrams shown in Figures 5-1 and 5-2. Notice that an arbitrary distance of 10 ft 6 in from the picture plane (P.P.) to the station point (S.P.) has been established (one will learn

how to plot the S.P. later) as well as the dimension of 1 ft 10 in for all cube dimensions which, coincidentally, equals the distance from the ground line (G.L.) to the bottom of the cube as shown in the elevation (Figure 5-1b). A height of 5 ft 2 in (average eye level) to the horizon line is plotted, but this, of course, may vary according to the desires of the illustrator. Eye level establishes the horizon line. Remember that this line is always parallel to the ground and should be thought of as a never-ending horizontal plane that reaches as far as can be imagined at a constant distance from the ground line (Figure 5-1a). It is on this horizon that the vanishing point(s) used to create perspective will be located. Notice also that because the horizon line is unending, it may be placed (as a line) on the picture plane (refer to Figures 5-1a, b and d) as long as this horizon line remains parallel to the ground.

The ground line (G.L.), as the name implies, is a horizontal line at the base of the picture plane. It is assumed that one standing at the station point is standing at the level of the ground line, and it is this line that is the base measure from which to establish the horizon.

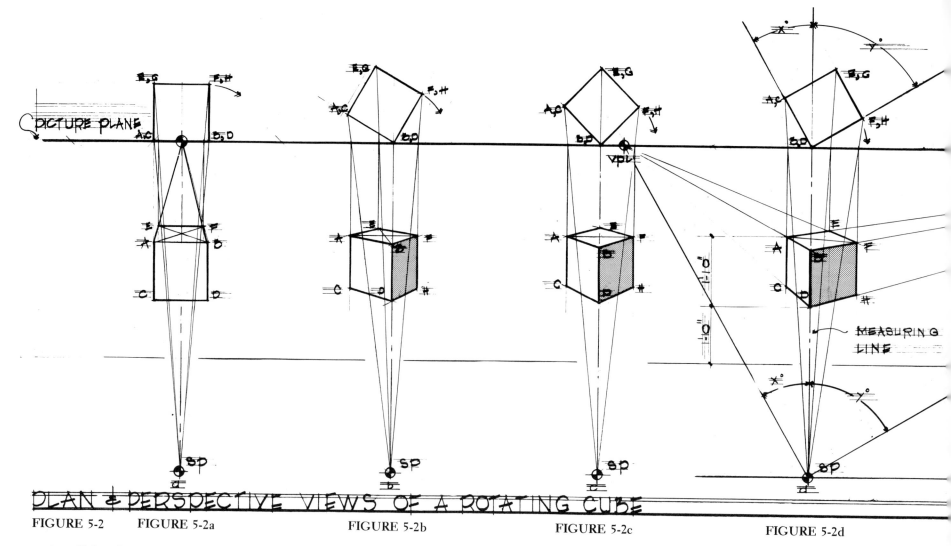

FIGURE 5-2   FIGURE 5-2a   FIGURE 5-2b   FIGURE 5-2c   FIGURE 5-2d

As will be observed, the picture that is capable of being produced in perspective depends on many things. The observer at the station point may look at an object straight on, or to the right or left (Figures 5-1c, d), or down at an object, or up at that same object (Figure 5-3a and c). All of the above conditions hold true for both one- and two-point perspectives.

ONE-POINT PERSPECTIVE

One-point perspective (Figures 5-1 a through d, 5-2a, and 5-2e) simply means that lines on all items within a drawing will converge to one point, except for vertical lines, and horizontal lines which are always parallel to the ground line. The main difference between one- and two-point systems is that in one-point perspective an entire plane of the subject lies flat on the rear of the picture plane (P.P.) and is the true measure. With a two-point drawing (Figures 5-2b, c, d) only the corner lies in contact with the P.P., creating a vertical line that is in true measure. True measure dictates that because the plane or corner (intersection between two planes) is on the

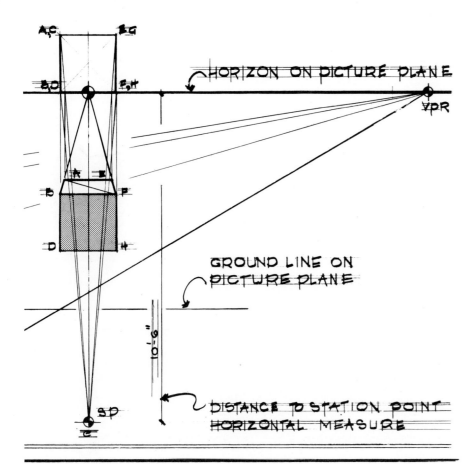

HORIZON ON PICTURE PLANE

VPR

GROUND LINE ON
PICTURE PLANE

DISTANCE TO STATION POINT
HORIZONTAL MEASURE

SP

FIGURE 5-2e

P.P. it can be measured and drawn to scale. This fact allows accuracy within a drawing as to width and height in one-point perspective and height only in two-point. All other forms, lines, and surfaces must be plotted with relation to the portions of the drawing that can be measured. Figure 5-1a shows clearly that the plane formed by A, B, C, and D of the subject lie on the P.P. Similarly, the shaded planes of three cubes (Figure 5-1d) viewed from one station point also lie on the P.P.

Refer again to Figure 5-2. This illustrates how the cube may be drawn

rotating about the true measuring corner, B, D on the P.P. Notice how plane B, F, D, H (shaded) changes position.

To review the process of establishing vanishing points on the horizon line (as in Figure 5-2d), draw lines from an established S.P. parallel to each plane of the cube *in plan* until these lines intersect the horizon line on the P.P. at V.P.R. (vanishing point right) and V.P.L. (vanishing point left). Once this simple procedure is understood, one can construct any cube in any relationship to the P.P. The student asking himself why cubes are so important should start thinking of these cubes as boxes made of clear plastic into which he, the illustrator, can place pyramids, cylinders, cones, conical solids, and finally, furniture and accessories.

ENVIRONMENT

Before explaining any additional drawing exercises, it would be good here to again note body position and drawing environment. No one can produce good work if he is not comfortable. One should sit at a table that is slightly slanted with light falling over the left shoulder (unless one is left handed). This will prevent shadows from being cast by the hand onto the drawing surface.

REVIEW PROCEDURE—TWO-POINT PERSPECTIVE OF A CUBE (Figure 5-2d)

1. Place the plan of a cube behind the P.P. with one corner touching the P.P. and in the proper angle of view based on what is desired to be seen in the finished drawing. Decide on the distance from the picture plane (in this case, 10 ft 6 in) to the S.P. and plot this point directly below the measuring corner along the measuring line.

2. Establish a ground line and horizon line in relationship to what is desired to be seen (Figure 5-1b). In this case, it is 1 ft 10 in above the ground line to the bottom of the cube and 5 ft 2 in to the horizon.

3. The cube is 1 ft 10 in high, so the corner B, D can be measured and drawn on the P.P.

4. Project lines to the S.P. through the picture plane from all corners of the object. Where these converging lines cross through the P.P., vertical lines may be dropped for an undetermined distance.

5. Measure the angles of the plan to the measuring line (angles X and Y), establish these same angles at the S.P. relative to the measuring line. Extend the leg of each angle from the S.P. These will then be parallel to the plan of the cube until they intersect the horizon at vanishing point left (V.P.L.) and vanishing point right (V.P.R.).

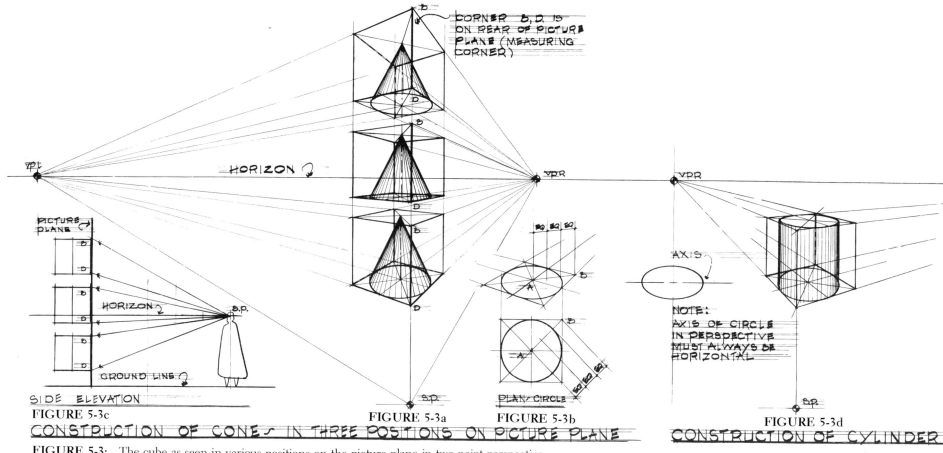

CORNER B, D IS ON REAR OF PICTURE PLANE (MEASURING CORNER)

HORIZON

VPL

VPR

VPR

PICTURE PLANE

HORIZON

S.P.

GROUND LINE

SIDE ELEVATION

FIGURE 5-3c

AXIS

NOTE: AXIS OF CIRCLE IN PERSPECTIVE MUST ALWAYS BE HORIZONTAL

EQ EQ EQ

A

B

A

PLAN CIRCLE

S.P.

FIGURE 5-3a

FIGURE 5-3b

S.P.

FIGURE 5-3d

CONSTRUCTION OF CONES IN THREE POSTIONS ON PICTURE PLANE

CONSTRUCTION OF CYLINDER

FIGURE 5-3: The cube as seen in various positions on the picture plane in two-point perspective.

6. Connect points B and D with both V.P.L. and V.P.R. Make a dot where these points cross the verticals (see Step #4) at F, H, A and C. Now connect point F to V.P.L.; then point A to V.P.R. Where these cross each other, point E is formed and the cube will be seen. Darken lines of the cube and your illustration should look like Figure 5-2d.

Procedure principles as listed above are true for all drawings in Figures 5-2b, c, and d.

Once the cube is mastered as seen from all directions, the student should begin to place simple items within the cubes, such as geometrical solids at first, and furniture, lamps, and other objects later. In these exercises, the formulation of geometrical solids may seem dull, but basic forms are the underlying principles behind more complicated drawings and must not be taken lightly.

28

Practice the construction of the following items within boxes. Remember, boxes must adapt to the shape of the item within. (See Figure 5-3a through d.)

Figure 5-3a denotes not only the construction of a conical solid, but also demonstrates how placement of the measuring corner B, D, with relation to the horizon, changes the image seen by the viewer at the S.P. Here we can view the cone straight on, from the bottom, or from the top. (See Figure 5-3c.) Figure 5-3d demonstrates the formulation of a cylinder in a box from which the cup (cylinder within a cube) sketch (Figure 5-3e) was established. Notice how a circle is formed in perspective (Figure 5-3b.)

To construct a circle in both one- and two-point perspective, first form a square as seen in the base of the cube (Figure 5-3e) and proceed as follows: Divide the square into eight equal sections using perpendicular, horizontal, and diagonal lines through the radius point. This should be done both in plan first, and then converted to the perspective views. Next, divide the diagonal A, B into thirds. As is shown in the plan circle, a diagonal A, B may be divided into thirds, one of which marks a point very close to the circumference line of the circle. This too can be found in a similar manner within the perspective dawing; and as points are plotted and connected, one will see the oval taking shape. A circle in perspective becomes an oval with its axis always parallel to the ground line.

Study the following examples of geometrical solids, furniture, light fixtures, and so on. Examine the perspective of each and how lines within boxes are formed to make up the illustrated items. Remember, break all complicated structures down into their least complicated forms where possible; i.e., cubes, pyramids, cylinders, cones, spheres, or other geometrical shapes. (See Figure 5-4a through 5-9.)

All of the previous examples, as one will observe, clearly illustrate objects positioned on the rear of the picture plane. This holds true for illustrating a single object; but when an entire interior perspective view is desired, the measured floor plan must be positioned in front of the P.P. (See Figure 5-5.)

As was mentioned earlier, it is assumed that the student reading this book has had some training in fundamental perspective theory. With that assumption and the foregoing short review of perspective theory, we will now begin a more specialized form of layout that is more directly related to interior design rendering.

PRACTICAL INTERIOR PERSPECTIVE

Practical office methods for producing perspective drawings in both one- and two-point systems are essential to the interior illustration. These, unlike the 30°, 45°, 60°, etc. grid charts that are commercially available, allow the artist to work from almost any station point he chooses without being tied to a rigid, preconceived system; hence, much more flexibility within drawings is possible. The restrictions of perspective station points are covered later. See Figures 5-25 and 5-26, p. 48. Basically, vanishing points, which are determined by the S.P., should not be within the picture area. The following procedure should be studied closely while examining the illustrations.

Please note that to maintain drawing clarity, in some instances lines to vanishing points have been suggested only, so as to clearly illustrate from where they originate without confusing the reader. Refer again to Figures 5-2 a through e. Here, only one cube (Figure 5-2d) has vanishing points and lines to the points plotted; but all of the remaining cubes were plotted in a similar manner and each has its own set of vanishing points (or one vanishing point, as in Figures 5-2a and e).

PROCEDURE FOR ONE-POINT INTERIOR

1. Begin by positioning the floor plan (Figure 5-5), drawn to scale, in front of the picture plane with the rear wall directly on the P.P. This plan should be complete with a series of grid squares marked to represent 1-ft increments over the entire floor plan (including furniture).

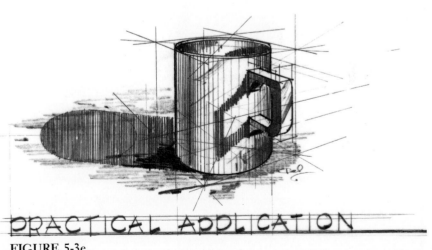

FIGURE 5-3e

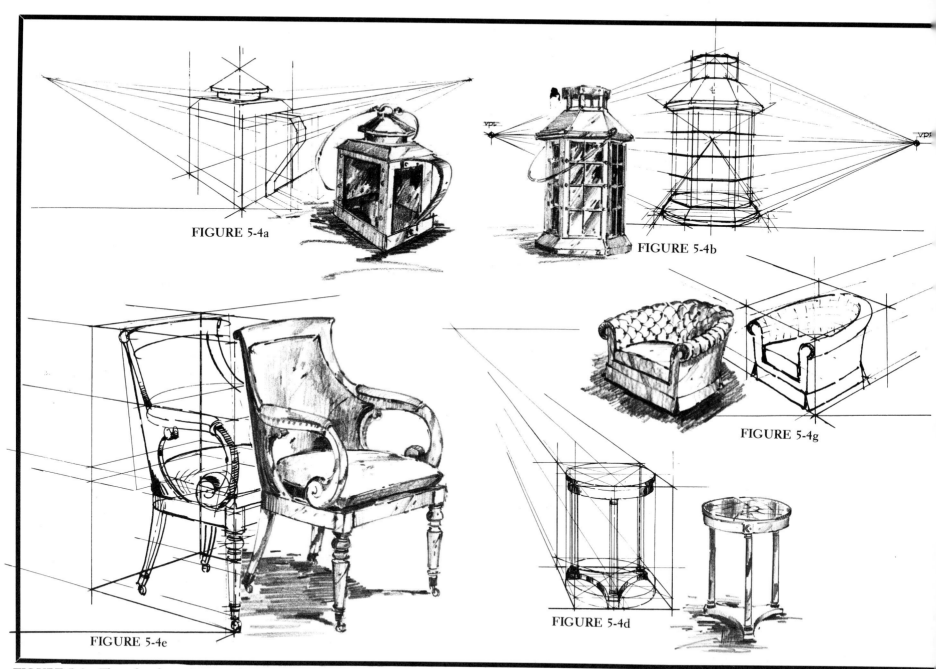

FIGURE 5-4a

FIGURE 5-4b

FIGURE 5-4g

FIGURE 5-4e

FIGURE 5-4d

FIGURE 5-4: The cube, drawn in two-point perspective, is used to contain familiar items found in interior design illustrations.

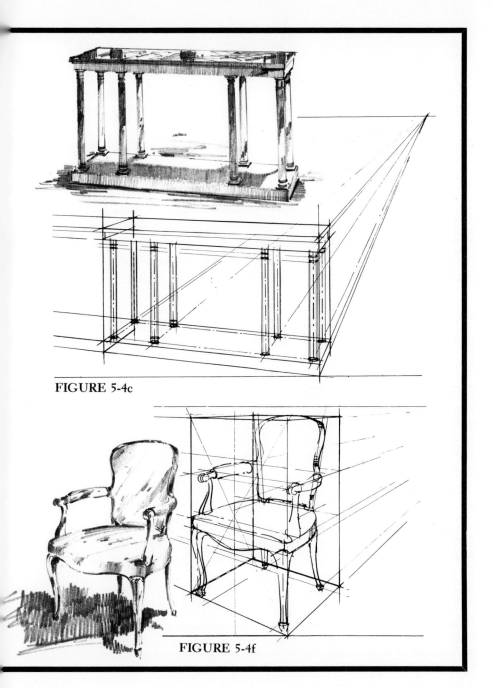

FIGURE 5-4c

FIGURE 5-4f

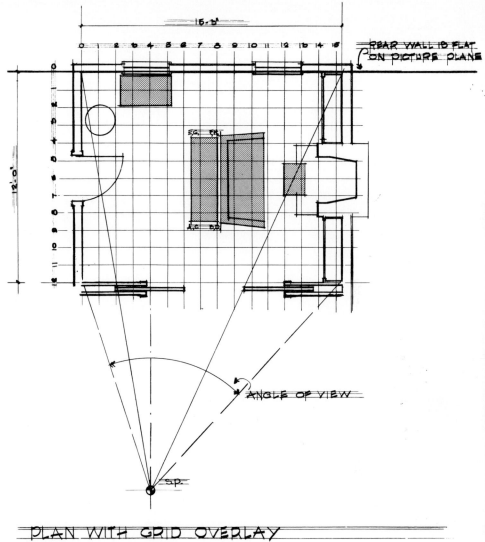

ANGLE OF VIEW

S.P.

PLAN WITH GRID OVERLAY

FIGURE 5-5: In one-point perspective of an interior, the floor plan lies in front of the picture plane with the rear wall of the room flat on the picture plane.

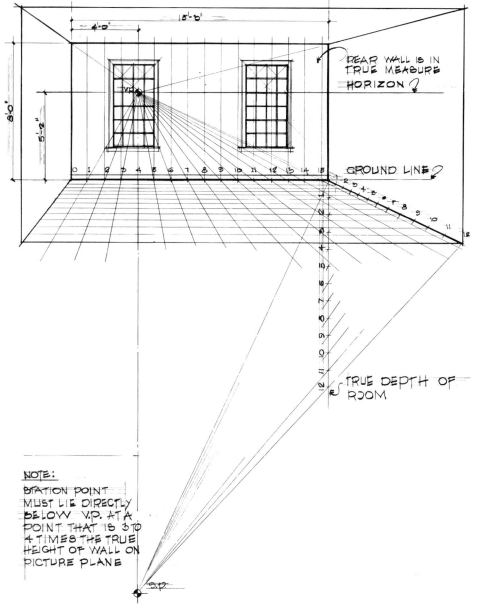

REAR WALL IS IN
TRUE MEASURE
HORIZON ?

GROUND LINE ?

TRUE DEPTH OF
ROOM

NOTE:
STATION POINT
MUST LIE DIRECTLY
BELOW V.P. AT A
POINT THAT IS 3 TO
4 TIMES THE TRUE
HEIGHT OF WALL ON
PICTURE PLANE

S.P.

FIRST STAGE OF ONE-POINT PERSPECTIVE / INTERIOR

2. Establish the station point a distance in front of the P.P., usually three to four times the measured height of the rear wall (that wall on the P.P.). The location of the S.P. may, at this distance from the picture plane, move right or left until it is felt a desirable picture would result. (See Figure 5-6a.) These small thumbnail sketches will help to determine angle of view depending on what elements within the finished illustration are most important.

3. Once the S.P. has been established, a second drawing must be done. (See Figure 5-6.) This one, an elevation of the rear wall in scale on the P.P., will be the beginning of the illustration. Draw all elements on this wall that are architecturally important and divide the floor line (ground line) into 1-ft segments. Draw a horizontal line 5 ft 2 in above the floor line. This will be the horizon line at eye level and it is on this line that the one vanishing point will be established.

4. Position the station point the selected distance forward of the picture plane (the G.L. is on the P.P., so this is the line from which this distance is measured) as was established in Step #2. The station point must be in the same relationship (right to left) as in the plan view (Step #2 or 4 ft from the left wall). (See Figure 5-5.) Once the station point has been plotted, one can position the one vanishing point directly above the station point and on the horizon line. The vanishing point is therefore plotted in Figure 5-6 to be 5 ft 2 in from the floor and 4 ft from the left wall.

5. Place a push-pin in the table through the V.P. This will serve as a pivot point to which all lines that are not horizontal or vertical will converge. This is true in this instance, because all furniture is parallel to both walls. If any furniture is at an angle to the perimeter walls, an added set of vanishing points for each piece of angled furniture must be established on the horizon line. This situation will be covered in a later section within this chapter. (See Figure 5-17, p. 42.)

6. Establish room boundaries by extending a line from the V.P. through the four corners (of the rear wall) in front of the P.P. (Do not at this time concern yourself with a stopping point for these lines.) Extend lines forward through each 1-ft mark along the floor line radiating from the V.P.

7. Extend the right corner of the rear wall vertically below the G.L. a

FIGURE 5-6 *Left:* One must first establish the station point in relationship to the view desired (see Figure 5-6a). This in turn will establish the position of the (one) vanishing point on the horizon.

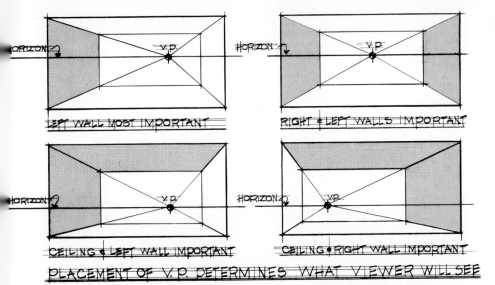

LEFT WALL MOST IMPORTANT

RIGHT & LEFT WALLS IMPORTANT

CEILING & LEFT WALL IMPORTANT

CEILING & RIGHT WALL IMPORTANT

PLACEMENT OF V.P. DETERMINES WHAT VIEWER WILL SEE

FIGURE 5-6a: Thumbnail sketches of interior spaces are very helpful when determining the view desired. These sketches in turn dictate the position of both the station point and vanishing points.

distance (in true measure) equal to the depth of the room, or 12 ft. Because the picture plane, like the horizon line, has no boundaries, this vertical extension in true measure is valid because it lies on the P.P.

8. Mark vertical 1-ft divisions on this extension.

9. Extend lines radiating from the S.P. (a pin pivot helps here also) through each mark on the extended vertical corner until they intersect the right wall/floor boundary previously established. Through each of these marks, horizontal lines parallel to the G.L. may be drawn to create a floor grid that is in scale and accurate to within acceptable standards. Note the front wall has been removed for clarity. (See Figure 5-6.)

10. Locate the floor plan area (Figure 5-5) to be covered by each piece of furniture or architectural feature. Letter each corner with the designation A, C—B, D, etc., as in plan of the sofa table. To explain this designation one must refer to Figure 5-8a. Notice that the vertical line formed by connecting points A and C would appear in plan as only a point; therefore, to locate both top and bottom points with letters, they read, A, C–B, D, etc.

11. It is now a simple matter to locate the floor-plan intersections of each piece of furniture and architectural feature in perspective as shown in the

shaded area of Figure 5-7. Note that from this step forward it is suggested that the student not draw on the floor-plan perspective drawing, but on successive overlays of architectural sketch paper. This will lessen confusion, as many lines will be required to complete a drawing.

12. Using the overlay sheet and Figure 5-7, trace the floor plan of each piece of furniture again and project vertical lines a short distance from the floor (see Figure 5-8). One does not know how high these lines must be drawn because these lines cannot be measured. Again, the only wall on which true measure may be taken is the wall on the picture plane. Assuming that the piece of furniture (in this case we will be concentrating first on the sofa table) is 2 ft 3 in high, find this dimension, L on the left rear wall corner, L (which you should divide into vertical 1-ft increments) nearest the piece of furniture. Project a horizontal line along the floor from D through C to J up the wall vertically until it intersects the 2 ft 3 in-high projected line on wall at K. At that point, a line parallel to line C, J should be projected from K until it intersects the line projected vertically from C, at A thus determining a height of 2 ft 3 in for the sofa table.

13. Using the preceding method and another tracing overlay, we can now plot all points on every architectural feature and piece of furniture, or rather, the packing boxes in which to later place the furniture. One can now see a practical application for the confinement of furniture within boxes in previous exercises (see Figures 5-8a and 5-4).

14. Now one may be able to see results of lines, picture planes, vanishing points, overlays, and the other aspects of perspective drawing, because depth finally begins to appear within the drawing. An overlay should be used to establish each piece of furniture roughly drawn within each box. Individual colored, ink, or pencil lines will help to separate all of the overlapping pieces.

15. After all pieces have been drawn, a final overlay will be needed onto which one should trace only those portions visible to the viewer (Figure 5-8b). This sheet is then used as an under-drawing from which a finished rendering can be made. A drawing on mylar is partially illustrated in Figure 5-9 (after completion of a value study). (Refer to Chapter 6, "Value Study of Shade and Shadows.")

PROCEDURE FOR TWO-POINT INTERIOR

1. Position the measured floor plan in front of the picture plane as was done in Step #1 of the previous example, except that in this case only one corner, not an entire wall surface, will be placed on the P.P. (Figure 5-10).

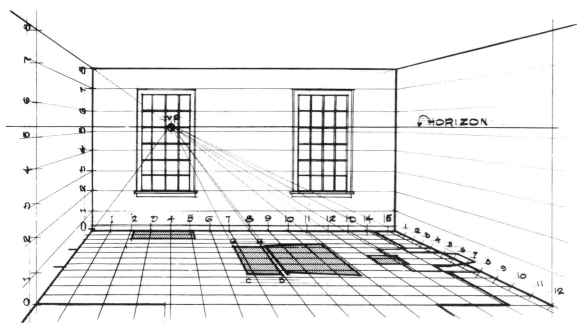

SECOND STAGE — LAY OUT FLOOR PLAN IN PERSPECTIVE

FIGURE 5-7

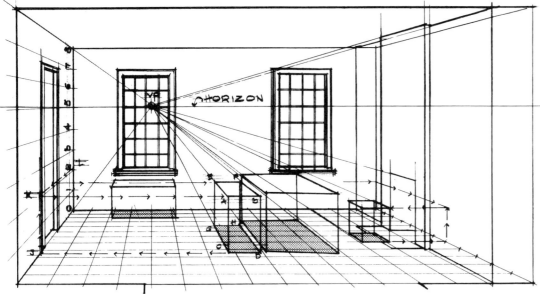

THIRD STAGE — CONSTRUCT BOXES TO CONTAIN FURNITURE

FIGURE 5-8a

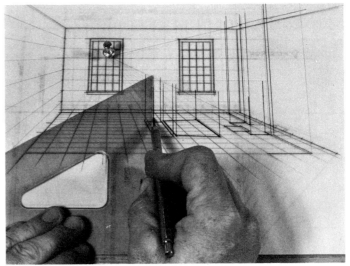

FIGURE 5-8: The placement of boxes that represent furniture is one of the most important steps in creating a perspective drawing of an interior space. The use of a T square and triangle is necessary for the production of accurate drawings (note the push-pin used as a pivot point).

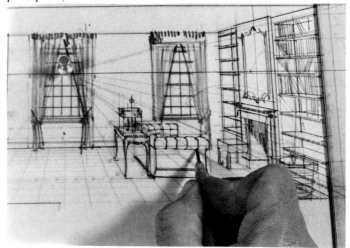

FIGURE 5-8b

34

FOURTH STAGE — RENDER FINISHED ILLUSTRATION

PARTIAL RENDERING / USE OF 2H PENCIL ON MYLAR OVERLAY NOTED

FIGURE 5-9: The final illustration may be delineated on a clean overlay sheet of mylar or Clearprint® tracing paper. Note the progression of pencil rendering strokes that have been worked from one side of the illustration to the other in order to finish all portions of the drawing in sequence.

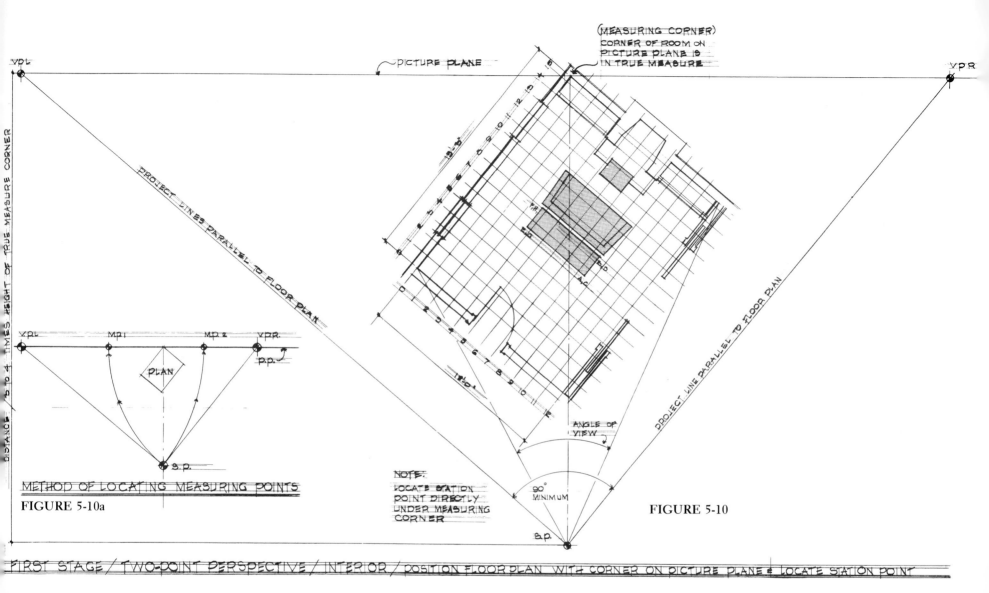

PICTURE PLANE

VPL

VPR

DISTANCE 3 TO 4 TIMES HEIGHT OF TRUE MEASURE CORNER

PROJECT LINES PARALLEL TO FLOOR PLAN

VPL   MP1   MP 2   VPR

P.P.

PLAN

s.p.

METHOD OF LOCATING MEASURING POINTS

FIGURE 5-10a

PROJECT LINE PARALLEL TO FLOOR PLAN

ANGLE OF VIEW

NOTE:
LOCATE STATION
POINT DIRECTLY
UNDER MEASURING
CORNER

90°
MINIMUM

FIGURE 5-10

s.p.

FIRST STAGE / TWO-POINT PERSPECTIVE / INTERIOR / POSITION FLOOR PLAN WITH CORNER ON PICTURE PLANE & LOCATE STATION POINT

FIGURE 5-10: Position the floor plan in front of the picture plane in direct relationship to the image desired. Note the angle of view. This will tell the illustrator what is to be seen from the station point. One corner of the plan must lie directly on the picture plane and will become the measuring corner.

FIGURE 5-10a: Measuring points MP-1 and MP-2 are located by swinging arcs from the station point using both VPL and VPR as pivot points. These will intersect at the picture plane. The intersection of these arcs with the picture plane establishes points MP-1 and MP-2. NOTE: These points should not lie within the desired picture.

FIGURE 5-11 *Opposite:* Using MP-1 and MP-2 together with VPL and VPR, construct a floor grid in perspective as shown, being extremely aware of the grid square (shaded in illustration) in the foreground. If this square becomes distorted, a reexamination of the placement of VPL and VPR is necessary. Remember that these are guidelines only. If rules must be broken in order to create a good drawing, then by all means, break them, but only with the knowledge and understanding of the traditional methods and the rationale for alterations.

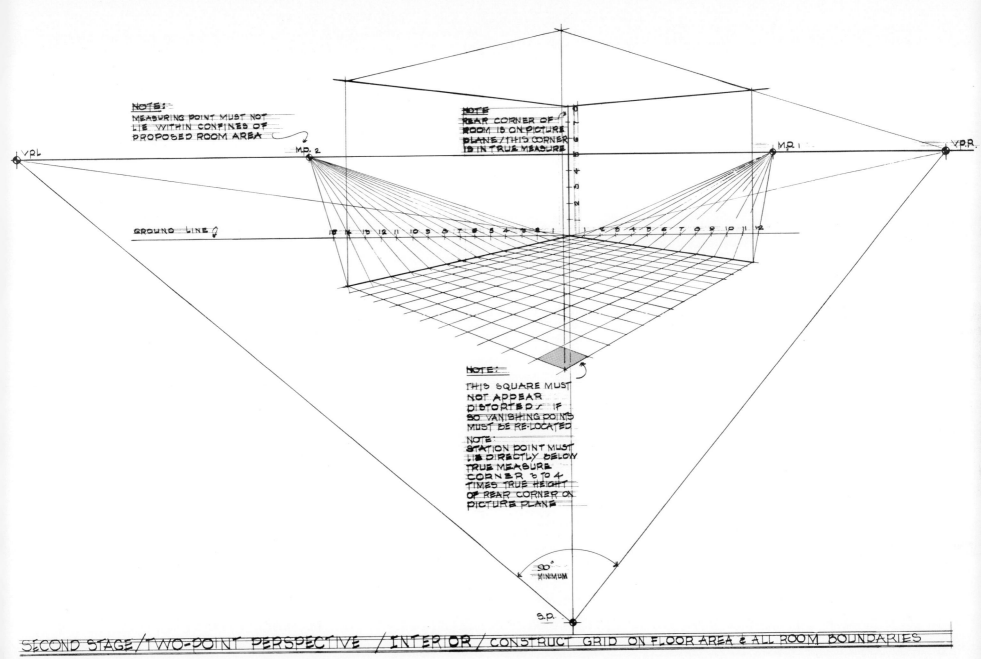

FIGURE 5-11

FIGURE 5-12: Accurate placement of furniture in perspective is aided by the grid system. Using many overlay sheets to create a gradual building process will minimize confusion for the beginner. Colored inks can also lessen confusion if overlay sheets are not available.

This corner will be used for true measure of height because it lies directly on the P.P. and can be measured. Mark 1-ft increments in scale along each wall in plan and divide the floor space into 1-ft squares. Plot the letter designations at the corners of furniture and architectural features projecting into the room. (See Step #10, p.33)

2. Find the station point by dropping a vertical line directly under the measuring corner on the P.P. downward to a distance equal to three to four times the true height of the room.

3. Locate the two vanishing points (as was done for Figure 5-2d, cube exterior) by drawing lines parallel to the floor-plan walls until they intersect the picture plane. (See Figure 5-10.)

4. Locate measuring points on picture plane as described in Figure 5-10a

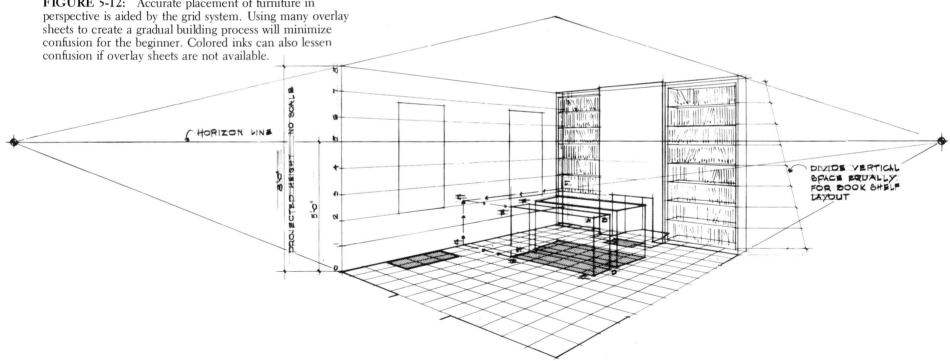

THIRD STAGE / TWO-POINT PERSPECTIVE / INTERIOR / LAY OUT FLOOR PLAN & CONSTRUCT BOXES FOR FURNITURE

FIGURE 5-13

by swinging arcs (using both V.P.L. and V.P.R. as radius points) from the S.P. until these arcs intersect the P.P. Mark these as measuring point one (M.P. 1) and measuring point two (M.P. 2).

5. Refer to Figure 5-11. On a separate sheet of tracing paper locate the horizon line complete with V.P.L., V.P.R., M.P. 1, M.P. 2, and the true-measure room corner. One must locate this measuring corner in proper height relation to the horizon line; in this case 5 ft has been chosen. This height may vary with the eye level chosen by the viewer.

6. Mark off 1-ft increments on the true-height wall (8 ft) and on the ground line. Note that because the room is 12 ft × 15 ft 3 in, horizontal divisions have been made along the ground line in each direction from the measuring corner as shown. For clarity, 15 ft 3 in has been rounded off to

15 ft, and this small variation in one dimension will not significantly affect the finished drawing. Care should be taken to make room dimensions in relation to what will be seen (angle of view) on the floor plan when standing at the S.P.; i.e., 12 ft to the right of the measuring corner and 15 ft to the left (see Figure 5-10). For purposes of clarity, the removal of two forward walls is a necessity.

7. Notice the position of the previously established measuring points M.P. 1 and M.P. 2 (Figure 5-11). If these fall within the space between the boundaries formed by right and left extremities along the ground line (15-ft and 12-ft marks) they must be moved so they are outside of what is to be the interior space occupied by the room.

8. Using pins as pivot points, extend lines from each vanishing point

FOURTH STAGE / TWO-POINT PERSPECTIVE / INTERIOR / PLACE FURNITURE IN BOXES

FIGURE 5-14: Once boxes are drawn, a piece of furniture can be constructed in each box, using a separate tracing paper overlay for each. Refer to Figures 5-4a through g.

PARTIALLY COMPLETED PENCIL DRAWING
DRAWN WITH 2H PENCIL ON DRAFTING MYLAR OVERLAY

FIGURE 5-15: Complete the final drawing using a clear sheet of mylar or Clearprint® tracing paper. Pencil hardness used will be dictated by the surface chosen. See Figures 10-4a through d for reference.

through the measuring corner extremities top and bottom, a distance close to the 12-ft and 15-ft marks on the ground line. This will form the boundaries (floor/wall and ceiling/wall lines). At this point, we do not know how far to extend these boundaries.

9. Extend lines from M.P. 1 and M.P. 2 through each 1-ft division on the ground line until these lines intersect the floor/wall lines. Place marks to plot these intersections. The extremities of the room width and depth in perspective are determined in this manner.

10. From each vanishing point, extend lines through each mark placed on the floor/wall boundaries across the floor of the room. This series of intersecting lines will form a true perspective grid covering all of the floor area, which is in direct relation to the P.P. and S.P. (See Figure 5-11.) Note the shaded square in the foreground. This must not appear distorted. If it does, the vanishing points are probably too close together. This can be changed by extending the distance to the S.P. in Step #2.

11. Next, using procedures previously established in Steps #10, #11, and #12 of one-point perspective, divide the rear corner wall with 1-ft divisions and plot all furniture and architectural elements on the perspective grid just completed. Do not forget to use an overlay for this to lessen confusion and to retain all work done to this point in case mistakes are made. (See Figure 5-12.)

12. Using the same piece of furniture as before (the sofa table) plot vertical lines and establish the height of boxes needed to contain the items to be included in the drawing (refer to Step #13 in the previous exercise).

13. Plot window placement, fireplace opening, and all book-shelf divisions by projecting height lines established on the measuring corner in Step #11. Vertical lines of these items are again brought up the walls from points located on floor/wall lines previously established on the plan (Figure 5-13).

14. Use overlay sheets to establish all elements within boxes as described in Step #14 of one-point perspective. (See Figure 5-14.)

15. All that is now left to do is to create a final drawing using an overlay of tracing paper or mylar. (Techniques of pencil rendering in final form as well as necessary value studies will be covered in depth in Chapter 6, "Value Study of Shade and Shadow," and Chapter 10, "Pencil Rendering".) Refer to the partially completed pencil drawing, Figure 5-15.

EXERCISES

Refer to Figures 5-16a through c for this exercise. This kitchen drawing

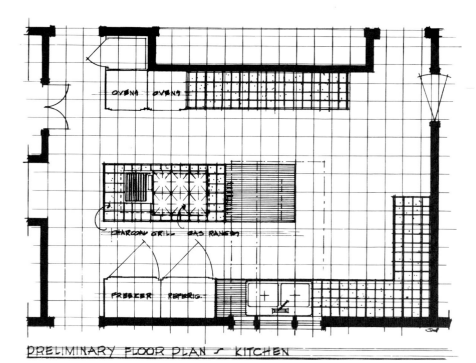

PRELIMINARY FLOOR PLAN — KITCHEN

FIGURE 5-16a *Above:* Lay out in scale a one-foot-square grid system on the floor plan. Observe how the angle of view chosen relates to the under-drawing (**FIGURE 5-16b** *Opposite Top:*) and finished illustration (**FIGURE 5-16c** *Opposite Bottom:*). The angle of view is *not* designated here in order to give the reader the experience of relating to both plan and perspective as a unit.

contains all elements parallel with the perimeter walls as in the previous exercise. The student should examine the floor plan (Figure 5-16a) with relation to the view shown in both the under-drawing (Figure 5-16b) and the finished pencil sketch (Figure 5-16c).

Trace the construction lines to the vanishing points (not shown) and become familiar with the direction of each element in relation to both V.P.L. and V.P.R. Notice how the counter top in the foreground gives depth to the room. There is a definite division within this sketch of foreground, middle ground, and background. Refer to Figures 8-11, and 8-11a. Chapter 8, "The Importance of Sketching," pp. 76 and 77.

OBLIQUE FURNITURE

Before discussing the last project, it would be well to note Figures 5-17, 18 and 19. The same drawings and elements of one-point perspective (Figures 5-3 through 5-9) will apply with the following special conditions.

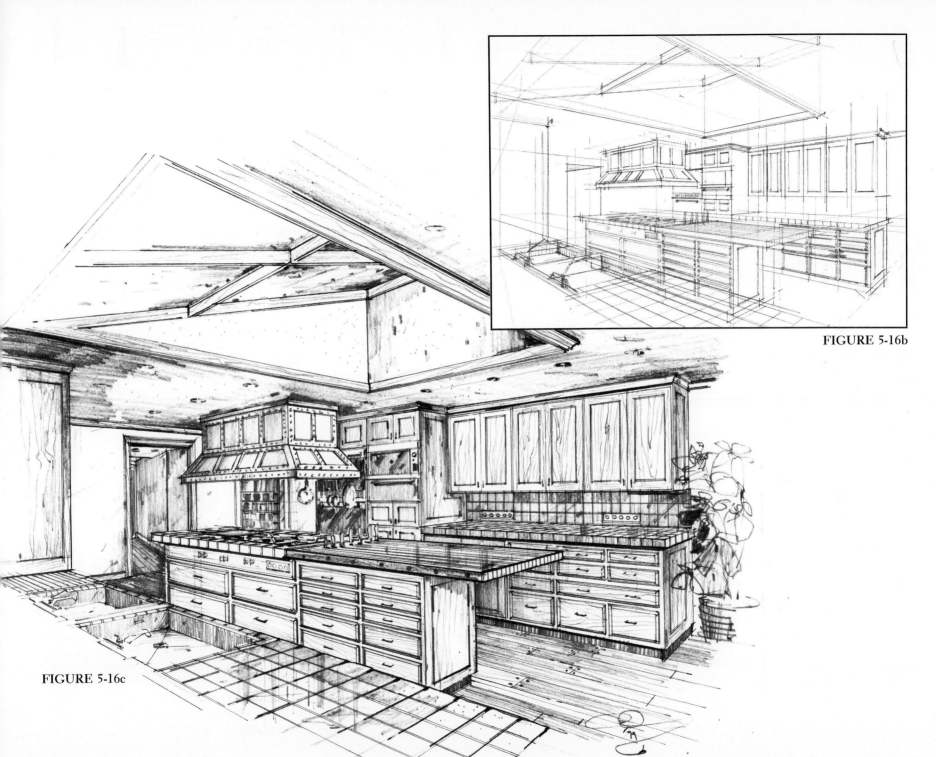

FIGURE 5-16b

FIGURE 5-16c

41

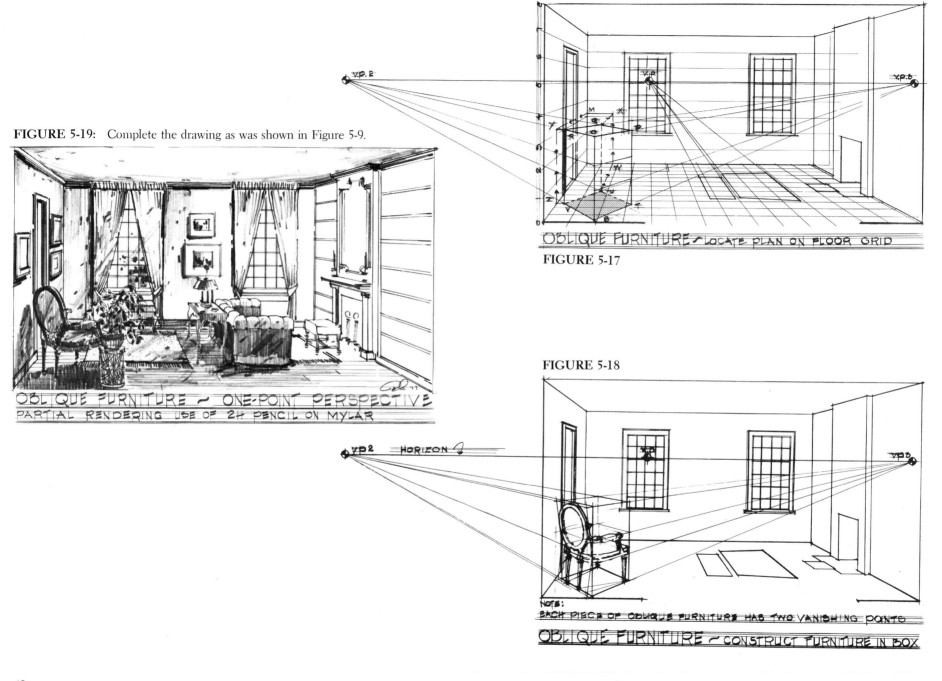

FIGURE 5-19: Complete the drawing as was shown in Figure 5-9.

OBLIQUE FURNITURE ~ ONE-POINT PERSPECTIVE
PARTIAL RENDERING USE OF 2H PENCIL ON MYLAR

OBLIQUE FURNITURE ~ LOCATE PLAN ON FLOOR GRID

FIGURE 5-17

FIGURE 5-18

NOTE:
EACH PIECE OF OBLIQUE FURNITURE HAS TWO VANISHING POINTS

OBLIQUE FURNITURE ~ CONSTRUCT FURNITURE IN BOX

FIGURE 5-20: This pencil rendering of a real estate sales-conference room will be used as the basis for the final perspective project, in this chapter. The student should retain the finished under-drawing for use in Chapters 6, "Value Study of Shade and Shadow," and 10, "Pencil Rendering."

In one-point perspective (Figure 5-17) if a piece of furniture is at an oblique angle to the room perimeter walls, this piece will have its own set of two vanishing points, each on the horizon line. After plotting the plan (shaded area), the perimeter heights of each box are plotted in the same manner as was discussed previously with reference to Figure 5-8a. (Note: with relation to two-point perspective, if a piece of furniture is at an oblique angle to either perimeter wall, it will have its own vanishing point or set of two vanishing points.)

Figure 5-18 and Figure 5-19 carry this exercise through to conclusion and each step should be studied carefully. It would be well to note here that many times one must "fake" position of an oblique object in order to make it read properly and not appear as though it were falling out of the picture. This "artistic license" is sometimes necessary and should not be overlooked.

EXERCISE—REAL ESTATE SALES-CONFERENCE ROOM

The last exercise for this chapter will be the construction of a basic two-point perspective drawing that will be referred to later on in this book in

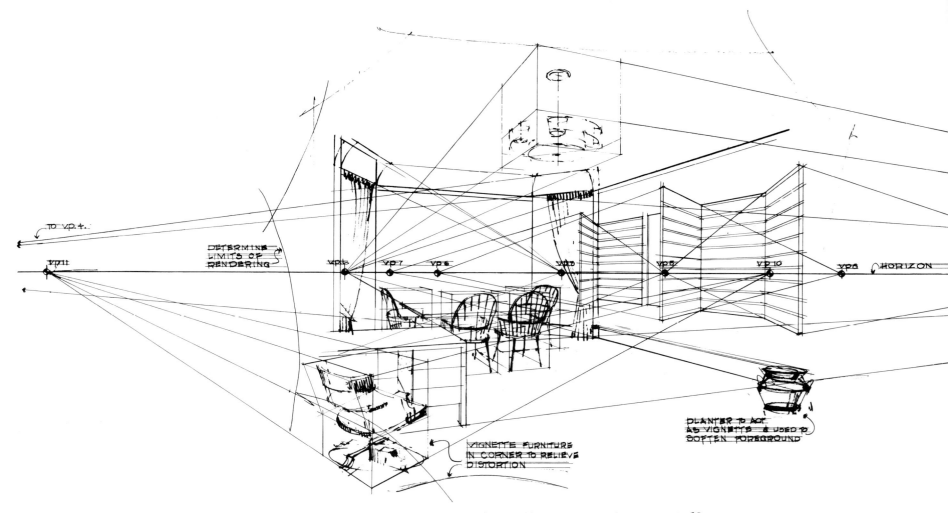

TO VP. 4.

VP 11

DETERMINE
LIMITS OF
RENDERING

VP 12   VP 7   VP 6   VP 3   VP 9   VP 10   VP 8   HORIZON

VIGNETTE FURNITURE
IN CORNER TO RELIEVE
DISTORTION

PLANTER TO ACT
AS VIGNETTE & USED TO
SOFTEN FOREGROUND

TWO-POINT PERSPECTIVE - REAL ESTATE OFFICE SHOWING MULTIPLE VANISHING POINTS

FIGURE 5-21: This master drawing shows all vanishing points in the drawing and is the final step before reaching the stage shown in Figure 5-22. Each of the following illustrations shows various stages of construction used to obtain this master.

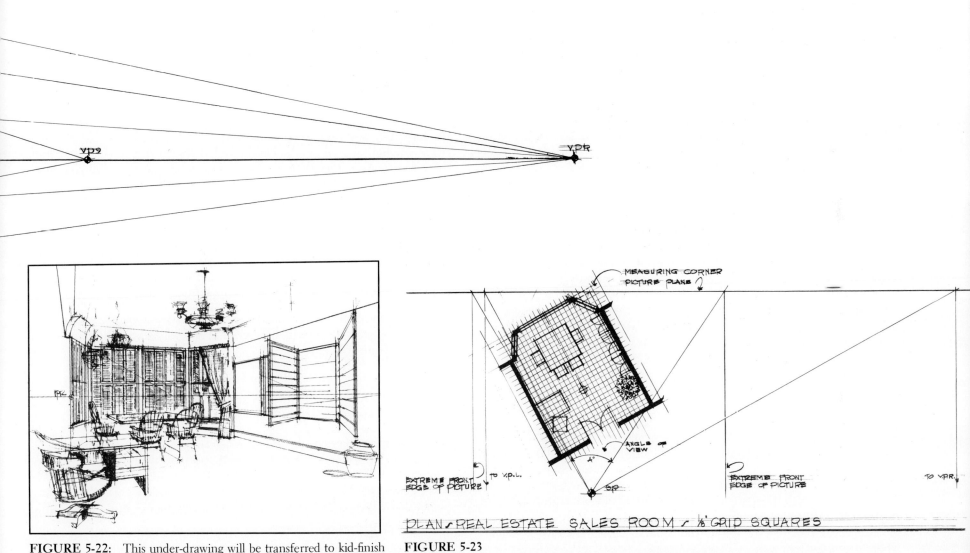

VP9

VPR

MEASURING CORNER
PICTURE PLANE

ANGLE OF
VIEW

EXTREME FRONT
EDGE OF PICTURE

TO V.P.L.

EXTREME FRONT
EDGE OF PICTURE

TO V.P.R.

S.P.

PLAN - REAL ESTATE SALES ROOM - ⅛' GRID SQUARES

FIGURE 5-22: This under-drawing will be transferred to kid-finish bristol board so a final pencil rendering can be made.

FIGURE 5-23

both Chapter 6, "Value Studies of Shade and Shadow," and Chapter 10, "Pencil Rendering," in which this construction drawing will be the basis for a final pencil rendering (see Figure 5-20).

In the last sections of both one-point and two-point perspective, we carried a very simple room layout from plan to perspective construction in steps that are almost always necessary when producing a finished drawing.

Often, the illustrator has the choice of the angle of view for a drawing, and designers usually trust in the illustrator's training to ensure that the view taken will result in a successful drawing portraying all aspects required to sell a project. In the case of the real estate sales-conference room we will be examining, prime importance was to be given to the display panels that contain photographs of property for sale by that company. The conference table was almost as important to the clients as was the desk and chair in the left foreground. Because this was an existing space in a Victorian house, traditional drapery treatment as well as the turn-of-the-century chandelier were carefully drawn to give a flavor of traditional architecture. Space was to be left in the foreground for copy, as the drawing was to be the basis for a publicity brochure.

The only thing that is unusual about this drawing is that there are *two* major vanishing points (these two vanishing points are referred to as V.P.R. and V.P.L. in this illustration) and *nine* minor vanishing points for items within the space. This drawing is not as complicated as it first may seem; and, if the student will approach the construction of perspective in steps using many tracing-paper overlays, confusion will be held to a minimum. Each vanishing point for items within the drawing will be referred to as V.P. 1 or V.P. 2, and so on; each will be given a number for easier reference instead of a designation for left or right vanishing points.

Refer to the over-all construction drawing showing V.P.R. and V.P.L. as well as all other vanishing points for items within. After studying this master drawing (Figure 5-21) and the finished perspective under-drawing (Figure 5-22), we will break down construction procedure into steps that are relatively easy to understand if overlays are used.

Refer to Figure 5-23 showing an over-all plan of the space. Note the angle of view, the placement of the station point, and the resulting vanishing-point placement. In most circumstances, vanishing points in a two-point interior perspective should never fall within the confines of the finished picture area. Here we are going to violate this principle to give the reader insight into two situations that must be dealt with sooner or later. Clients are always concerned about the visual image of the finished sketch. Therefore, if a client wants a two-point perspective that shows three walls instead of two, it may be possible to give the illusion of the third wall. In the

real estate sales-conference room, it will be the left wall. One may find that by placement of furniture on this wall and vignetting the foreground pieces enough to hide the distortion that always results when a V.P. is within the picture, a satisfying drawing will result.

The student, either when working for a firm or on a free-lance basis, is going to get into situations that require adaption, artistic license, and a good deal of faking before the required drawings can satisfy a difficult client. One must, therefore, remember that mechanical methods of laying out perspective drawings are only an aid in scale determination, depth perception, etc.; and if rules must be broken to achieve a result required by a client, then by all means break the rules. Always remember, however— *one must know all of the rules before one can successfully break them.*

The system by which measuring points were located on the horizon in the beginning portion of two-point perspective of an interior (Figure 5-10a) is a somewhat exacting method and is not always practical when time is of the essence. Also, the plotting of a station point and then drawing lines from the S.P. parallel to the plan until they strike the picture plane to determine vanishing points may not be practical if the plan is large and the drawing to be executed is also large. Drawing space required for this type of projection method can become too great for the small design office.

It is, therefore, logical to assume that shortcut methods should be found to create accuracy within a drawing without having to use all of the space-requiring steps of projection as studied in the previous exercises. Some steps have, therefore, been deleted to form the following method.

1. Draw a line that will represent the horizon. Below that (a distance to represent eye-level height) draw the ground line parallel to the horizon, 4 ft 6 in away (Figure 5-24).

2. Using the same scale (let us assume ⅜ in equals 1 ft), establish 1-ft horizontal dimensions from the measuring corner both to the right and to the left along the ground line, as was done in Figure 5-11; in this case, 21 ft to the right and 20 ft to the left (these distances represent the measure of each corresponding wall on the floor plan). Now, referring to the small diagrams from which the vanishing-point positions for the real estate sales-conference office were developed, examine how the angle of view establishes what is seen when the plan is positioned in this relation to the picture plane. (See Figure 5-25.) Note that these are diagrams only and are not the true floor plan as seen in Figure 5-23.

Figure 5-26 shows a small diagram of an ideal situation and it should be studied and compared until one is aware of the resulting picture when the

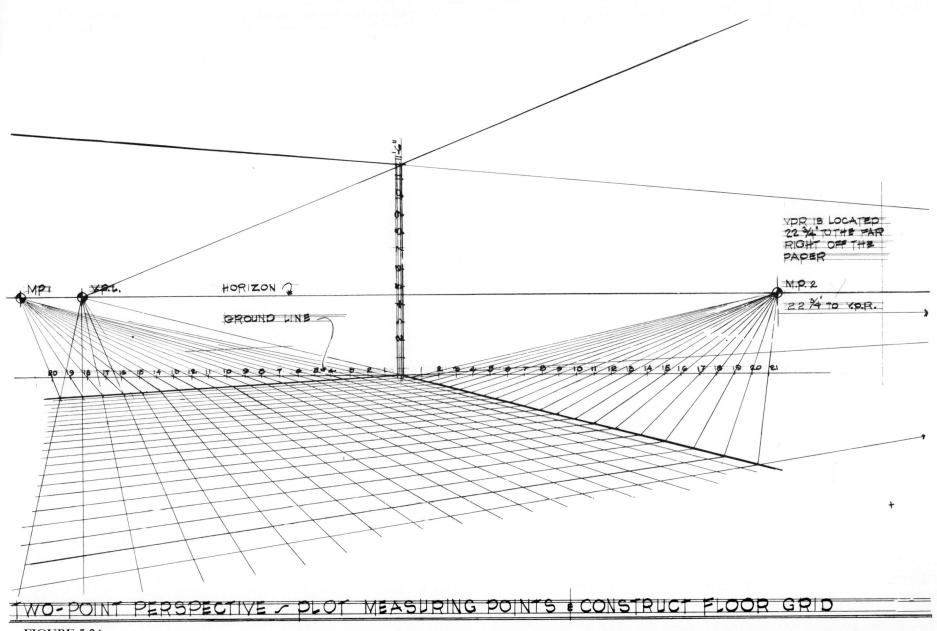

VPR IS LOCATED
22 ¾" TO THE FAR
RIGHT OFF THE
PAPER

MP1 V.P.L. HORIZON

GROUND LINE

M.P.2

22 ¾" TO V.P.R.

20 19 18 17 16 15 14 13 12 11 10 9 8 7 6 5 4 3 2 1 1 2 3 4 5 6 7 8 9 10 11 12 13 14 15 16 17 18 19 20 21

TWO-POINT PERSPECTIVE — PLOT MEASURING POINTS & CONSTRUCT FLOOR GRID

FIGURE 5-24

47

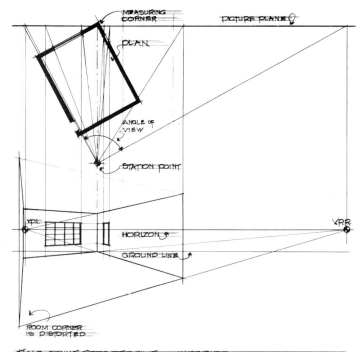

MEASURING CORNER

PICTURE PLANE

PLAN

ANGLE OF VIEW

STATION POINT

VPL

HORIZON

VPR

GROUND LINE

ROOM CORNER IS DISTORTED

TWO-POINT PERSPECTIVE / INTERIOR

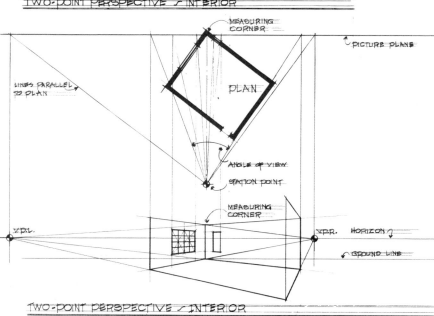

MEASURING CORNER

PICTURE PLANE

LINES PARALLEL TO PLAN

PLAN

ANGLE OF VIEW

STATION POINT

MEASURING CORNER

V.P.L.

V.P.R.

HORIZON

GROUND LINE

TWO-POINT PERSPECTIVE / INTERIOR

FIGURES 5-25 *Left Top:* **5-26** *Left Bottom:* Note the relationship of the vanishing points in each of the thumbnail sketches and how their placement is determined by the plan position rotating around the measuring corner using this corner as a pivot point. This is very much like the principle studied in Figures 5-2a through e. Figure 5-26 is the ideal situation, whereas Figure 5-25 is not so ideal because one of the two vanishing points (VPL) lies within the proposed picture area. We will be using a situation similar to Figure 5-25 for our experiences through Figure 5-29.

plan is rotated about the measuring corner on the picture plane. (This comparison was illustrated in Figure 5-6a and also in Figures 5-2 a through e where the plan was rotated about its corner on the opposite side of the picture plane.)

3. Because this drawing of a real estate sales-conference room is not an ideal example, let us compare the floor plan in Figure 5-23 with the simple plan shown in Figure 5-25. In each example the student should be aware of distortion resulting from the V.P.L. being inside the field of view (within the picture area). This distortion may be removed visually by "vignetting," as will be seen a little later. Note, too, that the V.P.R. is far off the drawing surface (22¾ in to the right of M.P. 2). (Refer to Figures 5-21 and 5-24.) It will be good for the student to have a long straightedge that will reach from the V.P.R. to the drawing in order to maintain accuracy of line. For most of the examples, line direction to this V.P.R. only will be noted.

4. Now that room perimeter dimensions have been marked on the ground line, place M.P. 1 and M.P. 2 on the horizon a short distance out of the resulting picture to the right and left of the last measurement marks (21 ft and 20 ft). Locate the resulting floor grid in perspective, as was done in Figure 5-11. Mark vertical height dimensions on the measuring corner (see Figure 5-24).

5. Plot the floor plan of each piece of furniture and of the architectural features of the room; i.e., two angled walls at the end of the room. (Figure 5-27.)

It will be noted that these angled walls may be plotted on the floor plan by location on the grid and projection up the walls until ceiling lines are intersected. Although this is a two-point perspective, these angled walls have their own vanishing points (V.P. 3 and V.P. 4), not too unlike oblique

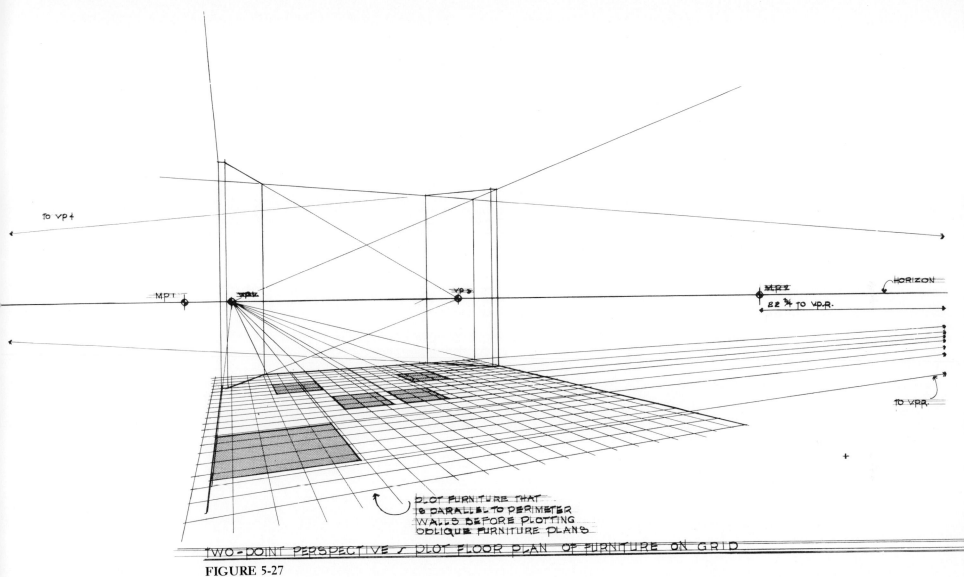

TO VP↓

MP↓

VP←

VP→

MP→
82 ¾ TO VP.R.

HORIZON

TO VP.R.

PLOT FURNITURE THAT
IS PARALLEL TO PERIMETER
WALLS BEFORE PLOTTING
OBLIQUE FURNITURE PLANS

TWO-POINT PERSPECTIVE / PLOT FLOOR PLAN OF FURNITURE ON GRID

FIGURE 5-27

49

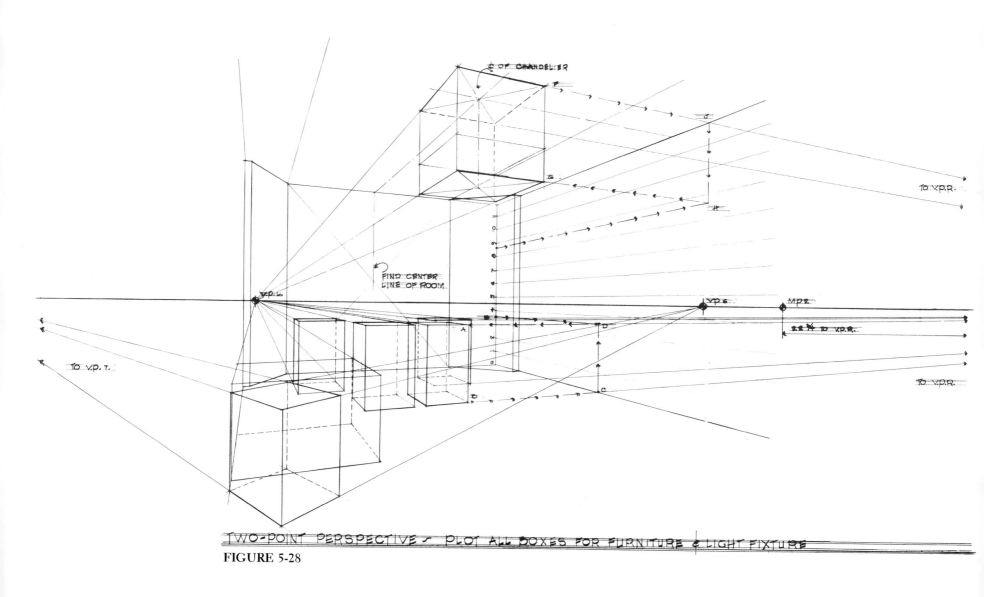

C OF CHANDELIER

FIND CENTER
LINE OF ROOM

V.P.L.

VP 6   MP2

22 ¾ TO V.P.R.

TO V.P.R.

TO V.P.R.

TO V.P. 7.

TWO-POINT PERSPECTIVE — PLOT ALL BOXES FOR FURNITURE & LIGHT FIXTURE

FIGURE 5-28

50

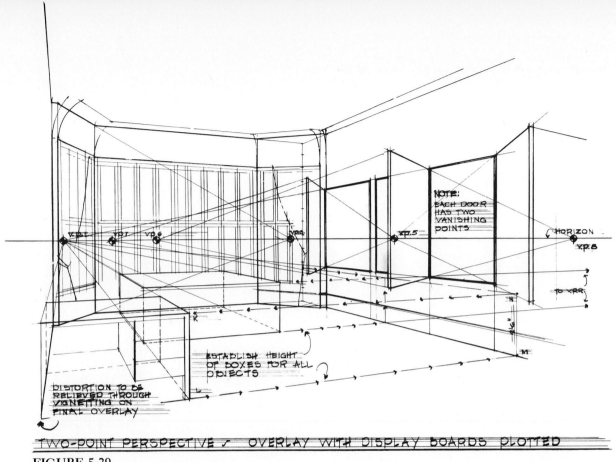

NOTE:
EACH DOOR
HAS TWO
VANISHING
POINTS

HORIZON

ESTABLISH HEIGHT
OF BOXES FOR ALL
OBJECTS

DISTORTION TO BE
RELIEVED THROUGH
VIGNETTING ON
FINAL OVERLAY

TWO-POINT PERSPECTIVE — OVERLAY WITH DISPLAY BOARDS PLOTTED

FIGURE 5-29

furniture (see Figure 5-17). These vanishing points are on the horizon line, as are all vanishing points in this drawing. It will be noted that this drawing is a good example of multiple vanishing points within one perspective. Draw boxes by projecting lines from the measuring corner, along the walls to establish height from which vertical furniture dimensions may be found, as was done in Figure 5-12 and 13.

Refer to Figure 5-28. Notice the large box at the ceiling that is to contain the chandelier. Observe how the center line of the window wall was divided into equal portions by use of intersecting diagonals, and how this center line was projected across the ceiling until it intersected the corresponding projections from the right wall.

Each step shown was drawn on a separate overlay to lessen confusion for the viewer. (See Figure 5-29.) When all overlays are superimposed over each other, a final tracing may be drawn to use as an under-drawing (Figure 5-22) by only drawing what is not hidden; furniture in the foreground is drawn first and what is not needed is omitted. If this were not accomplished by the use of overlays, confusion of line would result and the drawing would appear very difficult. By breaking down a very complex drawing into its smaller elements and then combining these elements, a better understanding of perspective will result.

6. Refer to Figure 5-21 and 5-29. See how the display boards each have their own vanishing points, V.P. 5, 6, 7, 8, and 9. Each board has two vanishing points, one each for the flat portion and one each for the thickness. Location on the wall for placement of these boards was plotted from the floor grid. Place furniture in the boxes on each overlay, drawing

51

the complete piece even though some will be hidden later by pieces in the foreground.

7. Combine all overlay sheets. (A light-colored table is helpful so lines below can be seen through the top tracing sheet.)

The resulting under-drawing is now ready for the value study and final rendering stages to be covered in Chapter 6, "Value Study of Shade and Shadows," and Chapter 10, "Pencil Rendering."

Value Study of Shade and Shadows

VALUE STUDIES ARE referred to in most chapters of this book. They are the basis from which the illustrator makes the rendering "live" and "read" as it is meant to do. Without value designation, a drawing does not have depth or object division. Without the presence of light, shade, and shadow, objects would appear flat and uninteresting, notwithstanding the fact that line division would be the only way to distinguish one object from another.

Chapter 3, "How to See," dealt with one's relationship to one's environment. In that chapter we learned how to analyze and relate what we see around us to a graphic representation of those objects. We only touched on the subject of light, shade, and shadow. This chapter is aimed at the deeper analysis of light, shade, and shadow, and how they relate to rendering and sketching done in both color and black and white.

LIGHT, SHADE AND SHADOWS

Light falls on all objects from one point or many and gives those objects the definition by which we determine their shapes. When some element comes between the source of light and a surface upon which the light rays are falling, three things take place: 1.) The element blocks light rays, causing a definite *shadow* on the surface. 2.) Those surfaces of the object not receiving direct light rays will be in *shade*. Shade is always part of the object casting the shadow. 3.) Light will be reflected back onto the object from the surface to form *reflected light*. (See Figure 6-1.)

CONVENTIONAL LIGHT

For our first exercises here, we are going to assume that light will be falling on objects from the right and front, each at a 45° angle to the horizon and picture plane. This assumption creates what is referred to as conventional light. To illustrate this, let us examine Figure 6-2, a cube (equal dimensions on all sides).

In this illustration, the light is falling from the right front and the rays are parallel to a line drawn from the right top corner through the lower left

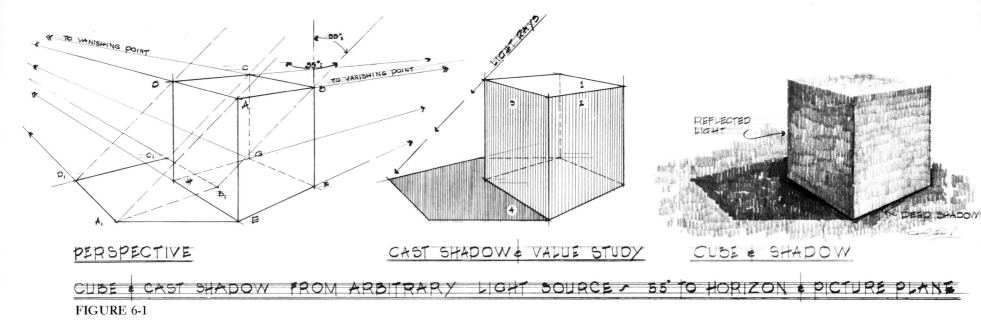

PERSPECTIVE   CAST SHADOW & VALUE STUDY   CUBE & SHADOW

CUBE & CAST SHADOW FROM ARBITRARY LIGHT SOURCE ~ 55° TO HORIZON & PICTURE PLANE

FIGURE 6-1

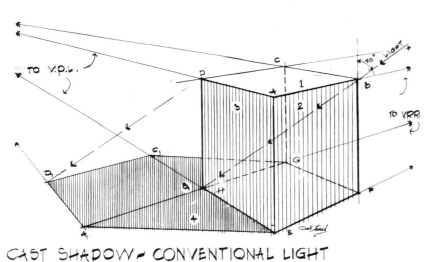

CAST SHADOW ~ CONVENTIONAL LIGHT

FIGURE 6-2: Note the square formed by points D_1, C_1, B_1 and A_1. This square is identical and parallel to the top plane of the cube D, C, B, A. After plotting this square in perspective (the lines for shadows also converge to both VPL and VPR), the base points C and G on the cube may be connected with points A_1 and E_1 to form the outline of the completed shadow. Note the value designations of the planes of the cube.

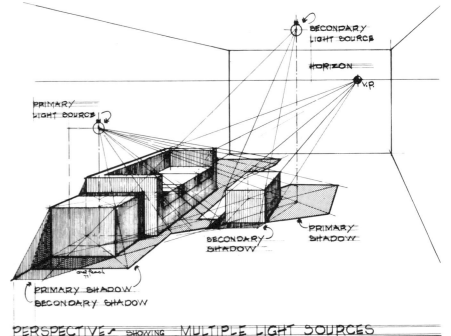

PERSPECTIVE ~ SHOWING MULTIPLE LIGHT SOURCES

FIGURE 6-4

54

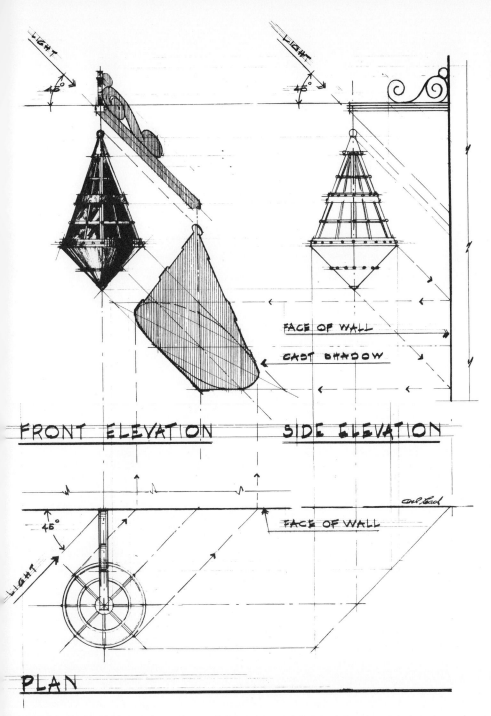

FRONT ELEVATION   SIDE ELEVATION

FACE OF WALL

CAST SHADOW

FACE OF WALL

PLAN

corner in the rear; again, conventional light. Once one is knowledgeable in the principles of light, shade, and shadow, and understands the conventional-light theory, one can move light about at one's own discretion within a drawing and the drawing will still read.

MECHANICAL DEVELOPMENT

Light, shade, and shadow can be mechanically plotted in both plan and elevation. Figure 6-3 is an example of this. Some illustrators plot all shade and shadow areas within a drawing using mechanical projection, and the student will do well to follow this procedure until he is familiar with the principles.

Unless the illustrator is locked into a light source predetermined by an architectural feature of the space he is representing (skylights, window areas, etc.), he may wish to establish his own light-source direction, use multiple light sources, or rely on "conventional light."

MULTIPLE LIGHT SOURCES

The same principles hold true in multiple light-source situations. (See Figure 6-4.) In these instances, it becomes necessary at times for the illustrator to emphasize one source and to deemphasize the other. This must be done with caution in order not to confuse the eyes of the viewer. A value study at the beginning stages of a drawing will solve many problems of this type.

EXERCISES IN LIGHT, SHADE AND SHADOWS

Study the following examples of shade and shadow principles. Each figure should be carefully examined before going on to the next. Note value designations as they pertain to each illustration.

FIGURE 6-4 *Opposite:* Light from more than one source must be analyzed by the illustrator. He must choose the one light source that is most advantageous for the illustration, emphasize this one source and minimize all others. Shadows of objects blocking the light rays follow perspective rules in the same way that furniture plans are located on the floor plan area; i.e. lines converge to the vanishing point or points used to construct the furniture. See also Figure 6-11.

FIGURE 6-3 *Left:* One may mechanically prove the plotting of shadows using a plan, front elevation and side elevation as shown above; the student should examine this illustration closely. Follow the directional arrows indicating lines of parallel light rays at a 45° angle to both horizontal and vertical planes, and their projected relationship throughout the three parts of this illustration, i.e. plan, front elevation and side elevation.

FIGURE 6-5, 5a: This drawing shows how light rays form shadows that are parallel and equal to both top and bottom surfaces of a cube when it is suspended above the surface receiving the shadow. The same principles examined in Figure 6-2 apply. Figure 6-5a The author has converted the lined portions of this exercise into a pencil stroke drawing to show an extension of the illustration in Figure 6-5.

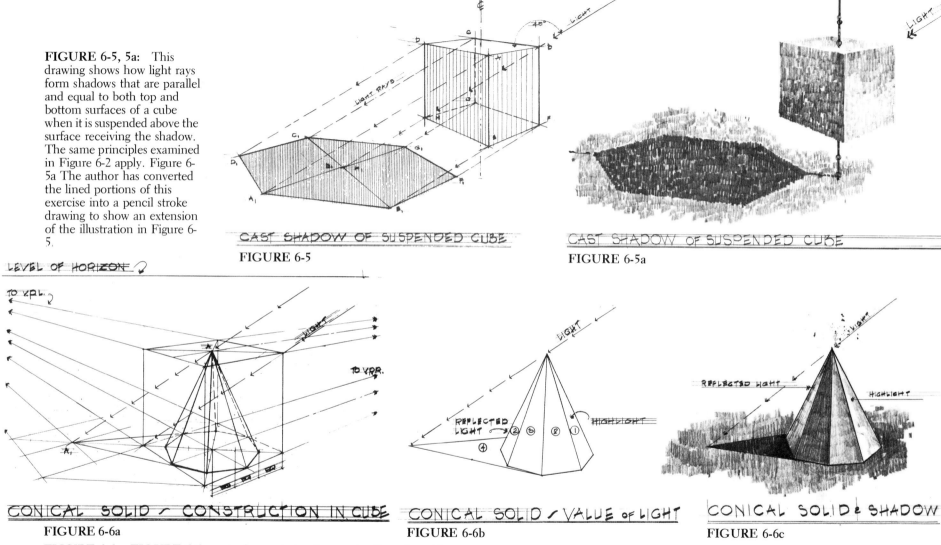

CAST SHADOW OF SUSPENDED CUBE

FIGURE 6-5

CAST SHADOW OF SUSPENDED CUBE

FIGURE 6-5a

LEVEL OF HORIZON

CONICAL SOLID / CONSTRUCTION IN CUBE

FIGURE 6-6a

CONICAL SOLID / VALUE OF LIGHT

FIGURE 6-6b

CONICAL SOLID & SHADOW

FIGURE 6-6c

FIGURE 6-6: **FIGURE 6-6a** again demonstrates the construction of an object within a cube. The base of this conical solid has been constructed in much the same manner as was the circle drawn in perspective as seen in Figure 5-3b of Chapter 5, "Perspective Theory and Practical Office Layout."
FIGURE 6-6a: Once the circle is formed, it is a simple matter to connect tangent points of intersection of this circle and the cube base perimeter lines. From this newly formed octagonal base, the conical solid is formed by connecting each intersection point along the base to the center point on the top plane of the cube.
FIGURES 6-6b and 6-6c carry the conical solid to its final rendered form. Note value designations on Figure 6-6b.

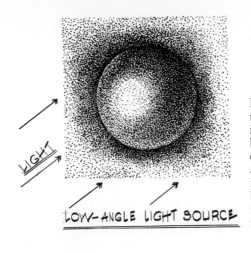

FIGURE 6-8: This illustration of a sphere shows parallel light rays striking the ball from a low angle. Although conventional light is used for most illustrations in this section, the student must become familiar with the effects of light sources from different directions. Note the hot spot created by the most intense light rays, and the gradual tonal gradation to the darkest area at the upper right. Reflected light causes the lower right and upper left areas to be one or two tonal values lighter than the darkest portion. This illustration was done on plate-finish bristol board using a medium-fine steel quill penpoint and waterproof ink.

LIGHT

LOW-ANGLE LIGHT SOURCE

PYRAMID & SHADOW

FIGURE 6-7a

FIGURE 6-7 *Below:* The pyramid (shown in **Figure 6-7a**) is the simplest of the solid shapes that can be constructed within a cube. All one need do is connect the four base corners to the center point on the upper cube surface. **Figure 6-7a** *Left:* shows a good pencil technique used to complete the exercise. Notice how the pencil strokes follow the slanted planes of the pyramid. Pencil techniques will be covered fully in Chapter 10, "Pencil Rendering."

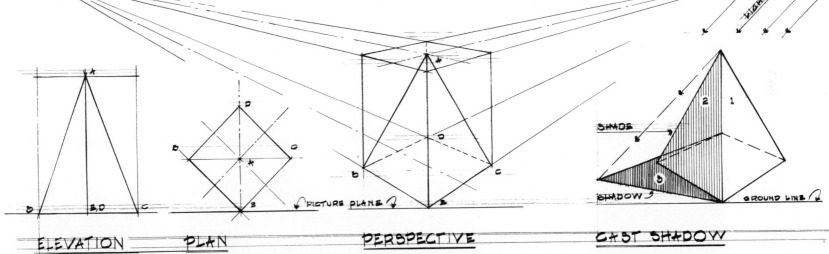

ELEVATION   PLAN   PERSPECTIVE   CAST SHADOW

FIGURE 6-7

57

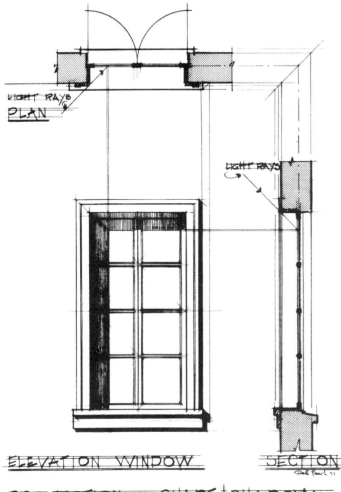

ELEVATION WINDOW   SECTION

PROJECTION OF SHADE & SHADOW

FIGURE 6-9: Here again, shadows may be plotted as was done in Figure 6-2. This treatment can be adapted for most any door or window illustration.

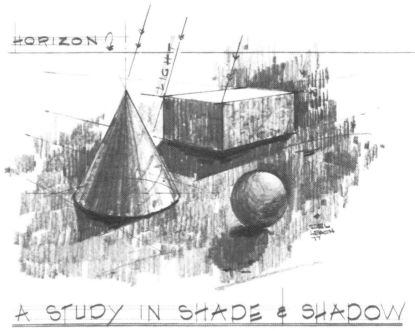

A STUDY IN SHADE & SHADOW

FIGURE 6-10: A 2H pencil on mylar was used for this study of various forms. The student should practice exercises such as this until light, shade and shadow principles are fully understood.

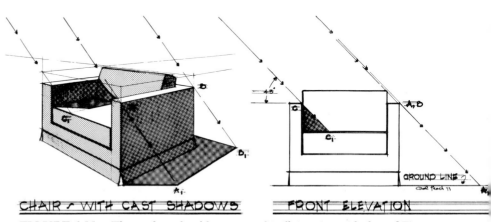

CHAIR WITH CAST SHADOWS   FRONT ELEVATION

FIGURE 6-11: The student should compare this illustration with that of Figure 6-1. The principles of shadow designation are the same although the light sources originated from different directions.

58

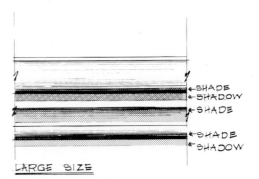

FIGURE 6-12 *Below:* Examine the molding detail section and elevation illustrated here and compare the details with the smaller-scale wall elevation at the left side of this illustration. It is easy to see how these principles apply to an interior rendering.

FIGURE 6-13 *Right:* Books on bookshelves are not usually illustrated completely, but are only indicated. This is done by darkening background shadow areas as shown and using some strokes that indicate diagonal books for interest. It is this darkened shadow area that gives the bookshelves depth and keeps the area from becoming static.

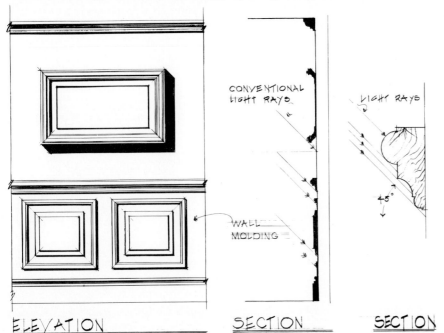

CONVENTIONAL LIGHT RAYS

LIGHT RAYS

WALL MOLDING

45°

SHADE
SHADOW
SHADE

SHADE
SHADOW

ELEVATION   SECTION   SECTION   ELEVATION-MOLDING

LARGE SIZE

FIGURE 6-14: This under-drawing of a real estate sales-conference room is the same as was created in Chapter 5, "Perspective Theory and Practical Office Methods," shown in Figure 5-22.

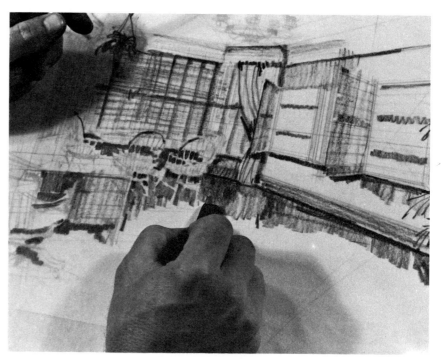

FIGURES 6-15, 15a *Above and Right:* A graphite stick and soft 2B carpenter's pencil are used to create a value study using an overlay of very thin architectural sketch paper.

VALUE STUDY OF AN INTERIOR SPACE

Now that basic principles of shade and shadow have been studied, the student is probably wondering what practical application all of the previous exercises can be made to create illustrations. Shade and shadow of each item whether exact or suggested, must be included in a finished illustration. The tying together of all of these shade and shadow areas within a drawing is accomplished with use of a value study.

EQUIPMENT

In order to create a value study, one will need light-weight tracing paper, a soft-lead carpenter's pencil, and a charcoal or graphite stick to cover large areas quickly and easily. These tools are inexpensive and expendable. Many times in the early stages, rendering lines or transfer marks are very faint and hard to read through heavier tracing paper. Light-weight architectural sketch paper is excellent for this because it is very thin and somewhat transparent. If the charcoal or graphite stick is soft enough, tears and rips in the paper will not be a big problem. Harder graphite does not perform as well; therefore, caution must be exercised.

PROCEDURE

In the following exercise, familiarity with the subject should be apparent. The real estate sales-conference room preliminary drawing from Chapter 5, "Perspective Theory and Practical Office Methods," will be carried one step further toward the finished stages of the illustration. A value study of this space must be done before the final drawing can begin. It is assumed that the student has created the necessary preliminary drawing as seen in Figure 5-22 in Chapter 5. (See Figure 6-14.)

As you will note, the preliminary drawing is now only linear in nature and nothing is apparent to emphasize depth except perspective. Windows are shuttered, so confusion as to light source is limited.

FIGURE 6-15A

FIGURE 6-16: Completed value study. Note space that has been left for copy, as this illustration was initially to be used for a publicity brochure.

Use a full-sized cover of tracing paper and tape it to the table directly over the preliminary drawing. Notice that the under-drawing is clearly visible beneath. Use a soft carpenter's pencil or graphite stick to build up value following both the illustration and what you know to be true based on the previously completed exercises. Do not forget "light (values) against dark" and "dark (values) against light." Sometimes, one must deviate from the rules in order to make the drawing have both definition and character; however, this must be done carefully and with knowledge. (Refer to Figure 6-15.)

In reality the oak chairs are dark but at this point the illustrator does not know if it will be advantageous to make them read light or dark. Notice how the area under the table is in deep shadow, and in order for the oak chairs to read they are left light. This must be done to minimize confusion for the viewer. If the oak chairs had been made dark, as they actually were, they would not stand out against the background. Also, if the background had

been left light, it would not appear correct because shadow would form under the table. Therefore, this area must be dark in value. Here we have a good example of the background principle referred to in Chapter 3, "How to See." The chairs are almost completely formed by their relationship to the background. No real outlines are needed, as is seen in Figure 6-16.

With a graphite stick of medium-hard lead, apply areas of graphite to the overlay sheet of tracing paper in varying tones of gray until, by squinting at this value study, you can determine where added tonal buildup may be needed in order for the drawing to read by itself. Work from light to dark very carefully, trying not to erase if possible. Remember, no lines are necessary for this study; only areas of lights and darks. (See Figure 6-16.)

Upon completion, this sheet should be tacked up in front of the illustrator for ready reference while working on the final illustration.

FIGURE 6-17a: Graphite from a lead pointer is sprinkled onto Clearprint® tracing paper. Notice the masking tape around the perimeter of the sheet. This will keep edges from tearing during constant usage.

FIGURE 6-17b: Lighter fluid is added to the graphite and rubbed into the paper surface with tissue paper. This acts as a binder to secure the graphite to the paper.

FIGURE 6-17d: Slip transfer paper between final under-drawing and illustration surface and secure with drafting tape.

FIGURE 6-17e: Transfer the drawing to an illustration surface by drawing over existing lines with either a fine point stylus or a dry ball-point pen.

FIGURE 6-17c: Burnish the surface using a clean tissue. This will remove surplus graphite and keep unwanted smudges from transferring to the illustration surface when this sheet is used.

SELECTING THE ILLUSTRATION SURFACE

Once the value study has been completed, the finished illustration can be considered. All that remains to be done before the final drawing is initiated is to decide upon methods of reproduction of the finished product. The two primary considerations are: 1.) will the drawing be made on tracing paper or drafting mylar for ease of reproduction or; 2.) will the drawing be done on opaque material such as kid-finish bristol board, thus determining photographic reproduction to be the only choice when copies are desired.

If transparent paper or plastic drafting medium is used, it need only be secured over the under-drawing to trace the elements, delineating the drawing completely as one works from one side of the illustration to the other. However, if bristol or illustration board is used, the image must be transferred to this new surface before delineation can occur.

TRANSFERRING

Transferring the line under-drawing to an illustration surface could be a problem without proper instruction.

COMMERCIAL TRANSFER PAPER

To find the most economical method of transfer for the student, one begins with the selection of transfer paper. This paper is coated with graphite (sometimes referred to as graphite paper) and is sold commercially by the roll in dark gray as well as other colors. Because it is graphite coated, the resulting transferred line will erase very much like pencil line.

DO-IT-YOURSELF TRANSFER PAPER

Students can make graphite transfer paper in the following manner. (See Figures 6-17a through e.)

Using a sheet of heavy tracing paper, begin by taping both front and back of all edges. Use ordinary masking tape for this purpose, reducing the probability of the paper tearing. One can and should use this paper over and over again before it wears out.

Obtain enough powdered graphite for the size paper you are using. Use about two teaspoons for a 24-in × 36-in sheet. Graphite from pencil-lead pointers works well for this. The only other items you need are lighter fluid (squirt-can type) and ordinary bathroom tissue.

Begin by sprinkling powdered graphite over the surface of your taped sheet. (See Figure 6-17a.) Squirt lighter fluid over the graphite and begin to rub the resulting paste in a circular motion into the surface of the paper. (See Figure 6-17b.) You will soon see the lighter fluid evaporating; squirt some additional fluid onto the area and continue rubbing. Work only on small areas at a time and work the graphite well into the entire surface. Upon completion, use a clean tissue to rub or burnish the graphite-coated paper. The transfer sheet is now completed and will be relatively smudge free. (See Figure 6-17c.)

PROCEDURE

Assume that for this pencil drawing we will be using three-ply kid-finish bristol board. Begin by taping the bristol board to a drafting table and place the under-drawing in such a position as to leave good negative space around the pencil-work portion of the finished drawing surface. Tape this under-drawing in place at the top corners only. Now, between the under-drawing sheet and the bristol board, insert the transfer sheet you have just made. Tape everything in place and you are ready to begin transferring. (See Figure 6-17d.)

A dry, ball-point pen (fine point) is a good stylus, or one can buy a stylus at any art store. Be especially cautious if a new ball-point pen is used; the ink will tend to smudge all over the under-drawing and your hands.

Press with the stylus as you would when drawing, using the T square and triangle to ensure straight lines. (See Figure 6-17e.) If you were successful constructing the transfer paper, the resulting transfer should be clean, sharp, and readable.

Before removing the under-drawing from the illustration surface, place registration marks at all four corners, far away from any area that might be a part of the actual drawing. Stick a pin through each registration mark into the illustration sheet. Circle these pin holes on the illustration board for ease of location later. These marks will serve to re-locate the under-drawing in the same position if additional transferring is required.

Further use of the under-drawing, value study, and bristol board onto which you have transferred the real estate sales-conference-room image will be needed to complete a portion of Chapter 10, "Pencil Renderings." The techniques you have learned up to this point are an integral part of all illustrations you will be doing both in color and black and white.

CHAPTER 7

Color

COLOR IS SOMETHING that is taken so much for granted by most of us. What if color did not exist and we saw everything in various tones of gray, such as we see when watching black-and-white film or television?

Color is beautiful and awe inspiring; it is something to marvel at and admire. As one develops the ability to see the environment around him, one will gain a much better understanding of color and what makes up the spectrum which, in turn, controls what one sees; i.e., as light falls on objects, certain light rays are absorbed and others are reflected, thus determining how we see the colors that we do.

Color, of course, plays an important part in the everyday work of both the designer and illustrator. It is that extra ingredient used to give the viewer added, instantly recognizable features that will make him want to relate more to an illustration and want to become part of it.

Color principles are the same in theory for most media used for illustrations, and only the application principles change. This book will be more concerned with these application principles than with actual color theory.

The subject of color as a science is too vast an area to cover completely within the scope of this book. Many books have been written on color theory and it will be assumed that the serious student of illustration will have had instruction in color theory and principles or will purchase books necessary to supplement the application techniques shown in this book. It is felt that techniques of brush handling, painting, drawing, sketching, etc. are as important to an illustration as is the color. Designers and architects usually select colors of paint, fabrics, carpeting, and so on. The illustrator, through practice, experimentation, and research must learn to reproduce these colors by learning to look into a color and see what basic colors are involved. Experience is about the only thing that will teach one exactly what colors to mix together in order to obtain a particular color.

Probably one of the most thoroughly thought-out and profusely illustrated books on color for illustrators is by Arthur L. Guptill entitled *Color in Sketching and Rendering*. It was published by Reinhold in August of 1935. In this book, Mr. Guptill discusses all aspects of color theory and shows many applications that are directly concerned with sketching and rendering.

Two other reasonably good books concerned with the illustrator and his art are written by Albert O. Halse, entitled *Architectural Rendering: The Techniques of Contemporary Presentation*, 2nd edition, 1972 and *The Use of Color in Interiors*, 1978. Both are published by McGraw-Hill Book Co.

In these books, we are learning techniques of illustration that deal with many media. Each medium has its own set of color names and designations. The student must experiment with the colors of each pigment form so he can visually relate a factory-given designation to its true color. Many derivatives of the basic spectrum colors are available, and certain color names are carried from one medium to another.

Mixing colored pigments together within each medium to form the various tones and colors will be covered later in this book.

It is unfortunate that one cannot provide a thorough study of a subject as all encompassing as color within this book, but such aspects are best left to those specialty books where space is adequate to cover the subject thoroughly.

CHAPTER 8

The Importance of Sketching

As ONE LEARNS how to observe, see, relate to, and remember his surroundings, more importance should be placed on graphically recording images of objects observed. The quickest, nonphotographic approach in this direction revolves around one's ability to sketch. Sketching, unlike the formal structure of renderings, is a fast, loose, graphic description of objects, landscape, people, and things relative to commercial ventures as well as leisure-time activities. That ability which enables one to pick up a pen or pencil and quickly delineate objects in a realistic and natural way is very satisfying indeed (see Figure 8-1).

This chapter is not so much concerned with the depiction of objects directly related to interior or architectural design illustrations, but is more concerned with instilling a desire in the student to explore the area of drawing for fun. This writer feels that such a desire is secretly hidden inside almost everyone, but the manifestation of the desire to draw is not proportional to the drive, determination, and practice required to accomplish such a goal. Drawing is fun; and when one is able to draw houses, barns, trees, landscapes, or anything else, rich and rewarding experiences await that person. But, again, let us remember the work and determination required.

If one is to succeed in the fields relating to graphic description and illustration, one must know and be able to represent nature as real, natural, and as inviting as possible. Because of this, all sketching discussed in this book will refer to and stress the reality of representation.

MATERIALS

Drawing from nature means just what it says. One carries with him tools and devices that enable a quick set-up, comfortable atmosphere, and adequate material selection when sketching. The following is a list of materials required for the student when outfitting for out-of-doors sketching, but it is assumed the student will make substitutions that suit his personal tastes. Comfort devices such as stools, cushions, or ground cloths

FIGURE 8-1: Sketching out of doors is an excellent learning experience and it is also very enjoyable. Here the author is sketching the brewery in Figure 8-8.

FIGURE 8-2: The author's sketch case has a top that tilts to almost any angle covered with white linoleum. This forms a cleanable working surface that is excellent for use in sketching with pen, pencil or water color.

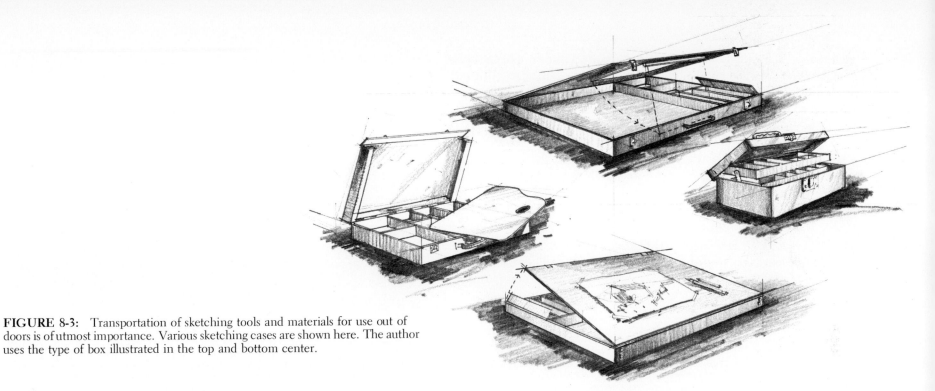

FIGURE 8-3: Transportation of sketching tools and materials for use out of doors is of utmost importance. Various sketching cases are shown here. The author uses the type of box illustrated in the top and bottom center.

are suggested, but these items tend to get heavy if carried over long distances. *Proper prior planning applies here as in any form of illustration.*

One should also concern oneself with choice of media and work around the special needs of that medium.

The following items are needed:

1. Pencils: H, 2H, HB, 2B, 4B, 6B,
2. Pen, points, charcoal, conté crayon, graphite stick
3. Sanding block
4. Ink: choose the right ink for pens selected
5. Erasers: pink, art gum, ink, or white
6. Illustration board or paper
   a. Kid-finish bristol board (heavy weight)
   b. Plate-finish bristol board (heavy weight)
   c. Drawing pad of all-purpose drawing paper
   d. Water-color board (if required)

7. Masonite sketch-paper holder. One should obtain the type with a cut-out handle (for ease of handling), metal clips (to anchor paper at the top) and a rubber retaining device (to keep paper from flapping in strong breezes). (Note: strips cut from rubber inner tubes or surgical rubber tubing knotted behind the board work well for this.)

8. Carrying case for papers, drawing surfaces, and other supplies (see Figure 8-2). In lieu of the masonite unit previously described, the author uses a wooden box large enough to hold all items needed. The lid is linoleum covered and tilts to form a slanted drawing surface. (See Figure 8-3.)

9. Metal box (if desired) to carry pens, pencils, erasers, etc. A fisherman's tackle box is perfect for this. The compartmentalization of these boxes tends to keep one organized as well as to separate items from one another, thus keeping a cleaner environment in which to work.

10. Dry cleaning pad and drafting brush. These are important items with which to keep a clean drawing clean. Rubber powder within a porous cloth bag is used to both aid in hand movement when sketching

(the hands glides on beads of rubber, thus keeping dirty fingers from touching the drawing surface) and as a dry, light-duty eraser. It is not meant to erase lines, but it is convenient for removing smudges of graphite. *Caution*: oil from fingers creates invisible fingerprints on smooth surfaces such as plate-finish bristol board. When graphite is laid over these prints, the oil will tend to repel the graphite and a light fingerprint will show through.

11. Plastic drop cloths. These are a must. Do not include the flimsy painter's drop cloths found for less than a dollar at most paint stores; these are so thin that they can become a problem in the wind. Builder's Visqueen® is best and, in small sheets, is not too bulky.

12. Water containers. If one choses to sketch in color, he must decide if water is needed. If not available within the sketching vicinity, it must be transported. Expanding plastic bottles are good for this purpose as they may be reduced in size as water is used.

13. Plastic sketch cover. Again, do not use the thin plastic referred to previously. A shower curtain sewn to a continuous strip of elastic is good to cover the sketching surface in case of sudden rain. Plate-finish bristol board will be completely ruined in moments if just a few sprinkles hit the surface. Water drops expand surface fibers which do not return to their original pressed state.

14. A small sketch book should be carried to quickly record scenes of nature. These thumbnail sketches are a helpful way to dissolve some of the fears the student may have from being intimidated by vast, unending, natural space. Many artists who sketch from nature use these small sketch books to aid in later studio drawing and composition of larger studies and finished drawings. (See Figure 8-4.)

SKETCHING

One will tend to be overwhelmed with the choices of subject matter upon first venturing into the out-of-doors burdened down with carrying box, paper, tools, drop cloths, and other paraphernalia. As one studies perspective in the studio, all of the subjects are neatly and simply contained within the restricted view the example illustrations portray. Quite unlike this restricted representation, nature is all encompassing, endless and, at first, overwhelming.

As explained in Chapter 3, "How to See," the reader must first reduce what he sees to its basic forms. In the first awareness exercise, let us examine a tree. Trees appear as they do because of their composite makeup, consisting of many branches and leaves. In order to be able to

FIGURE 8-4: The artist and student shown here are using small sketch pads to record information to be used at a later date. Notice the tripod stand incorporating a sketch table. This is a highly portable unit and should be considered for purchase by the serious student.

completely read a tree, one must study the following: tree shape or silhouette; the bark and form of the trunk; leaves; how the tree grows out of the ground; shape, size, and texture of the trunk (small and straight, large and grotesque, smooth or rough); whether the roots run exposed on top of the ground; how far the trunk extends above the ground before any branches appear; etc. It may seem involved to examine each part of nature in such detail, but it is necessary if one is to record what really exists. The student cannot abstract nature until he or she knows the importance of realism. Knowing what to leave out is just as important as knowing what to put into the sketch.

FIGURE 8-5 *Left:* Basic nature studies are an important part of sketching. They help the student to simplify the complexities of nature into understandable elements. Drawing courtesy of Mr. and Mrs. Stephen D. Blacker.

FIGURE 8-6 *Below:* Even free-form elements of nature may be broken down into planes. Note the circles drawn in perspective; they become oval in shape when viewed in various positions.

Such is the case with everything one may choose to portray, whether it is a weathered wood fence, barn door with rusted and broken hinges, a majestic stand of aspen trees, or a gnarled, old, oak tree. Each portion of each item must be examined and reexamined and then examined once again; drawn, sketched, and sketched again. The process of learning to remember and record what one sees is a very long and involved, step-by-step venture and must not be taken lightly.

As one examines objects in the out-of-doors he will find that the perspective theory learned in previous chapters is more difficult to visualize than it was when dealing with very limited subjects. Each item drawn had its visible horizon, vanishing points, and borders. Vanishing points were easy to establish because one could trace lines back to points of intersection, working with flat, two-dimensional surfaces as we were. Now, however, one must establish horizon lines at eye level, vanishing points by examination of real objects, and size by estimation and containment of objects within the bounds one creates. All of this will come to the diligent student only through practice. The beginning artist should not believe any sketch or illustration is sacred. Each practice sketch is only a learning experience, and paper is the most expendable supply in this training.

PRACTICE EXERCISES
Practice drawing the items shown in this section, sketching and delineating as close to the illustrated technique as one is able. Only after mastering a technique by copying, should one begin to think about developing one's own. Of course, no two people draw exactly alike, so just by copying one

will tend to develop shading methods, vignetting form, and a style of laying down strokes.

VIGNETTING
Study very carefully in each case how vignetting is carried out without the perimeter of the illustration becoming too obvious. Examine the negative space outside this perimeter also. *The purpose of vignetting is to separate an important object or portion of nature from its immediate background, thus making the point of interest obvious to the viewer.* The viewer should

FIGURE 8-7: Once basic elements are understood, further development of these elements should be studied and practiced.

not be totally aware of this fact. Very seldom is a sketch ever carried to the extremities of the paper, and one should not depend on the mat (if one is used) to cover up border mistakes.

Vignetting also helps lead the viewer's eye into the picture. Use of a mat is still advisable but should not be depended upon for the end result. Again, study how vignetting helps create bounds within the perimeter of the area to be covered by a mat.

EXAMPLE #1

In Figure 8-5, aspen leaves were chosen by the author as a study in basic nature forms. As was stated earlier, reduction of all objects to basic forms is the only way to understand the basis for reality and life in nature drawings. This branch was selected at random and was drawn very carefully under natural sunlight (in this case, a one-directional light source). The branch was placed on a medium-gray background to avoid an overabundance of reflected light. Definite shadows were purposely left out to decrease confusion. Complexity of shapes casting hard-edged shadows on a background as well as flat or curvilinear shapes can create confusion in the eyes of the viewer. This is a prime example of knowing what to leave out.

Kid-finish bristol board was selected as the drawing surface in this instance and four grades of pencil lead, 2H, HB, 4B, and 6B were used.

Basic structure was first examined and planes were established. Study the under-drawing as to plane direction and preliminary leaf characteristics. (See Figure 8-6.)

The viewer should notice the white vein lines within each leaf in the finished drawing. These veins are part of the leaf structure and cannot be left out. A fork tine was used in this instance to score all vein lines in the paper before applying graphite. The grooves, being below the surface, did not pick up graphite and were thus left light in tone. This is, of course, an illustrator trick, but the results created speak for themselves. Both fine and wide vein lines were created by turning the tine point while engraving each leaf structure.

Lighter leaves were created with 2H lead strokes; medium tones were made by first burnishing the entire leaf surface with 2H or HB; and a final darkening was made with 4B and 6B leads. If the 4B or 6B leads had been used directly on the rough surface of kid-finish bristol board, too much graphite would have been scraped into the vein channels and these channels would not read as clearly as required. Not all veins need be the same tone, however; just as in other line work, variation in tone, width, and character create interest and reality within the total picture.

Background as well as shadow was left to the viewer's imagination since it would have detracted from the subject as well as created confusion.

EXAMPLE #2

Refer to the drawing in Figure 8-7. In this sketch, the wagon was obviously the main source of inspiration; but notice the aspen trees. Each tree is made up of many branches like that shown in the previous illustration, and here the author has carried the nature study one step further. Examine bark direction indications, tone, and the presence of numerous accent marks (old branch connections) around the trunks. Observe how much trunk extends above ground before the limbs become prominent, and the fact that trunks grow straight out of the ground with little or no root-system exposure. As you study these illustrations, more of what was learned in Chapter 3, "How to See," will become apparent.

This wagon caught the eye of the author not far from Aspen, Colorado. Obviously it had been many years since this antiquated piece of transportation had seen service. Overgrown with vines and plants, it was a beautiful, hard-line contrast to its free-form background.

Here, plate-finish bristol board was chosen as a drawing surface to create a smoother appearance. The pencil softness was increased to 3B, 4B, and 6B in order to maintain darkness of values within the required areas. An HB pencil was used to burnish the water area and create reflections. Most of the boards and wagon structure were done using 3B and 4B pencils, and a 6B pencil was used in dark shadow areas. It was observed that this entire sketch was not a deep in over-all tonal value because of the smooth plate surface. The absence of tooth on this particular surface lends itself to pen drawings more than to pencil.

EXAMPLE #3

In this sketch (Figure 8-8), an old brewery in Telluride, Colorado, was chosen as the subject matter. Kid-finish bristol board was selected as were 2H, 4B, and 6B pencils. An HB pencil was also used to create some dark areas where burnishing was desired, thus obtaining a dark area without an overabundance of graphite buildup.

The reader should examine particularly the technique used to vignette the subject matter. "Dark against light and light against dark" work extremely well for the foreground vignette techniques. Notice how background was added to allow the artist to leave the fence rails light so as to accentuate each marking, typical of aspen branches.

Squint and examine the sketch as a whole. *Squinting reduces all of the details to a value study.* Examine the photograph of the brewery and preliminary drawing (Figure 8-9). As one will observe, light does not fall

equally on each side of the brewery or the cube. This building can be reduced to the simplicity of a block and a pyramid.

Notice at the leading corner of the building the intersection of two unequally lighted planes. So as not to lose detail in the left plane, this surface was made darker than the right plane, beginning at the leading corner and gradually getting lighter as it recedes back from this corner. Notice also the rock-corner building method. One must examine building methods in order to draw them adequately.

Dark-gray openings portray the unlighted interior seen through the barred windows and the jagged opening in the rocks. Rafters are visible but

---

FIGURE 8-8 *Left:* Compare this finished drawing with the preliminary drawing in **Figure** 8-9. Note the simple cube and pyramid that form the basic shape of the main structure.

FIGURE 8-10 *Below:* In order to compensate for the lack of foreground as seen in the photograph of the buildings that were drawn in Figure 8-8, artistic license was used by the author to create the needed interest in this area. Refer again to Figure 8-8.

FIGURE 8-9: This preliminary perspective and value study was used to develop the drawing in Figure 8-8.

are only suggested in the darkness. This darkness was first burnished with an HB pencil and worked over with a 6B.

All of the background is only suggested, as is the aspen tree to the left. This is a good example of how a tree can be the boundary on one side of the subject, whereas the opposite boundary is not as pronounced. Suggested roofing and shutters end the right side and are more subtle than the middle-ground tree. Because the tree is in the middle ground, it does not become too important, although it is highly detailed.

FOREGROUND, MIDDLE GROUND AND BACKGROUND
In each sketch, whether it is of a few objects or a landscape, one finds certain techniques that work better and make the drawing look more believable. Divisions of area within a picture separate it into three definite stages: *foreground, middle ground, and background.*

"Foreground! Don't forget foreground!" These are words spoken by a beautiful and wise friend. Foreground is, of course, much more detailed than either middle ground or background.

The photograph of the Telluride Brewery (Figure 8-10) clearly depicts an absence of foreground. It was felt by the artist that more emphasis was needed to push the main building mass to the middle ground; therefore, foreground taken from adjacent fenced areas was included in the sketch. ("Artistic license" is the term generally referred to when substitutions in nature are made merely to make a drawing or sketch read well.)

Be extremely careful to select just the right amount of foreground. Too many things too detailed with strong contrasts of value and color can be harmful to the entire sketch. The eyes of the viewer must enter the picture and not be redirected elsewhere. Diagonal lines, as learned in basic design, can lead one's eyes out of the planned direction. Foreground acts as the vignette border at the bottom of the sketch.

In the next sketch of an old, weather-beaten, mining cabin (Figure 8-11) observe how a weak foreground becomes part of the middle ground and needs the addition of a strong element closer to the viewer (See insert photograph Figure 8-11a). Using this technique, the house, rock, and debris areas will be pushed deep into the picture in Figure 8-12 by adding a strong foreground element.

FIGURE 8-11   *Below:* Compare this illustration with that of Figure 8-11a and 8-12 and observe how the cabin is pushed into the middle ground with the addition of a foreground element.

FIGURE 8-11a   *Left:* This photograph clearly indicates the need for a strong foreground element in the sketch.

FIGURE 8-12: In order to retain continuity in the drawing, a large pine tree was introduced as the foreground element. This free-form, natural element serves as a good complement to the hard lines of the structure and tends to act as a vignette in the right foreground area.

FIGURE 8-13: It is often necessary to introduce abstract areas into a sketch to counteract visual elements that appear too strong. Cloud indications were used here to counteract the strong directional element created by the windmill blades.

FIGURE 8-14 *Opposite:* Strong foreground is very evident in this water-color painting. Vignetting with the use of natural elements provides not only a soft approach into the picture, but also creates a way of terminating the painting at the bottom.

The foreground in Figure 8-12 was added to the value study after the finished drawing (Figure 8-11) had been completed, because the artist was not satisfied. This added element was then introduced into the finished sketch.

This mining-cabin sketch is a good example of single and multiple pencil-stroke techniques used to depict lumber and boards. Each group of strokes was carried the full length of a particular board without the chisel pencil lead leaving the paper. The sharp point formed with the chisel edge, or a separate sharp-pointed HB pencil was used to darken cracks between lumber and create shadows under the upturned ends. For clarity, the inside of the cabin was left dark. Background was only suggested. A thorough study of additional pencil techniques will be found in Chapter 10, "Pencil Rendering."

COLOR

If color is to be used, all of the same rules hold true for value representation except that the simulation of sky may form the completion of the vignette. Sky in the previous pencil sketches was left up to the viewer's imagination.

FIGURE 8-16: The quick-drying ink used for this sketch is waterproof, smudgeproof and completely indelible. This technique lends itself to quick sketches as well as any the author has used. Refer to the illustration in Figure 11-6 showing the type of pen used to create this sketch.

Refer to Figure 8-13. In this drawing of a windmill, sky has been indicated by the introduction of cloud patterns. These have been abstracted in order to soften the visual power of the windmill blades. Direction of line here has been interrupted, and a more pleasing result is evident.

Examine the water-color painting of a small church found in Canada. (See Figure 8-14.) Strong foreground gives this drawing great depth. Notice how the tones of foliage were painted leaving the fence outlined against a very strong background. The fence becomes a design element used by the artist to guide the eye of the viewer into the picture. The brilliant blue of the church roof has been softened by the pine-covered hills of the background, and the jagged silhouette of this hilltop intersecting the strong, straight lines of the church roof tend to soften angular structures such as this. Sunflowers in the foreground add a happy thought to the very colorful painting. Transparent water color was used on rough water-color board; no opaque colors were added.

In the example of a quick, on-the-spot drawing of an old farm house in northern Minnesota (Figure 8-15), interest has been created by two ele-

FIGURE 8-17: Comfort while drawing can be thought of as warmth as well as drawing position. Here, warmth was considered the most important element of comfort out of necessity.

FIGURE 8-18 *Right:* A quill pen, although a nuisance on a windy day, can be an exciting medium in which to sketch. Line weight variation within this sketch speaks for itself.

ments. First, the main tree mass was left a very light value to show good detail in the balance of the house. Second, vignetting in the form of fence posts and wire form a good, readily identifiable foreground to which the viewer can relate. This sketch was done on a bond sketch pad with pencils available at the time, and is a good example of quick pencil work done with no special tools—only a drugstore-variety pencil and pad.

A note should be said here about fast-drying ink for sketching. Up to now, pencil has been the primary medium involved in quick sketches. Although pencil is most often available, another medium is worth consideration; that is the plunger-type felt-tipped pen. Ink is dispensed from a felt-tipped point as pressure is applied to it; it dries immediately, and is smudge-proof and indelible.

In the illustration of a half-timber house in Chartres, France (Figure 8-16), all construction lines are visible and add to the sketch, as do the suggestion of people. This type of sketch is very quick and spontaneous because permanence of the ink allows no margin for error.

Earlier in this chapter we stressed comfort for drawing out of doors. When the situation arises that requires one to sketch something fast and the desire to capture the object is strong enough, comfort is not usually of the utmost importance. In Figure 8-17 one should notice that the primary comfort thought was for warmth, and drawing position was secondary.

A quill pen was used to execute the sketch of a wagon on kid-finish bristol board. The fast drying of ink in a quill pen on a windy day is a real nuisance but does not need to deter one from using a quill pen. Here, the variations in strokes not possible with a technical type of pen having reservoir ink supply are worth all of the problems encountered in its use.

Sketching is ever so important in the visual learning process. The ability to remember what we see can be greatly improved through practice. Remember, drawing is fun and the more accomplished one becomes, the more rewarding will be the results.

CHAPTER 9

The Interior as Seen by an Illustrator

INTERIOR DESIGNERS AND architectural and commercial art illustrators are all creators of illusions—illusions of products that do not exist except in the mind of the designer or architect. The creation of illusion through expertise in techniques is only a part of the total rendering experience. Rendering requires more than skill in drawing and painting.

Knowledge of the subject matter being presented is an essential part of each rendering project. The artist, like the designer, must know and understand materials, fabrics, textures, and lighting, and all other aspects of an interior and be able to faithfully reproduce these to the satisfaction of the designer.

STYLE

If two artists are illustrating the same subject matter, each will represent that subject matter in a different style. Each will see differently and will, therefore, interpret what he sees just as differently. Style is somewhat the same as technique except that many techniques may be involved to make up an artist's style. (Refer to Figures 9-1 and 9-1a.)

Each student will want to develop his own style. This will happen in due time if he is aware enough to realize how important basic techniques and design principles are. Awareness is the key. (See Chapter 3, "How to See.") Individual style can only be developed after one learns to faithfully represent all those elements that comprise an illustration. Practice in representation of elements done within a prescribed technique will give the student the confidence and knowledge required to develop his own style. A successful abstract painter must be an accomplished draftsperson within his chosen medium before he can become accomplished in the abstract. One cannot successfully deviate into the abstract without fully understanding reality. So it is with interior design rendering. One must learn to reproduce reality within accepted commercial standards before developing his own special style.

FIGURE 9-1

FIGURES 9-1 *Opposite,* **9-1a** *Above:* Compare the two renderings and notice the completely different styles used to illustrate the same subject matter. Each illustrator, after years of practice, will develop his own distinctive style that will set him apart from his peers.
Interior Designer: Anthony Hail; Interior Design Consultant: The Author; Illustrators: Figure 9-1—The Author, Figure 9-1a—Larry Bratton; Project: Best Friend Bar—Mills Hyatt House, Charleston, SC.

Figures 9-2 *Left*, **9-2a** *Right:* After a style has been adopted by the illustrator, he may be called upon to provide renderings in his style, but completely different in terms of mood. Examine these two illustrations closely to see how this has been accomplished successfully.

Interior Designer: Anthony Hail; Design Consultant/Illustrator: The Author; Project: Lounge—Mills Hyatt House, Charleston, SC.

MOOD

Each illustration the student does will incorporate certain characteristics that make up the mood of the illustration. Mood is that certain atmosphere which makes the viewer want to identify with and become a part of the illustration.

Lighting, angle of view, medium and technique used, use of scale figures, etc., all contribute to the finished mood. The illustrator can, using the same elements, angle of view, and medium, create two renderings that are entirely different in atmosphere. (See Figures 9-2 and Figure 9-2a.) Artistic license, as a term, can sometimes be used when referring to this creation of atmosphere.

The successful renderer must be able to understand what his client

(usually a designer or architect) requires in terms of mood. Even if all necessary elements within a space are carefully and faithfully reproduced, the client may not be happy with the illustration if the agreed-upon atmosphere is not represented. Many times the artist sees a space differently from his client. Adequate communication about the look of the resulting illustration must be carried out before any sketches or layouts are begun. Samples of the illustrator's work must be discussed along with any special effects required by that designer.

Renderings are sales tools, and each designer will require somewhat different aspects of sales representation. The total look of an illustration must be geared to complement the product being sold by your client. Unsatisfactory renderings are usually the result of poor communication.

FIGURE 9-3: Light sources must be controlled so as to lessen confusion. Multiple light sources must be reduced to one dominant source with other sources of light being secondary in importance. See also Figure 6-4 to study this principle further.
Illustrator: Larry Bratton

LIGHTING

An interior design illustration, unlike a rendering of the exterior of a building, depends entirely on manufactured lighting for its atmosphere. One does not have sky, trees, landscape, and single-source sunlighting to help create the necessary illusions. One must establish light directions first. Notice that this writer uses the plural "directions." By examination of most interiors lighted by man-made light, the presence of multiple light sources becomes very apparent (See Figure 9-3).

These multiple light sources create multiple shadows for each object within a space; these shadows are not all uniform in intensity, direction, or shape as light is reflected, absorbed, and broken up to a much greater extent than is apparent in an exterior situation. The student must be aware of exactly what does happen to light in situations of multiple light sources. (See Figure 6-4, Chapter 6, "Value Study of Shade and Shadows.")

In order to create illusions of reality, the beginner must be familiar with not only environmental conditions, but with all of the individual elements that comprise a finished design project. Furniture of all periods, from historic to contemporary, must be learned as to lines, fabrics, wood used, and construction methods. Thorough knowledge of period and contemporary background settings is a must. The successful interior renderer must be able, on request, to graphically reproduce such elements as English Tudor panelling, French carved doors, and windows, drapery treatments, rugs, and chandeliers true to the period, as well as all contemporary architectural forms, surfaces, and corresponding furniture. For the illustrator to acquire a knowledge only of period furniture is not adequate for purposes of accurate representation. Here, again, atmosphere is very meaningful. One would not, and should not, employ the same atmosphere or mood techniques to illustrate an English Tudor interior as would be used to create a clean-line, light, contemporary interior of concrete, chrome, and glass. Perhaps the above statement seems very elementary; but, basically speaking, it usually holds true for all illustrative purpose.

CHOOSE A MEDIUM TO FIT THE JOB

The medium chosen for illustrations is a governing factor in the creation of proper mood. Light-hearted as well as somber moods may be created in all media, although some techniques work better in certain instances. Use of color is a prerequisite when presenting an interior that depends highly on color to create atmosphere. In some instances, black-and-white illustrations just do not tell the entire story. Likewise, complete absence of color may create the best possible atmosphere for a drawing in which architectural detail, line, and, form are much more important than color. (See Figure 9-4.)

ANGLE OF VIEW

When examining an interior space and discussing the aspects of it with the client, angle of view is most important. The same space viewed from various angles becomes entirely different in look, feeling, and, most of all, content. The illustrator must establish content within a rendering so that the selling tool he is creating can do the job it is expected to do.

Examine Figures 9-5 and 9-6. These two preliminary drawings were needed in order for the client to decide on the angle of view for the finished illustration. Figure 9-5 is a photostat positive print of a pencil drawing on tracing paper. Figure 9-6 is pencil on drafting mylar.

FIGURE 9-4 *Left:* The use of color in this illustration of a bar that has been designed almost totally in wood, could do little to add to atmosphere. This type of line work tells an adequate story to the viewer. In instances such as this, one must decide just how important color is to the total design.
Designer/Illustrator: The Author; Project: Preliminary Presentation for The Big Four Restaurant, San Francisco, CA.

FIGURE 9-5: Preliminary sketch used in meetings with the designer/client to establish the angle of view.
Designer: Anthony Hail; Design Consultant/Illustrator: The Author; Project: New York Residence.

FIGURE 9-6: Alternate view of the room seen in Figure 9-5. The designer in this case felt that more interest would be gained from a rendering based on this revision.
Designer: Anthony Hail; Design Consultant/Illustrator: The Author; Project: New York Residence.

Consider the decorator who employs the services of an illustrator to create a rendering for client presentation. In an illustration, it is very important that the illustrator emphasize whatever his client requires, and to minimize those items that are not so important. The illustrator who gets carried away rendering automobiles in a newly designed auto showroom and de-emphasizes the architecture, may not satisfy his architect client. Mutual agreement of all concerned as to angle of view and content is a must.

SCALE FIGURES

More often than not, scale figures do more harm than good in an interior rendering. Unless the illustration is of a space usually inhabited by many people, overuse of scale figures may become a negative factor. Scale figures are exactly what the name implies—figures in proper scale relation to different areas within a rendering, thereby giving the viewer instant size and scale relationship within that drawing. Figures can date a rendering because of clothes style, hair length, etc.; and renderings should not be so dated. (See Figures 9-7 and 9-7a.)

Color illustrations containing scale figures can become very confusing because of clothing color. One must remember that the designer-client is not interested in viewing figures clothed in bright colors; he wants to see a representation of an interior that will sell his ideas—not clothes. Brightly colored clothing will cause the viewer's eyes to bounce from one figure to another, thus by-passing the atmosphere required to make the viewer identify with the drawing. Clothing of figures must be subdued enough not to become obvious. They should blend into the illusion being created and

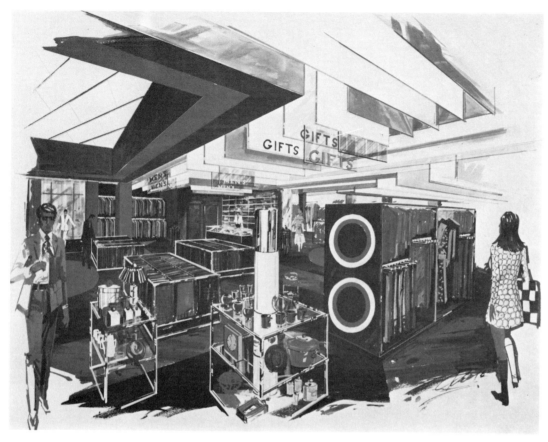

FIGURES 9-7, *Left:* 9-7a *Opposite:* Scale figures should complement an interior rendering without distracting from it. They should accomplish exactly what the term implies, i.e., establish human scale relationship and no more.
Project: Joseph Magnin Store; Architects: Chatham and Sehulster, Thomas Sehulster; Architect Graphics: Sheri Sehulster; Illustrators: Umberto Baldini/Sid D. Leach.

should complement it to the extent required by the client. If the illustrator will experiment using colors within the palette of the illustration, he will see that figures clothed in the colors used in other portions of the rendering will be more pleasing and complementary to the drawing. Scale figures should not be noticed except to add atmosphere to a rendering.

ILLUSTRATOR / DESIGNER COMMUNICATIONS

Some interior designers approach their projects in the same manner as do architects; i.e., the project is designed, and complete working drawings are done before the final presentation renderings are commissioned. However, most designers do not function in this manner.

In the residential interior design field, renderings are used only on jobs where the budget allowance is adequate enough to cover the costs of such drawings because many items within residential drawings are not chosen at the time of client presentation and must be shopped for, allowances in the rendering must be made. After discussion with the interior designer, the illustrator must, in many cases, fill in voids left undecided. Such items as lamps, paintings, plants, and other accessories not yet chosen can either "make or break" the look of a rendering as well as the finished design. Designers add accessories, as needed, after the main items are in place. The design illustrator must also be able to add those items to the drawing that will complement the interior and give it that special touch of personality each designer gives his own work.

Both designers and illustrators are usually chosen by their clients because of that special *look* they are able to give to a space. The illustrator must gain as much information from the designer as possible. The more

FIGURE 9-7a
Interior Design: Barry Brukoff; Project: New Varsity Theatre; Illustrator: Umberto Baldini

93

pertinent the information given the illustrator by the designer, the more accurate will be the artistic interpretation of that designer's ideas.

Thumbnail sketches done in the presence of the designer can be a good method by which ideas may be agreed upon. It also offers the illustrator a good opportunity to establish lighting sources and the finished look of the drawing. In these small vignettes, it is easy to establish all aspects of perspective, content, and atmosphere without going to the trouble and expense of constructing a complete perspective layout. Thumbnail sketches can save you time; and "time is money."

Architects usually require very precise delineation of all items, whereas interior designers usually favor a looser approach. A loose rendering technique can suggest many things without the exact representation of the items. This approach gives the delineator and interior designer the latitude required when all items are not as yet chosen. Items of unsure nature or source are indicated and suggested without tying down the designer to an exact object he may never be able to find.

Many factors govern the finished look of a design-presentation rendering. The more aware the illustrator is of the specific needs of the designer, the more successful will be the finished product—a selling tool to sell design.

In many cases, the decorator assumes the illustrator to be an accomplished interior designer. To be a successful interior designer illustrator, this, of course, is not mandatory; but it certainly does help. One must ask himself, "how much should I, the illustrator, design for the designer before charging an extra design fee?" The amount of added information included in the drawing by the illustrator should be discussed with the client. He must realize he is buying either a design service or an illustration of *his* design, and he should reimburse the illustrator accordingly.

CHAPTER 10

Pencil Rendering

THIS CHAPTER WILL BE PROBABLY one of the most useful in this entire text. Because of the universal appeal and availability of pencil, the illustrator, if trained in its use, need never be wanting for an illustration tool to help convey his ideas. A pencil is probably one of the most universally available illustration tools one can master. Many selections of lead hardness and width provide for an almost limitless variety of lead/paper combinations, as the matching of lead hardness to paper surface gives the illustrator many choices within which to develop his style (see Figure 10-1).

Pencil is a fun instrument with which to draw, as most corrections are easily made and reproduction does not need to be a problem. Photographic reproduction, if one uses continuous-tone film, can create an almost identical duplicate of the original. Ozalid® reproduction is a much less expensive method, as it uses a direct-contact, nonphotographic approach.

The student should not skip over any of the succeeding exercises to save time. Each portion of technique feeds the next, and to let any one area go unstudied will leave gaps in his training.

If one masters the techniques used in all of the illustrations in this chapter, a rewarding experience in the creation of beautiful pencil drawings will be the result.

MATERIALS

In order to complete the exercises in this chapter, you will need to obtain the following materials:

1. Drawing surfaces
   a. Kid-finish bristol board
   b. Plate-finish bristol board
   c. Heavy-weight, hot-pressed, illustration board (smooth)
   d. Heavy-weight, cold-pressed, illustration board (rough)
   e. Clearprint® 1000 H tracing paper
   f. Typing bond for practicing
   g. Mylar drafting medium

2. Pencils
   a. Graphite drawing pencils in the following grades: 4H, 2H, HB, 2B,

FIGURE 10-1: This pencil drawing was done on mylar drafting medium using 2H, 2B, and 4B pencils.

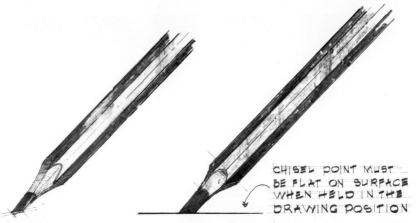

CHISEL POINT MUST
BE FLAT ON SURFACE
WHEN HELD IN THE
DRAWING POSITION

PENCIL SHARPENED PROPERLY

FIGURE 10-2 *Left:* Good pencil technique depends on proper pencil lead shape. A chisel point (refer to Figure 10-3) is formed by cutting away enough wood to allow final shaping using a sanding block as shown. Correct sharpening techniques must be employed in order to create a tool that will give the proper shape of stroke at all times.

FIGURE 10-3 *Above:* The normal angle at which the illustrator holds the pencil determines the angle to which the lead must be sharpened.

3B, 4B, 6B (graded from hardest to softest)
  b. Flat-lead carpenter's pencils in hard and soft lead
  c. Black, nongreasy pencils, medium-hard to soft

3. Sharpening instruments
  a. Utility knife or X-acto®-type knife (very sharp mat knife)
  b. Sanding block
  c. Carpet square for cleaning lead

4. Preservatives
  a. Spray fixative with workable mat surface

5. Erasers
  a. Pink pearl
  b. White vinyl (preferably electric type)
  c. Kneaded type
  d. Dry cleaning pad

PREPARATION

Before one can effectively use the pencil to communicate, correct sharpening techniques must be mastered. Divorce from your mind, if you will, the long-standing method of sharpening with the mechanical or power sharpeners. The type of point they create has its use, but it is very limited in our exercises and in doing a final drawing it is limited to layout.

Begin by sharpening your pencils in the manner shown above in Figures 10-2 and 10-3, being very careful to form a chisel point that will lie flat on the drawing surface when held normally in your hand. Use the mat knife to trim away just enough wood to expose the graphite rod without reducing the effective support of the wood. Exposing too much graphite will weaken this support and, especially in softer grades of pencils, cause breakage. After this initial trimming has been carefully done, use the sanding block to further shape the rod into a chisel point.

Now that your pencils are sharpened correctly, the drawing surface

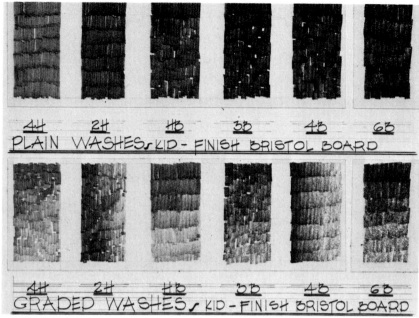

FIGURE 10-4a

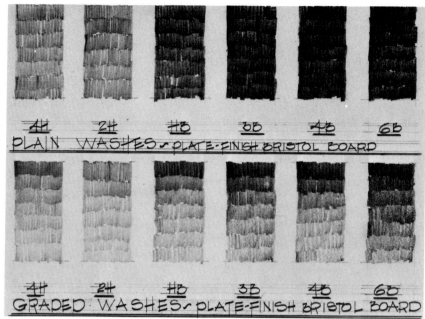

FIGURE 10-4b

FIGURE 10-4: Lead hardness should be matched to the drawing surface selected. Comparisons of several combinations are illustrated here. It is essential for the student to be familiar with the results obtained by practicing each combination shown.

must be matched to the proper pencil. It will be observed that many combinations of effects can be achieved by proper matching of lead hardness to the drawing surface.

Every drawing surface has a tooth that scrapes the graphite from the pencil and holds it intact. The rougher the surface, the more graphite will be scraped from the pencil. Also, the softer the lead, the more graphite will be scraped onto the surface.

For instance, a hard lead (3H) will produce a clean, smooth, light gray stroke on smooth plate-finish bristol board; a medium dark-gray stroke on mylar drafting medium; a light-gray stroke on heavy tracing paper; and a much darker gray, rough-edged stroke on a rough-surface illustration board. Soft lead, such as a 6B or 4B, will produce a dark-gray stroke on smooth bristol board and a very dark to black stroke on mylar and tracing paper. If 6B is used on rough bristol board, a fuzzy-edged line of exceed-

ingly dark value will result, but stability of the graphite will be lacking. Much experimenting must be done so that the student is familiar with the many combinations of effects obtainable.

The following are some of the factors which must be considered when choosing the right combination of pencil and drawing surface:

1. Size of finished drawing

2. What the drawing is to be used for

3. How it is to be presented to the client

4. Whether the drawing is just a quick sketch or a finished selling tool

5. Whether this drawing is to be easily reproduced and, if so, should it be drawn on tracing paper or mylar for easy Ozalid® printing.

Many times this information will be given you by the client. If not, you must make your own intelligent decision. Don't be afraid to experiment. *Your drawings are expendable but your clients may not be.*

PRACTICE EXERCISES

For these exercises, let us experiment with different grades of pencil

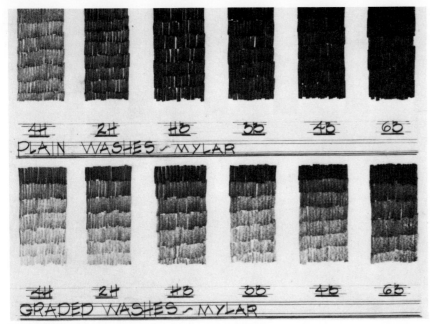

FIGURE 10-4c

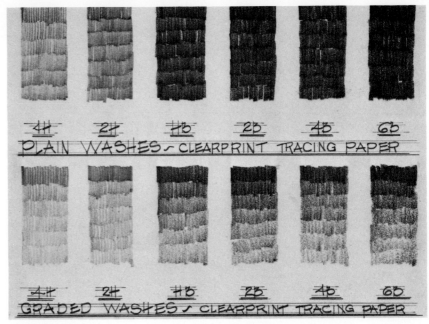

FIGURE 10-4d

hardness and drawing surfaces. Do not be too concerned about making mistakes. Try to control your tendency to erase but be as spontaneous as possible. This will keep the drawing fresh and interesting.

WASHES

The term "wash" has validity in pencil drawing as it does in water color, pen, opaque color, and acrylic painting. *A wash is merely a uniform tone used to cover a surface;* the only difference is the medium being used and the absence of color. A graded wash consists merely of covering a surface with a tone that graduates from light to dark, or dark to light, whichever is appropriate.

Washes in pencil differ from water-color washes in another way. Because one is working with a dry medium and there is no liquid to float the pigment or graphite on the surface, individual strokes, side by side and end to end, must be laid down to give an over-all effect of a wash. These strokes must be firm and even. The student must try to maintain a uniform line width even though the pressure of the lead on the drawing surface will vary in order to obtain lighter and darker tones. (Refer to Figures 10-4a through d.)

The student should be very firm and sure in his placement of each

stroke whether it be light or dark. Refrain from indecisive scribble and wishy-washy strokes. Form your strokes from the wrist to the elbow, letting your arm do the work, not your fingers (see Figure 10-5).

Remember: The beauty of a pencil drawing is in the quality of the strokes. They should say to the observer, "I am a stroke made with a pencil and I am proud of it." Never try to imitate another medium—let the pencil be true to itself.

LINE WEIGHT AND CHARACTER

The beginning student usually gives very little importance to line character. One reason for this is that from grade school on, you were taught to draw everything by outlining the form. While the importance of line cannot be disputed (see Chapter 11, "Pen Renderings"), sometimes we tend to depend on line rather than shade and shadow to define an object. (This was covered more fully in both Chapter 3, "How to See" and Chapter 6, "Value Study of Shade and Shadows.") A line is not of paramount importance; however, lines that are a necessity in any drawing must have character. (See Figure 10-6.)

Never let lines become static and uninteresting. By varying the pressure of your pencil on the drawing surface this can be alleviated. Do not let any

FIGURE 10-7

LINES MUST NOT BE STATIC OR UN-INTERESTING

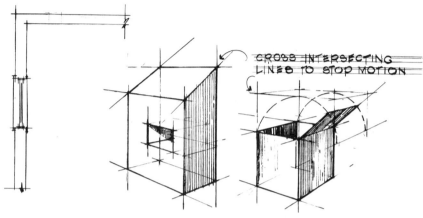

A LINE MUST HAVE A DEFINITE BEGINNING & END

FIGURE 10-8

REST HAND ON SCRAP PAPER

FIGURE 10-5: Strokes should be formed from the wrist to the elbow letting your arm do the work. Rest your hand on a piece of scrap paper to avoid smudges.

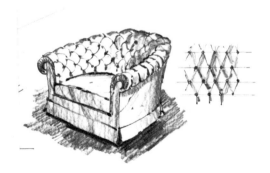

FIGURE 10-6: Lines of importance must have character. Note the tufting layout demonstrating the organized pattern one sees when tufted items such as this are examined closely.

line progress very far without something happening to it. Let it get lighter, darker, thinner, wider, or disappear altogether. (See Figure 10-7.)

Lines should have a definite beginning and a definite end. Learn to press down much harder at the beginning and end of each stroke and soon it will become a habit. (See Figure 10-8.)

Preliminary construction lines, such as lines to vanishing points and horizon lines, if interesting and very light, can sometimes even add to the visual quality of a drawing. These construction lines have been used to great advantage as a part of finished art, especially in the fields of industrial design and technical illustration. (See Figure 10-9.) This is all part of the individual technique, and as you progress, you will find out more and more that knowing what to leave out is as important to a drawing as what you put in.

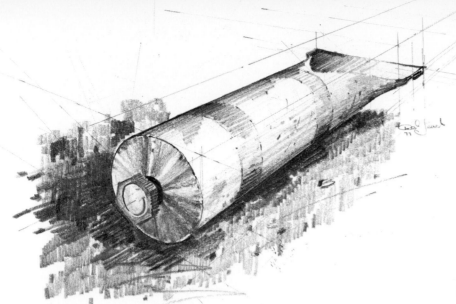

FIGURE 10-9: Preliminary construction lines will often add character to a pencil drawing.

SHADE AND SHADOWS IN PENCIL

As in pen illustration, crosshatching is sometimes used for shade and shadows as well as over-all tonal value in pencil renderings. This is covered quite extensively in Chapter 11, "Pen Renderings"; and, because the technique for this is similar for both media, it will not be covered at this time.

Deep, dark shadows can be obtained with line-and-wash combinations. Shadows should never be so hard-edged and definitive as to appear boring. If one is observant, one will note that shadows from an object are often cast from numerous light sources and are, therefore, not too definitive. (Refer to Figure 10-10.) In cases such as this, contrast is more important than hard and exact shadows.

Usually, direction of light will be of primary importance and will dominate. So it is with the rendering of these shadows. One should lead into a shadow with lighter, less important strokes and, finally, define shape and position by laying down that final, hard, dark stroke that will say, "I am a shadow and I give this drawing dimension." (See Figure 10-11.)

Now that you are more familiar with this medium, go on to more difficult exercises. Before starting these, however, practice again using different-weight pencils and drawing surfaces in varying combinations; again, refer to Figure 10-4. Lay down strokes side by side and end to end to

form a continuous tone. This is usually more difficult than graded washes because of the precise control required.

Combine the skills you have already learned in this chapter with your new knowledge of drawing and value relationships. Begin with simple shapes such as cubes, cones, and spheres. Establish a light source (see Chapter 6, "Value Study of Shade and Shadows"), use kid-finish bristol board or Clearprint 1000 H® tracing paper, and 2H, hB, and 4B pencils.

FIGURE 10-10: Light values against dark values and vice versa is the rule when definite shadows are not apparent. Light sources casting shadows in many directions from one object may form shadows that are not definitive. Here, contrast of value plays an important part in making this drawing read. 2H pencil on mylar drafting medium was used to create this drawing. With this type of drawing surface, deep shadows as well as light washes are possible using one hardness of lead. The surface must be fixed upon completion in order to avoid smudging.

FIGURE 10-11: This formal living room was illustrated using 2H and 2B pencils on Clearprint® tracing paper. The shadows under tables, chairs, and within drapery areas give the drawing depth and help to tie down objects to their surrounding environment. 2H and 2B pencils on Clearprint® tracing paper will give good shade and shadow possibilities, but the use of a 4B pencil is usually necessary for the addition of final deep-shadow areas.

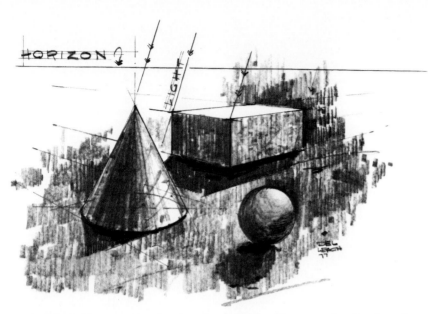

FIGURE 10-12: Practice drawing these simple volumes and notice how the pencil strokes follow the direction of the planes and surfaces they define. This illustration is shown also on p. 58, Figure 6-10.

Draw the basic outline of each object shown above, keeping the character of line all important. Plan ahead. Know where your shade and shadow will be laid down and be firm. Don't forget the importance of a preliminary value study for reference. Using good, positive strokes give the shapes dimension. Refer again to your previous exercise on graded washes and tonal value. Don't forget the final dark shadow at the base to *tie* the object to its resting place (see Figure 10-12).

MATERIALS AND MOODS OF A RENDERING

Every interior drawing has representations of many combinations of construction materials used in conjunction with each other. You, as the illustrator, must learn to create the total mood, feeling, and image required by the designer, using a total absence of true material color, delineating surfaces and textures using only tones of gray. Tone, surface representation, line weight, shade, and shadow, or the total absence of any of the above, are the illustrator's tools used in creating the visual illusion required.

The drawing of a lantern constructed of iron and glass is of particular interest, as it demonstrates how shapes may be simplified to basic forms. Notice particularly the technique used to suggest glass and how a sugges-

tion of shadow is all that is required to tie the subject to its resting place. (See Figure 10-13.)

Figure 10-14 shows examples of a few primary construction materials and interior surfaces that must be represented in renderings. Care should be taken to study the numerous pencil drawings showing items in large and small scale. Note the construction of each and the quick shading methods used. The drawings of all items shown should be copied diligently by the student, noting patterns of wood grain, marble, brick, wood panels, shutters, window panes, drapery, etc. Character of individual strokes is of utmost importance in these exercises. (See Figure 10-14.)

Figure 10-15 demonstrates many pencil techniques used to create illusion. Shelves filled with volumes of books can become very static if not handled properly. Only the shadowed areas behind the books have been emphasized. Hence, shapes of different-sized volumes are determined by background relationship (light against dark). Variation of book placement, such as some placed diagonally, adds interest and keeps the area from becoming monotonous.

Reflections in both table and floor surfaces in Figure 10-15 are suggested only. Here is a good example of knowing when to deemphasize areas of little importance to the immediate selling job; in this case, furniture and drapery were more pertinent.

Shutters are relatively simple to indicate; the determining area is, of course, the jagged shadow along the right side of each panel. Here, shadow alone determines what we see.

Drapery may be as simple as that in Figure 10-16, or as flamboyant as in Figure 10-17. Much use was made in these illustrations of HB, 4B, and 6B pencils on Clearprint® tracing paper. Note the suggestion of door moldings and frames behind the somewhat transparent Austrian curtains. This gives depth to both the drapery and the curtains. A suggestion of mirrored walls flanking the drapery offers a good opportunity to vignette the drawing.

FIGURE 10-13: A cone on top of a cube forms the basic shape of the lantern shown at right. Most items can be easily broken down into simple shapes if the student trains himself to see "into" complicated forms. This is the same illustration as Figure 5-4a—a metal and glass lantern.

WOOD PLANKS WINDOW BRICK-SMALL

MARBLE SHUTTERS PANEL BRICK-LARGE

FIGURE 10-14: These are a few examples of typical surface designations that must be mastered by the illustrator when using pencil as an illustration tool. Illusion of patterns representing such things as wood grain, building materials, and construction methods can be illustrated only after the student is learned in the appearance of these items as seen in reality.

FIGURE 10-16

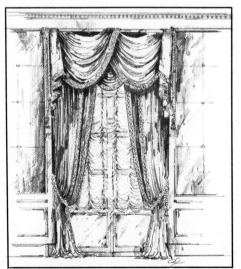

FIGURE 10-17

FIGURE 10-15   *Above:* This pencil illustration was done using a 2H and a 2B pencil on Clearprint® tracing paper for ease of reproduction. Note particularly the method used to illustrate books. Do not draw each individual book; the shadows are much more important to the illusion than individual book designation. A detail of this illustration may be found on p. 59, Figure 6-13.

FIGURE 10-16   *Top Right:* Sometimes a suggestion of background is required to illustrate the transparency of window glass. In this case, the background was minimized in order to make the drapery most important.

FIGURE 10-17   *Bottom Right:* Austrian curtains must show a certain transparent quality while still retaining fullness. This may be done by suggesting window mullions behind the curtains. In this illustration much importance has been given to the elegance of over-drapery which contrasts successfully with the filmy quality of the curtains. The student should examine the drapery and realize that shade and shadow representation gives this drawing dimension and reality.

FIGURE 10-18 This under-drawing for the real estate sales-conference room developed in Chapter 5 will be used as the basis for our last project in this chapter. The student should review both Chapters 5 and 6 before continuing with this illustration.

FIGURE 10-19 The drawing shown has been transferred to a kid-finish bristol board for final pencil delineation. Notice particularly that the dark shadow areas have been chosen as a starting place for the final illustration procedure. Some illustrators prefer to work from lightest to darkest, but this is a personal preference. If a proper value study has been made, it really doesn't make any difference, as long as a definite procedure has been established.

All of the preceding examples must be mastered before any room drawings can be successfully completed. Practice drawing all of the items faithfully over and over; do not be afraid to copy the illustrations as you see them. The importance of this exercise cannot be overemphasized.

After you have learned the techniques shown in these drawings, you should have the skills to faithfully reproduce materials so that the observer will recognize them immediately, and, most important, your drawings will have character and appeal. It is this instant appeal that can make the observer feel a part of the environment you are creating.

CREATING THE FINISHED DRAWING

Our last exercise of this chapter will be a continuation of the real estate sales-conference room previously studied and partially completed in both

Chapter 5, "Perspective Theory and Practical Office Methods," and Chapter 6, "Value Study of Shade and Shadows."

An under-drawing (Figure 10-18) has been made; but, if this drawing has not by now been transferred to kid-finish bristol board, it should be done at this time using the techniques discussed in Chapter 6. If the resulting transfer was executed as instructed, it should be clean and sharp. Figure 10-19 shows this transferred drawing after finished pencil work has commenced.

Study Figure 10-22. This finished illustration encompasses many of the techniques studied previously in this chapter, so nothing new to the training process has been introduced. The student should copy the style illustrated as closely as possible, keeping in mind that individual technique and style will develop as one proceeds with study and practice.

Begin by taping the bristol board to a drafting-table surface that can be rotated if possible. (A piece of ¾-in plywood is good for this.) Turning the drawing while working gives one the added flexibility needed at times.

Pencil selection should include 2H, H, 2B, 4B, and 6B, leads.

In order to keep your drawing clean, sprinkle some dry powdered eraser from the dry cleaning pad onto the surface. These granules must not be left on the surface area where the pencil strokes are being placed, as they impede the adhesion of graphite to paper and produce small specks of dark

gray if ground into the sketching surface. Brush the granules around on the surface so that only the portion actually being worked on is not covered. A good practice also is to rest the drawing hand on a sheet of clean, white paper. This is done in conjunction with the powdered eraser, not in lieu of it. (See Figure 10-20.)

The student must now study his recently created value study in order to preestablish lights and darks. The value study should be placed in a vertical position in front of the student for ready reference. (See Figure 10-21.)

FIGURE 10-22: This is how the finished pencil illustration done on kid-finish bristol board should look. Notice that space for copy has been purposely left in the carpeted area. Refer to the value study and notice that this area has been so marked. This helps to keep unwanted pencil strokes out of this area during the illustration process.

Begin with a chisel-pointed 2H pencil. Starting at either the right or left side of the carpet, construct a graded wash. Notice that strokes become darker around the perimeter of the floor, under the chairs, and under the desk. Observe also how dark this graded wash becomes as it recedes under the table. The pencil softness was increased to 2B in this case, with a 4B and 6B used for the final dark tones. All strokes were laid down in a vertical manner to further suggest the texture of the carpet. For the shuttered areas, 2B pencil was used; and the addition of 4B over the previously drawn 2B strokes both darkened areas as needed and gave them a much softer feeling.

The dark shadow in the drapery and plant areas was made with 4B and 6B pencils, while H lead (because of its firm quality) was used for all dark, fine, line work.

Study how the carpet strokes created the vignetting. (See Figure 10-22.)

Desk outline was purposely omitted to relieve distortion. Had the desk been completely drawn in, wall suggestion on the left side of the drawing would have been necessary and distortion of perspective would have been overwhelming. (Refer to Chapter 5, "Perspective Theory and Practical Office Methods.")

FIXING

Hopefully, you now have a believable pencil rendering, tastefully done and faithful in its reproduction of the example in Figure 10-22. All completed pencil drawings must be "fixed" in order to prevent smudging. Pencil is, of course, made of graphite and wood; graphite is very unstable and tends to smudge if abraded. Fixative is usually sprayed on the surface of the drawing to form a uniform, clear film that helps to stabilize the graphite and keep the drawing clean. A mat, of course, is needed to finish the presentation.

CHAPTER 11

Pen Rendering

"Pen and ink" are two terms that, through function and time-honored convention, seem to naturally belong together. The pen is a tool, said to have been developed centuries ago. There is early evidence of this instrument having been used to apply ink (colored liquid) to papyrus writings more than 4,000 years ago. In addition to the written language, pictorial evidence has been found indicating that "pen-and-ink" illustrations of people and their surroundings were also used to graphically tell a story.

The student must be aware that every medium with which he will come into contact has certain restrictions and advantages that apply only to that medium. As a result of this, certain conventions in working with each medium have been developed over many years. These conventions are called techniques, and must be mastered before an individual style can be considered. To illustrate this, consider a sculptor's representation of an object. He may use plastic materials to build up a three-dimensional object. However, the absence of color is a definite limitation. The painter who transfers the three-dimensional object to a two-dimensional canvas must rely on color, shade, and shadow to develop the three-dimensional illusion that is so natural for the sculptor. The artist that puts large masses of color on a canvas using a brush has a definite advantage over an illustrator using pencil to cover the same amount of surface; but, the illustrator using pencil has the added advantage of a sharp point when required, even if he is limited to tones of gray. Each medium demands its own treatment and should not try to emulate another. Some schools of thought do not require the student to master time-honored traditions, so as not to destroy that person's artistic individuality. This author does *not* agree with this. It is to be remembered that by mastering the basic techniques taught here, one can produce believable illustrations that will sell one's product or design. Then, and only then, should one be concerned with developing one's own particular style within the limitations of a medium.

The pen is a linear tool. This means that all representation must be in the form of a line equal to the size of the penpoint, or nibs. The line may vary in width if the nibs are forced apart as pressure is applied to the pen, as when using a quill-type point, or it may be a constant width, as when using

a technical drawing pen (this particular pen has a drawing cone and a self-contained refillable ink-supply cartridge, in lieu of the nib found in ordinary pens). Most quill points hold only a small amount of ink and must be refilled constantly, while other pens of the fountain-type have a built-in reservoir that constantly feeds the point as lines are set down. The fact that each pen stroke covers so little space as compared to a pencil or brush predetermines that pen work is very tedious when covering a large surface.

We know that a point of a specific size will produce a line of a specific size (narrow point—narrow line; wide point—wide line). We can assume that a drawing must then be made up of a series of lines of different sizes, directions, and spacing. To this premise, let us add another aspect. If a specific point transmits the same amount of ink to the surface with each stroke, then each stroke will be the same darkness or value (usually totally black). This is unlike pencil where different strokes have varying degrees of darkness determined by pencil hardness, paper type, and pressure of application. Pen drawings must depend upon line placement to achieve shade, shadow and, hence, form.

The reader should examine Figure 11-1. This portion of a photograph, to be used in a printed brochure, has been enlarged many times. Notice

FIGURE 11-2: Compare this pen illustration to the photographic illustration shown in Figure 11-1. It becomes apparent that by placing black dots of ink that are spaced as shown in this illustration, the same kind of illusion shown in **Figure 11-1** is possible.

FIGURE 11-1: This half-tone photograph is an enlarged section taken from Figure 10-22, p. 108 and has been screened before printing, i.e., a line screen is used in the camera during the shooting. It is apparent that the image appears to have been formed not with tones of gray, but with black dots spaced unevenly. It is this uneven spacing along with the variation in the size of the dots that give the viewer the illusion of dimension and value.

that the entire photograph is made up of dots placed far apart and close together, not of wash values of gray. Each dot is black ink and each dot is, therefore, as dark as the adjacent dots. Value is created by the spacing of these dots; the more space between dots, the lighter the value, and the closer together the dots, the darker the value. Of course, this dot principle is created in photographs through the use of screens in the photography process. We, however, when drawing in ink, may apply this dot theory to linear theory. As with the dots, lines close together will produce darker value, and widely separated lines produce a lighter value. An additional technique employed by pen illustrators is direction of line. Line direction may be used to change value by superimposing opposite diagonal strokes within an area. This is referred to as "hatching" or "crosshatching." The more crosshatching, the darker the value will be.

Penpoints are capable of applying dots as well as lines. As in the enlarged photograph, dots may be used in pen drawings to produce value. (See Figure 11-2.)

Each line and dot must be painstakingly applied to a drawing to produce the final illustration. If a technical pen is used instead of a quill type, points of different sizes must be used for the size of dots to vary. Pen work is very tedious and is, therefore, expensive to produce. Consider also that once

FIGURE 11-3 *Left:* This piece of furniture was sketched freehand by the author as a student. Notice how many weights of line work go into its make-up. There is practically no limit to the lightness and darkness possible when crosshatching (many lines of different direction superimposed on each other) is used.

FIGURE 11-3a *Above:* This pen illustration was delineated using a fine-point technical pen. The delicate line formed by this point is apparent. Here again, values are created by the use of multidirectional crosshatching. Unlike Figure 11-3, which was executed without aid of T square and triangle, this illustration depends greatly upon these tools for straightness of line.
Interior Designer: Val Arnold and Associates; Architect: Donald James Clark, AIA; Illustrator: Robert Sutherland; Project: Master Bath in House Designed for Mr. and Mrs. John A. Burris, Hillsborough, CA.

pen lines or dots are placed, they are very difficult to remove. Even with the use of an ink-removing eraser, "ghosts" are likely to be apparent in the final work.

Because of all of the technical difficulties of working with ink and a fine-pointed tool, it is practically impossible to reproduce all of nature's textures, colors, light, shade, and shadow with this medium. Therefore, one must disregard or merely suggest those parts of nature that seem less important to the illustration and emphasize those more important parts.

If color is to be disregarded and values alone are to give the viewer an accurate illusion, we must resort to the use of time-honored techniques to achieve our final result. The use of outlines (though we must realize that in nature outlines do not really exist) is a very common method of separating two adjacent objects of equal value. Pen is an excellent instrument for outline work. Not only is the pen line constant in value, but many variations may be achieved that give much interest to the viewer. This use of outline, together with dots, lines, crosshatching, and often ink wash (done with ink, water, and a brush) give the illustrator many and varied combinations with which to achieve a pleasing illustration.

One must remember at all times that in order for an ink illustration to excel in its presentation to the viewer, it must be true to the medium. This means that one must not disregard the size relationship of the rendering. If one forces the medium beyond its capacities the end result will show lack of understanding on the part of the illustrator.

This does not mean that individual styles must be ignored; however, only when the traditionally accepted methods of delineation are mastered, can the illustrator become as individual in his work as he likes. (See Figures 11-3 and 11-3a.) Like handwriting, no two people will achieve the same result given the same tools. Even though you may be hesitant about copying a traditional approach to the subject, it must be noted that each student will develop a specific style as he practices the exercises set forth in this chapter. Compare the free-hand quill pen technique of Figure 11-3 with the structure method used in Figure 11-3a where a technical pen was employed in the delineation. It is presupposed that the student of pen drawing is serious because of the complexities in the execution of this medium. A word of encouragement to the beginner: if this written text sounds confusing, do not be too concerned; the practical aspects of this medium have been so highly conventionalized and structured that execution is more or less the application of tricks and each of these tricks must be mastered. Do not despair. Many artists who excel in other media fail miserably with pen. It is a very difficult medium to master; but with practice and guidance, excellent results can be achieved.

FIGURE 11-4: A pen drawing photographically reproduced onto clear mylar may be used as a line overlay when colored backgrounds are desired. Alternate color schemes are possible using this method without having to create separate color renderings. In this illustration, the right half of the mylar overlay has been registered over the colored background. The left side has not been brought into contact with the light Ozalid® print lines below; hence the lack of clarity. *Architects: Moulton and Clark, Inc.; Illustrator: Chun/Ishimaru; Project: Outdoor Restaurant and Street Scene—Bavarian Village, Twin Canyon, UT.*

FIGURE 11-5: Compare the two drawings that have been reduced to a much smaller size. The pencil drawing above, does not retain the clarity as does the pen illustration on the left. The width of each original drawing was 24″. The pen drawing was executed in ink on Clearprint® tracing paper using both technical and quill pens. The pencil drawing was illustrated on Clearprint® tracing paper using 2H, H, and HB pencils.
Figure 5: Architect: Michel Marx, AIA; Illustrator: The Author; Project: Residence, Piedmont, CA.
FIGURE 11-5a: *Developers: The Hofmann Co.; Illustrator: Umberto Baldini; Project: Condominium Project, Walnut Creek, CA.*

ADVANTAGES OF ILLUSTRATING WITH PEN AND INK

What are the advantages of using pen illustrations instead of pencil, water color, pastel, marker, or other media? If the techniques are difficult to master and the production time required is excessive, what is so great about pen illustration?

Pen drawings are created with ink, which is generally waterproof and is, therefore, stable on the surface. If care is taken in the execution, clear, concise, clean drawings will be the result. When dry, ink does not smudge and is easy to handle without fear of destroying the lines. Pencil under-drawings may be used successfully on the same surface and erased upon completion without fear of damage to the final ink drawing.

Sharpness of line makes this medium excellent for photographic reduction and reproduction. Shade and shadow are just lines, dots, or solid value, and will reduce proportionately to the space between. This ensures that upon reduction, the same degree of value will be as apparent as in the original.

Pen drawings on tracing medium, such as drafting mylar, tracing vellum, and Clearprint® tracing paper may be printed cheaply and efficiently.

Many times the designer will be required to give prints of an illustration to contractors or suppliers, and at the same time, present to the client a full-color illustration. Pen illustrations may be printed (contact copied) onto clear mylar, as this line drawing on clear film makes an excellent line and texture overlay. (See Figure 11-4.) If colored backgrounds are done, this line overlay can be used to view alternate color schemes without doing many full-color illustrations of the same subject matter. If the drawing is reproduced by the Ozalid® process, black-line prints can be colored with transparent colored markers, providing these prints have been dry mounted and no original black lines are destroyed. One can photographically reproduce a drawing onto special water-color paper (mural-paper), and then color directly on the print without losing any line definition. This is certainly the most satisfactory of the fast coloring processes.

Clarity, again, is one of the best aspects of pen drawing. Reduced to business-card size, an 18-in × 24-in pen drawing has excellent definition. Pencil drawings, on the other hand, do not reduce as well as pen. (See Figures 11-5 and 11-5a.) Because a pencil drawing is made up of values of gray, these values tend to flow together when photographically reduced, making clarity of line and value a definite problem. Fuzzy reductions will result if the original is not very sharp.

Contrast within pen drawings is clear and concise. Light against dark and dark against light is very apparent. Remember that ink, being black, is very stark against a white background, unless of course a tone paper is used.

Many times illustrators will render a subject directly onto an illustration board. This board may be white, or it may be a value of gray, or a tonal coloration of an earth color. Earth colors or warm colors tend to lend themselves more to universal acceptance than do colder colors. Illustration board is generally available in sizes of 30-in × 40-in, more or less. Different manufacturers offer slightly different sizes, but all are within this maximum size range. A larger 60-in size is available in some illustration surfaces.

One may think at first that because black ink is being used, the finished illustration may become somber and heavy. This may be true in the beginning. If variation in line width, contrast, negative space, shade and shadow, and vignetting are all handled properly, pen illustration can be very delicate in nature. The fineness of line weight delivered by the penpoint, together with heavy outline and concentrated points of interest, can give renderings in this medium vitality and life.

DISADVANTAGES OF PEN ILLUSTRATIONS

The student of pen drawing must be patient and, above all, diligent. The process of execution is slow. As we discussed earlier, it takes many lines and dots to cover a large area. Time required to produce a finely executed drawing is great even for the accomplished illustrator.

"Time is money," and the more time required to produce a drawing, the more that drawing should cost. Finished ink drawings in today's market are not as common as they were when labor was not so expensive. If one chooses to use pen to illustrate an interior, careful selection of rendering style is very important. One must take enough time to produce a satisfactory result in a given style. Rendering time is directly related to the style of drawing.

Corrections on ink drawings are very difficult to accomplish, and sometimes impossible. Depending on the drawing surface, even the lightest lines become difficult to remove without traces.

Ghosts, as previously mentioned, are those areas remaining after corrections have been made that do not have the same look as the untouched portions of the illustration surface. Faint lines may still remain on the surface of the paper and will reflect light differently, thus becoming very obvious when viewed from different angles. As we discuss materials, the reader should make note of and experiment with different surfaces and how they respond to corrections.

MATERIALS REQUIRED

Materials required for illustration in pen and ink are relatively few. Basically one needs a pen, ink, and paper. Within these three areas there are many selections. We will examine each and give the student recommendations that have been proven through the years. One should be aware, though, that quantity of art materials does not necessarily predetermine the creation of good illustrations. Quality must be the governing factor when choosing supplies. One cannot do good work, either beginning or advanced, using poor materials.

THE QUILL PENPOINT

"Penna," the latin term meaning a feather or plume, seems to be the origin of the simpler word, "pen." Split-feather quill points with feather intact were used for many centuries. We have all seen early stereotyped illustrations of a bespectacled old gentleman writing in his large ledger book with a feather-quill pen. This type of pen is virtually unknown today due to the advent of steel penpoints. The first steel points were introduced to the world in 1825 by Joseph Gillott, an English manufacturer. His split-steel "quill" was the forerunner of today's metal penpoints. The market is varied today, and numerous manufacturers supply penpoints of almost any variety; small to large, fine point to wide point, ball-tip point to the wide, lettering penpoints.

All metal penpoints have two things in common; they hold a limited supply of ink and must be continually refilled, and they must be inserted into a holder in order to be used properly. Examine the illustrations of both penpoints and holders. (See Figure 11-7.) Notice that the holder has a cork barrel at its base. This is not only a cushion for the hand, but in most cases will slide down far enough to protect the delicate point. After purchasing penpoints (three sizes are sufficient) and holders, it is recommended that designation markings of some type be affixed to each holder in order to identify penpoint, style, and size. Some illustrators choose to notch each holder with varied numbers of notches or to color each with a different color. Both of these methods offer ease of identification.

INK

Most of the accepted inks favored by today's illustrators are commercially available in glass containers suited to the function of dipping or filling. Waterproof drawing inks are now manufactured by a number of houses and are made especially to correspond with particular penpoint types and drawing surfaces. As the pen developed from the split-point quill to the fountain pen, inks had to be developed that would not dry inside of

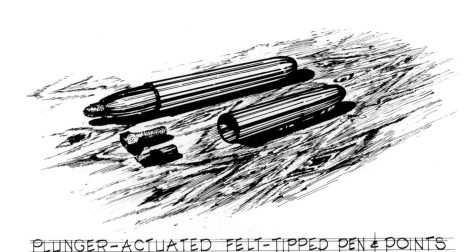

PLUNGER–ACTUATED FELT–TIPPED PEN & POINTS

FIGURE 11-6: This illustration of the pen type used to sketch the room shown in Figure 11-9 clearly shows how proper line weight and character can give impact and interest to a pen rendering. Notice the break-up of lines indicating reflection of light from the pen's shiny exterior. If these lines are continuous, much of the character of the illustration is lost.

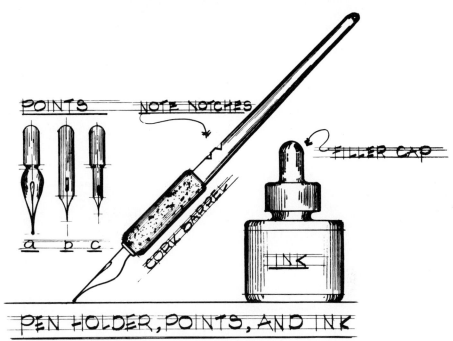

PEN HOLDER, POINTS, AND INK

FIGURE 11-7: Proper selection of pen holders, points and ink are important. Note the wide-base bottle. This bottle shape has been introduced by ink manufacturing companies to prevent the possibility of overturning the bottle and spilling ink. A more reliable solution to this spilling problem is to cut a round hole in a small, wide box and insert the ink bottle into this opening. Notches on various pen holders can be used to indicate penpoint size used with that holder.

this new, self-contained inking instrument. Recent years have seen the invention of the technical-drawing pen. This type of pen is of the self-contained ink-supply variety, and many architects and designers prefer this type of tool for quick sketching as well as for finished art. The disadvantage to this particular type of pen is that different-sized points are required for different line widths. Special waterproof inks have been subsequently developed for this type of pen. Previously, when using this type of pen with standard waterproof ink, in-point hardening would result if the pen were not used for a few days, and cleaning was a considerable problem. Even removal of the point for cleaning or to substitute another point size became an annoying situation. New inks tend not to harden within penpoints and the waterproof characteristics still remain.

Inexpensive pens manufactured outside of the U.S. were introduced in this country under various brand names all incorporating either a hard or soft fibrous tip and a self-contained quick-dry ink supply. Since the advent of this quick-dry and inexpensive writing and drawing instrument, many varieties of pens have been introduced. Porous penpoints of nylon and felt, inks that are waterproof and water soluble, fine points, wide points, soft and hard points, all are offered in this type of pen. These pens offer the illustrator many varieties of line, ink color, and permanence, with the added consideration that they are inexpensive and disposable. This type of pen can be bought cheaply and will not dry out within a reasonably long time period if the cap is kept in place when not in use.

Refer to Figure 11-8. This interior sketch was made on architectural

sketch paper with a felt-tipped pen. The author favors pens that are in various stages of drying out. The lack of full ink flow to the tip allows one to create many values of line. Instead of all lines being totally black, as is the case when pen lines are made with a technical pen, various tones of gray (if black ink is used) are possible. This added advantage is apparent in Figure 11-8 where not only line width, but intensity of tone, play an important part in the look of the finished product.

One of the author's favorite sketching tools is the variable ink supply plunger type of pen. (See Figure 11-6.) This pen has a refillable, self-contained, pressure-controlled ink supply, and a large, hard, rounded felt tip. A valve governing ink distribution to the tip is actuated when a plunger is pushed by the felt-tip. One can create large flat strokes (alternate shape points are available) of an infinite variety with this pen. It is an excellent traveling partner for those who like to do quick sketches. (See Figure 11-9.) Instant drying of the ink prevents smudging, but mistakes *cannot* be corrected. The ink is indelible. Value studies are made quickly with this pen. Many large-sized points are available, as well as very small points contained within a metal adapter. The two colors of ink preferred by this author are black and sepia. (See Figure 11-6.) Notice the particular pen technique used for this illustration. Heaviness of line used to illustrate this pen is combined with the light strokes used when illustrating the wood surface. This technique is frequently used in both industrial design and commercial art.

DRAWING SURFACES

When selecting a drawing surface, one must consider whether the illustration will be reproduced by a direct-contact print (Ozalid®) method, or it will be reproduced by the photographic method.

All the preceding really means is that one must choose a drawing surface that is either translucent or opaque. Varieties of translucent drawing surfaces are many. To list a few favorites here will be sufficient for the student, until such time as he expands his own horizons and experiments with different surfaces.

Mat-surface mylar drafting film is the first choice of this author. It takes and retains regular waterproof ink. Some acetate film requires special acetate ink for a good bond. This ink will clog most pens if they are not

FIGURE 11-8 *Opposite:* Original size (18″ × 24″) was illustrated using an inexpensive felt-tipped pen (sometimes referred to as a fibrous tip) on light-weight architectural sketch paper.
Architect: Phillip Wasserstrom; Interior Design: Noal Betts Designs, Inc.; Illustrator: The Author; Project: Preliminary Design for Pool Enclosure—Mariott Inn, Berkeley, CA.

FIGURE 11-9: Plunger-activated felt-tipped pens are excellent for quick sketches of interiors. Quick-drying ink is available in various colors although the author prefers sepia or black. These inks are very permanent, and when dry cannot be erased. The ink from this pen produces a softness of line that cannot be achieved with any other pen and ink tool.

cleaned immediately after use. Engineers, surveyors, and architects use mylar drafting film for the permanent drawing surface required by city and county offices for all registered survey documents. Cost is about double that of tracing vellum or Clearprint® tracing paper. Corrections are easier with this medium than with any other this author has used. Reproduction clarity is excellent, and this product resists wrinkling from moisture, expansion and contraction due to humidity, and will not easily tear.

Some quality tracing papers that have been a favorite of draftsmen using pencil have a waxy surface that is resistant to certain types of ink. The varieties of this type tracing paper that do not have the waxy, ink-resistant surface are obviously superior to those that resist waterproof drawing ink. Even the rapid-drying inks do not adhere well to some types of paper. Drafting pounce may be used to scrub the surface enough to create a tooth onto which the ink will adhere. Many illustrators prefer architectural sketch paper for finished ink drawings. This is certainly within individual

FIGURE 11-10: Sepia ink is being applied with a small lettering brush. Washes of transparent water color or diluted ink tend to unify a drawing. It is imperative that this technique be employed only over waterproof ink drawings or photo-reproduction of ink drawings. Water-soluble-ink line work will bleed if a diluted ink wash is applied over it.

Living room within a house for Joseph Delvalle and David Davies, Marin County, California; Architect/Designer: David James Clark, AIA; Illustrator: Jerry Taylor.

taste, but low resistance to tearing, and susceptibility to moisture and wrinkling make this author shy away from it.

Of the opaque variety of drawing surfaces, kid-finish and plate-finish bristol board are favorites that have withstood the test of time. These boards are available in different weights and surfaces. They are thick enough not to "telegraph" pin holes or other surface imperfections from a drafting table, but not so heavy as to be awkward and cumbersome. As was mentioned earlier, if colored background is required, an infinite variety of colored mat boards are available. These offer a reasonably good drawing surface but are not considered illustration boards, even though excellent results can be obtained by their use.

INK ERASERS
Ink erasers are a required item but should be used very sparingly. It is the feeling of this writer that spontaneous drawings are the result of not relying on erasure as a way out when mistakes are made. The electric variety offers the most control, and with use of a metal eraser shield, minute corrections are almost undetectable. Soft-pink or art-gum erasers should be employed to remove pencil lines.

BRUSHES FOR INK WASH
Many times in a pen illustration it may be felt that tones of gray would help otherwise dead areas. In order not to overwork an already busy drawing, water-diluted ink wash may be used. Flat, medium- to light-gray washes of waterproof ink tend to pull together previously ununited areas. (See Figure 11-10.)

Water-color brushes may be used for this wash technique, providing that they are cleaned immediately after usage. Ink hardened within the brush will ruin it. Chinese writing brushes are also a good tool for applying washes, but control within a given area is more difficult because of the irregular shape of this brush. Fantastic effects not possible with any other type may be made using this brush to illustrate plants, trees, patterns of fabric and carpet design, etc. The soft bristles that rapidly come to a point are well adapted to this delicate and free-form part of an illustration.

PEN TECHNIQUE
The student of pen rendering must master basic strokes as a prerequisite to anything else. Without basic pen control, future applications of technique are impossible. One must know what the pen will do under all circumstances.

The following exercises are basic and might appear to be boring and

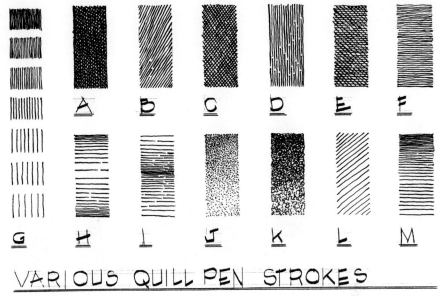

VARIOUS QUILL PEN STROKES

FIGURE 11-11

unexciting. Do not skip over these exercises. They are fundamental and must be mastered before one can continue with this chapter. These flat and graded washes were made on plate-finish bristol board and demonstrate many various stroke combinations using the quill penpoint. (See Figures 11-11 through 11-b for practical application.)

LINE WORK AND PEN FAMILIARITY USING CROW QUILL AND WATERPROOF INK.
Examine the illustrations (Figures 11-11, 11-12 and 11-13) in detail. Each stroke has direction. Each stroke must be laid down with determination and preplanning. Let the penpoint glide over the surface. Notice the difference between the strokes made using even pressure and those made using varied pressure. (See Figure 11-13.)

If one will compare the freehand approach with that of using ruled lines, he will notice how uninteresting the ruled lines can become. Practice each exercise.

Strokes can be laid down in an endless variety of directions and line widths. Predetermined limits should be first lightly laid out with a soft pencil. This will help one begin to feel the starting and stopping points of each stroke. The pen should be held as it would be if one were doing

FIGURE 11-11a *Left:* This illustration clearly shows how the various strokes shown in Figure 11-11 may be used to form shade, shadow and a suggestion of surface texture within a finished drawing.
Project: Master bedroom for Mr. and Mrs. Andrew Johnson, Tilburn, CA. Architect/ Interior Designer: Donald James Clark, AIA, Illustrator: Jerry Taylor.

FIGURE 11-11b *Above:* Pen strokes of an almost infinite variety may be used to indicate carpeting, blinds, and other features. This practical application of the exercise shown in Figure 11-11 also shows how vignetting with pen and ink can be done successfully.
Project: Lobby of a medical office building, Burlington, CA.

FIGURE 11-12: Examination of these three cubes indicates how outlines can be successfully left out of a drawing. Values created by lines drawn freehand, either continuous or broken, as well as crosshatching, create the boundaries of planes within the drawing as well as perimeter designations.

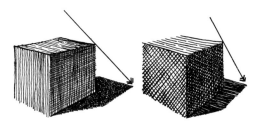

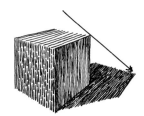

SOME VARIOUS STROKES DRAWN IN PERSPECTIVE

VARIOUS QUILL PEN STROKES

FIGURE 11-13

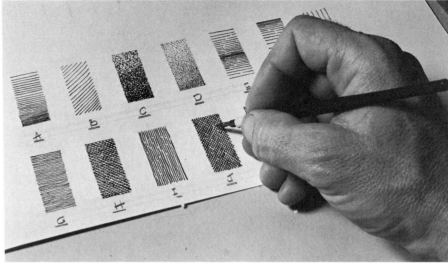

FIGURE 11-14: Proper hand position is important to the formation of pen strokes. One must practice strokes in various directions in order to become familiar with pressures needed to create desired results when using a quill pen.

normal handwriting, but the direction of strokes must be preplanned. (See Figure 11-14.) The nibs of split-steel crow quills will tend to jab into a toothed surface if normal direction is not maintained. If the nibs do dig into the surface, they will throw ink in front of the point as the nibs "let go," causing unsightly splatter within the drawing area. Care must be maintained to keep the surface clean at all times. Erasures of pencil lines should be attempted only after the ink has sufficiently dried.

The student should at this time compare the versatility of line work using the crow quill to line work done by other types of pens previously mentioned. Variation of line when using the fibrous-tipped variety can be obtained by line breakup (lines are not continuous, but are interrupted), by doubling up on line work (placing lines close together to make the total line created appear wider), and by using a combination of new, sharp points, and flat, worn-out points. Refer again to Figure 11-8 p., 116.

Crow quills offer the most varied form of line character, but they must be refilled often. Be certain not to overfill these points, or a black ink spot may suddenly appear on your clean drawing. Care must also be taken if, instead of filling these points, they are dipped into the ink bottle. It is easy to rub the cork holder on the bottle edge, thus covering the cork and one's hands with waterproof ink. It is always a good practice to place a clean sheet of paper under the drawing hand to protect the drawing surface.

Now that you have gained some familiarity with the crow-quill pen and can visualize the advantage of varied line weight, consider using one of the increasingly popular technical pens. These offer the illustrator the use of waterproof ink in a reservoir within the pen, and many line widths by changing the size of the penpoint. Each point does, however, only maintain one constant line thickness, and the only method of varying line width is through the doubling up of lines or the use of a crow-quill pen as well.

121

FIGURE 11-15 *Right:* Compare the strokes in this illustration to those in Figures 11-11a, 11-12, and 11-13. Notice how the practice strokes have been used to create values of various surfaces. Note how the absence of strokes form the suggestion of a tree.
Illustrator: Umberto Baldini

FIGURE 11-16 *Below:* Lines, crosshatching, dots and outline have all been used successfully within this one rendering. Notice how the square-edge format has been relieved by the overlay of some foliage in the foreground and the tree foliage in the upper portion of this illustration.
Illustrator: Umberto Baldini; Project: Condominium Project—The Hoffman Co., Walnut Creek, CA.

FIGURE 11-17:
Architect: Moulton and Clark, Inc.; Illustrator: Chun/Ishimaru; Project: Outdoor Restaurant and Street Scene—Bavarian Village, Twin Canyon, UT.

FIGURE 11-18:
Architect/Designer: Donald James Clark, AIA; Illustrator: Jerry Taylor; Project: Kitchen in a house for Joseph Delvalle and David Davies, Marin County, CA.

The illustration of an exterior courtyard (refer again to Figure 11-5a as well as Figure 11-15 and Figure 11-16) demonstrates, within one illustration, most of the techniques of crosshatching, dot pattern texture, and line variation and breakup, that were studied in the previous exercises. A technical pen and ruled lines were also employed in its execution. Notice in the enlarged portion (Figure 11-15) how line patterns are left out of the area occupied by the tree. The tree is only suggested by its relationship to its background, and not by a definite outline. It is very difficult for the untrained eye to visualize objects that are not surrounded by lines.

The overhanging portions of the roof in Figure 11-16 show how various dot-pattern densities have been used to define shape.

This drawing is a very good example to copy for techniques of both quill and technical-pen illustration.

The following illustrations encompass many techniques of pen strokes, line width and ink wash. In both cases, a good balance of lights and darks is very apparent. Ink, while very black, needs a complete range of tones to keep the intensity of value from overpowering the drawings. The beginner should not be afraid to use black. He should only be aware of how powerful its intensity can be. A note worth mentioning about black areas within a drawing—if the areas are not totally black (a few patches of lighter paper are left uncovered) this black area will appear much more interesting and not overpowering to the viewer.

Study these illustrations and do not be afraid to copy illustration methods. Remember, after one is proficient in the techniques as shown, one will soon develop the techniques to make drawings as original in style as the illustrator wants them to be.

FIGURE 11-19:
Architect/Designer: Donald James Clark, AIA; Illustrator: Jerry Taylor; Project: Entrance Lobby—Kaiser Permanente Hospital, Terra Linda, CA.

CHAPTER 12

Opaque Color Rendering

COLOR RENDERINGS may take many forms. They may be fast wash drawings, colored marker sketches, opaque water-color renderings, or pastel drawings. One must choose the particular technique that will best suit both the nature of the project the renderings are to illustrate, and the client to whom they are to be presented. One must also consider at this time the value of the project in terms of dollars to be earned in proportion to dollars spent on presentation. (Refer to Chapter 2, "Use of Renderings in Design Presentation.")

One of the most sought-after techniques of contemporary high-budget projects is the familiar, large, opaque water-color rendering. This form of rendering will give the best color and mood representation, texture delineation, and photographic reality of all of the other forms of graphic illustration.

Opaque water pigments are available in many forms. Those to be covered in this chapter will be:

1. Bottled (opaque) Water Color (poster color and tempera)

2. Designer's Colors (gouache in tube form)

3. Casein Colors (casein in tube form)

4. Acrylic Colors (polymer the tube form)

All of the preceding types of colors are usually used in an opaque manner. However, acrylics may be used both as transparent and opaque colors and are fast replacing the other forms of opaque water colors because of their distinct advantages. (See Figure 12-1 and Figure 2-3, which is on p. 7 color plate.)

All opaque pigments offer the illustrator many desirable characteristics: i.e., excellent, sharply-defined photographic reproduction; ease of workability; accurate color match; and good mood description possibilities. An added advantage, not to be found with transparent water color, is that of the ability to correct most mistakes without them being noticeable. One can, after a rendering has been approved, make changes without losing the freshness of the original painting. Many times architects and designers, because of budget limitations and client desires, are required to make

FIGURE 12-1: Acrylic polymer plastic colors may be used in both an opaque and transparent manner. Here, where the transparency of color was desired, acrylic colors were chosen because they do not lift other colors during the glazing process. This is particularly important when illustrating such a complex subject. Opaque white is added in the final stages of a rendering such as this to create the fine lines that represent window divisions.
Architect: Garo Dorian, AIA and Assoc.; Illustrator: Umberto Baldini; Project: Phillippine Trade and Cultural Center, San Francisco, CA.

FIGURE 12-2: Interior designers usually request renderings in a very loose style when suggestion of items rather than a carefully delineated representation is required. See also p. 14, Figure 12-25 for color plate.
Designer/Illustrator: Michael Zokas

changes in materials, colors, furniture, or accessories. Rather than redo an entire illustration, it is desirable that changes be made on the previously finished product. With opaque water color this can be accomplished with the least amount of effort.

Residential interior designers usually require a much looser approach to renderings than do architects. Many items in a design are not chosen at the time renderings are commissioned. It is, therefore, most often the case that interior designers do not like to be obligated to use specific items. The interior designer usually requests that the renderer be very loose in the treatment of the art work, as a certain mood should be created, rather than an architectural, pictorial, or photographic picture. (See Figure 12-2.)

The student will learn to create a mood or feeling in his renderings using opaque water color which, if handled properly, can complement any interior design presentation.

The illustrations within this chapter will be depicted rather loosely and the reader should realize this is not the only approach. It should also be realized that there are many techniques to be learned, and through

practice, each can be mastered. There must be a starting technique if one is to be an accomplished illustrator. One will learn to do satisfactory and commercially acceptable renderings using this loose manner, and it will be up to the individual's desire to practice other more hard-line illustrating procedures and to develop his own techniques and procedures. After all, it is the individuality expressed in a particular artist's work that gives him that all-important reputation, thus keeping him busy and financially stable.

MEDIA COMPARISON

At this time, let us compare the opaque water colors listed previously. Techniques for these media are very similar, but there are definite advantages and disadvantages to each. For comparison, let us take the liberty of combining bottled colors, designers' colors, casein, and tempera into one group. This group shall be referred to as soluble opaque water color. Many manufacturers refer to designers' colors and bottled poster colors as tempera, but tempera has been traditionally a pigment mixed with egg, intended to increase adhesion qualities. In the case of the following

126

FIGURE 12-3: Detail of chandelier shown in Figure 12-4.

FIGURE 12-4:
Interior Designer: Anthony Hail; Design Consultant: The Author; Illustrator: Larry Bratton; Project: Lounge— Mills Hyatt House, Charleston, SC.

drawings, designers' pigments or bottled colors can be made adhesive by mixing them with casein titanium white. Casein gives not only adhesion characteristics but will increase both body and workability.

Acrylic colors, on the other hand, are a more recently developed medium and are sometimes referred to as acrylic polymer plastic color. The pigments used in acrylic colors are mixed with polymer and are thinned, if desired, with water. These colors are extremely workable as well as completely insoluble to water when dry, setting them apart from the other opaque media mentioned. As previously stated, acrylics can be used as both transparent and opaque colors, an added advantage over other opaque water colors. Notice the illustration Figure 12-4. Here acrylics are used as opaque water color. (See the detail of the chandelier in Figure 12-3.)

The following chart (Figure 12-5) will give the reader an idea of the advantages and disadvantages of each medium. It will be up to the individual to experiment and to find how each works.

MIXING SOLUBLE OPAQUE COLORS
The most difficult paints to mix and master are the bottled varieties. These must be mixed first in containers, further mixed on the butcher's tray, and tested on a scrap piece of water-color board before one is ready to paint onto the final illustration surface.

Our discussion of paint mixing in this section will be primarily concerned with bottled opaque (poster colors) water color mixed with casein. Mixing techniques for gouache, casein, and acrylics are much simpler and

COMPARISON OF WATER-COLOR PIGMENTS

CHARACTERISTICS	OPAQUE	TRANSPARENT	ACRYLIC/POLYMER
AVAILABLE IN TUBE OR BOTTLE	YES	YES	YES
MUST BE FIXED BEFORE PAINTING OVER WITH A LIKE MEDIUM	YES	WATER COLOR WILL NOT TAKE OVER FIXATIVE	NO
WILL THIN WITH WATER	YES	YES	YES
COMPLETELY INSOLUBLE TO WATER WHEN DRY	NO	NO	YES
ARE PLIABLE WHEN DRY, I.E., WILL NOT CHIP FROM A SURFACE SUCH AS ACETATE	NO	WILL NOT TAKE ON ACETATE	YES
WILL MIX WELL WITH CASEIN	YES, CASEIN ACTS AS A BINDER	NOT RECOMMENDED	NO
MAY BE USED BOTH TRANSPARENT AND OPAQUE	YES, WITH CERTAIN COLORS	TRANSPARENT ONLY	YES
WILL BUILD UP THICKNESS IF VISCOSITY IS HEAVY	YES	NO, PAINT WONT DRY IF USED TOO THICK	YES
MAY BE USED IN CONJUNCTION WITH MASKING MEDIUM	YES, IF VISCOSITY IS LIGHT	YES	YES, IF VISCOSITY IS LIGHT
BRUSHES MAY BE CLEANED AFTER PAINT HAS HARDENED IN BRISTLES	YES	YES	ONLY WITH USE OF A SPECIAL CLEANER
WILL GLAZE OVER IF LEFT UNCOVERED / SKIN FORMED WILL NOT DISSOLVE IN WATER	YES	NO	YES
WILL "TAKE" ON SMOOTH SURFACE (HOT PRESS) ILLUSTRATION BOARD	YES	NO	YES, BUT WILL NOT COVER WELL
CAN ONLY BE USED ON WATER-COLOR PAPER OR WATER-COLOR BOARD	NO	YES	NO
CORRECTIONS ARE EASILY MADE	YES	NO	YES
COLORS WILL NOT "BLEED" THROUGH SUCCESSIVE GLAZES IF COLORS ARE ALTERED	NO	NO	YES
MAY BE LEFT TO HARDEN IN CUP CONTAINERS FOR USE AT A LATER DATE (WATER SOLUBLE)	YES, IF THEY ARE KEPT AIRTIGHT	YES	NO
COLORS WILL LIFT IF WASHED WITH SUCCESSIVE GLAZES	YES, DARK COLORS WILL LIFT	YES	NO
PAPER MUST BE WASHED WITH WATER BEFORE PAINTING	YES	YES	YES

FIGURE 12-5

128

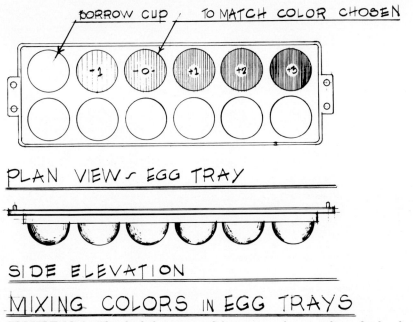

PLAN VIEW - EGG TRAY

SIDE ELEVATION

MIXING COLORS IN EGG TRAYS

FIGURE 12-6 The shaded portions of the egg tray denote values of color that should be mixed in each cup. Note the "borrow" cup from which white pigment is taken to mix with each value if needed.

FIGURE 12-7 *Below:* This value chart of colors mixed in the egg tray (Figure 12-6) goes beyond the +3 value mentioned in the text to illustrate how the progression of values may get either lighter or darker than the chart, depending on the requirements of the illustration.

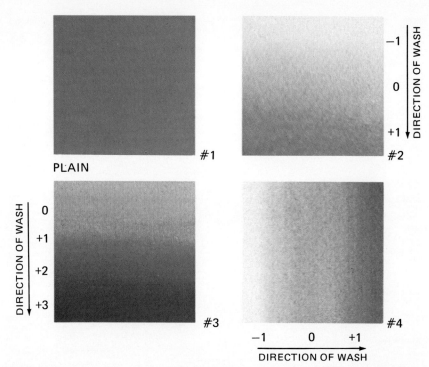

FIGURE 12-8: These squares were painted using the method described on the adjacent pages. Square #1 has a constant tonal value throughout. Square #2 has an excellent example of a graded wash. Square #3 has a graded wash of poor quality; the −1 tone has been left out, the +3 tonal value has been added, and the wash changes too abruptly from light to dark. Square #4 has a tonal wash that is graded unevenly. Notice the streaks. This is caused by the board being too dry when making the final passes of the brush.

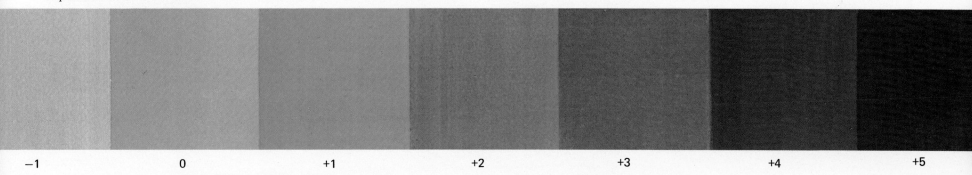

| −1 | 0 | +1 | +2 | +3 | +4 | +5 |

FIGURE 12-9

are done on the butcher's tray, similar to the way an oil-color artist would mix tube colors onto the palette.

PREPARATION

An inexpensive, #11 round wash brush is to be used in the mixing process. This will be a useful tool. It does not have to be a good brush, but the hair must not fall out. (See Chapter 4, "Materials.") Place an egg tray, bottled colors, diluted casein, old brushes, butcher's tray, and water on a table adjacent to an adjustable working surface. The surface must not slope too much and should be cleanable; it will get dirty. A plywood board with a covering of linoleum will be adequate, and it should have square edges so a T square can be used when needed.

LIGHTING

When working in any medium, be certain to select an area that has a great deal of light, preferably natural north light. Colors tend to change when viewed under different types of light. To illustrate this to yourself, observe a red carpet under natural daylight, incandescent light, and fluorescent light. Notice how the color changes under each condition.

Most important, one should use an area that will give enough light and has a working surface at which the artist is as comfortable as possible. Comfort is very important in all aspects of illustration.

MIXING PROCEDURE

Begin by first diluting white casein pigment. This casein will act as a mixing white as well as a binder between paint and illustration board. Squeeze into a small, 4-in-high bottle with a tight-fitting cap, enough casein to fill the jar about one-half full. Add enough water to produce a cream-like consistency when stirred or shaken vigorously. This will now serve as a base with which colored pigments can be mixed to obtain tonal values of each color as required. Be certain to let this mixture settle before use to remove the many air bubbles which have formed. Casein pigment used directly from the tube is unworkable for use in renderings because of its consistency; therefore, it must be diluted before use.

FIGURE 12-9: Study the values of the carpet color in this rendering and note the value designations as shown. These correspond directly with values that were mixed in the egg trays for previous exercises. Here, though, instead of blue being the base color, yellow ochre was chosen. The student should note that +4 is the darkest value noted, although darker values of +5 exist under the table. This example relates well to the pencil exercise in Figure 10-22 in Chapter 10.
Interior Designer: George Onhauser & Associates; Illustrator: The Author; Project: College Food Service—Kalamazoo College, Kalamazoo, MI.

Pour the diluted white mixture into one cup of your egg tray until it is about one-half full. This will serve as a "borrow cup."

Now, using the #6 mixing brush, distribute a small amount of the diluted white pigment into four additional cups of an egg tray adjacent to each other. Obtain a sample of blue carpeting to act as a color reference. Into the middle cup, drop some blue pigment. Mix this blue pigment with the white and add other colors as necessary until a perfect color match is obtained of the sample selected. This will be the base color, or -0-. (See Figure 12-6 and Figure 12-7.)

Begin with -0- and, working each direction, mix the values of −1, +1, +2, etc. in adjacent cups already containing some white by adding pigment as required. Add more colored pigment or white, as the case may be, to darken or lighten tone. It will be noted that as bottled colors are mixed together with casein, the paint tends to thicken greatly. This gives body to the paint, but the consistency must be kept to that of cream by adding water, or too much buildup will occur on the final illustration.

One will find that to obtain a darker tone of blue, as in a shadow or shade area, the complement of this color, orange, and sometimes burnt umber or black, must be added. This will give a deeper tone of blue while keeping the same chroma or color range. If more blue is added instead, the tone you are creating will merely appear more blue and will not look like a grayed shade or shadow tone. The darker tones of color in shade and shadow are grayed down so they are more intense in value but less intense in color. The same principles apply to other colors as well. Be careful; too much black added to blue when trying to achieve a darker or grayed-down color will make the color lifeless and uninteresting. The addition of the complementary color, orange, should be sufficient for all but the darkest values.

Mixing to match a specific given sample is always somewhat of a trial-and-error process until the renderer has trained himself to see into a color of any sample (carpet, wood, wall covering, etc.), and read all of the colors used in its make-up. This process takes a great deal of practice and should not be expected to be perfected on the first try.

At first one must use the trial-and-error method to perfect color match in all problem cases. Refer to books on color theory mentioned in Chapter 7, "Color."

COLOR TESTING

After mixing the four or five values of the blue carpet color, try each one on scrap water-color board and examine the drying characteristics. Often the color you mixed will look different in the cup than it does when dry.

Some will dry much darker or much lighter than they appear when wet. If you desire to speed up the drying process, an inexpensive hair dryer will do nicely for this. Caution: *do not use a hair dryer on large areas or for water-color washes because it causes uneven drying.*

The above process can now be repeated for all colors you are likely to use. The only exceptions to this would be wood tones. No white is used in the mixing of wood tones. Colors as they are used directly from the bottles or tubes provide the most realistic wood tones; and when applied in the correct manner, they can simulate with surprising exactness the color, texture, and grain of all types of wood. If one has studied various grain patterns this is not as difficult as it first seems.

STORAGE
After all colors to be used in a rendering have been mixed (with the exception of colors needed for small items, accessories, and plant colors) they must be kept moist during and after use. They may be needed for later changes or touch-up. Storage is accomplished by either stacking or nesting the trays, or covering the trays with a product such as plastic food wrap or a similar plastic material. This material forms an airtight cover while enabling the observer to see the colors in the trays.

Acrylic colors will harden to an insoluble state if not kept covered while working with them. Therefore, mixing cannot be accomplished in the same manner as soluble colors. Brushes, too, must be kept moist, or ruined brushes will result.

Colors previously mixed will tend to separate in the cups unless they are stirred. After storage for any period of time, stir to be certain of the color you think you are using. If not, you may get a surprise at a most inopportune time.

After a color has hardened in a tray, it cannot be reused by adding water. It may partially dissolve but will not return to its original mixed consistency and, therefore, must be remixed.

EXERCISES—BRUSH TECHNIQUES
Brush techniques for both soluble and acrylic colors are very similar. Therefore, we will be considering all forms of opaque color when referring to rendering techniques; only the mixing section of the text is limited to bottled colors.

For this exercise, we will examine the rendering in Figure 12-9, p. 130, noting particularly the carpeted floor. This carpet was rendered with at least five variations of tones of the base *yellow ochre* being required.

As was shown in Chapter 6, "Value Study of Shade and Shadows," actual shadows (as opposed to 45°-angle, conventional, single-light-source

shadows) are cast from many directions in varying intensities. These shadows must take on many tonal variations to make them interesting. The five tonal variations you would mix would be: (Note designations of value in Figure 12-7.)

1. *Base value -0-, the color that is to be matched to the carpet sample.* This color, or tone of color, is used on the greatest area of the carpet shown.

2. *One tone or shade lighter than base value, −1.* When sunlight or artificial light falls on a carpet or any object, the reflected light reaching the observer's eyes overpowers the true color of the rug. Thus one still reads ochre, in our case, but it is a considerably lighter value than the actual color of the carpet. This color is represented by value −1.

3. *Medium to darker tone, +1.* This tone is blended on the illustration board with the base color "*wet into wet*" (a wet brush painting into a wet area) to create many of the intermediate darker tones leading into shadowed areas.

4. *Dark tone, for blended shade and hard-line shadows, +2.* Observe the light play again on a soft surface such as a carpet. Shadows are cast by many light sources that overlap each other. (See Figure 6-4 in Chapter 6, "Value Study of Shade and Shadows.") Only with a strong, single-directional light source does the shadow actually conform to the shape of the object casting the shadow. Tone +2 will be used to create the illusion of these shadows.

5. *Finally, an even darker tone, +3.* This can be almost as intense as dark gray. This tone is used to tie down objects by giving them that last important shadow line at their base and for the deep shadows under the table. This tone is not mixed at this time because of the small quantity involved. It will be mixed only at the time it is needed. Note that a darker value of +4 is used only slightly and it is of importance to mention this only for reference to the illustration.

We recommend that the student use water-color board for his practice exercises just as he will use this same surface for final renderings. One must get used to the way in which the water and pigment react with this surface. If, in order to save money, the student uses another type of painting surface for practice and then invests in a large water-color board on which to do the final drawing, he may be surprised at the difference in results. The water-color board will have different acceptance characteristics than the practice board, as each paper surface has different drying, absorption, and color-acceptance characteristics. One must become familiar with these as they are among the basic painting skills that must be mastered.

Begin preparation by washing a small piece of water-color board, both front and back, lightly with water, using a soft natural sponge. Be careful not to scrub the surface of the paper as the wet paper is very delicate and imperfections will be left in the surface. Weight the board with a heavy object and let dry. Washing removes any surface impurities that may hinder color absorption. The back of the board should be washed to relieve uneven surface tension as the board dries. If only the front surface is washed, the board will cup, or "dish," as it dries.

Now, using drafting tape or masking paper, lay out a number of 3-in or 4-in sq areas to keep the color confined. Remember, masking is used more with lighter-bodied paint than with heavy-bodied paint due to edge buildup at the taped line. You will be able to observe this in this exercise.

Place the tray in which you have previously mixed pigment adjacent to your work area, along with a ¾-in flat-tipped brush and a ½-in flat-tipped lettering brush, a butcher's tray, paper towels, and some water. We will again use a value of blue, as in our mixing exercise.

PLAIN WASH
In the first square on our board (see Figure 12-8, p. 129) we are going to paint a constant color wash of tone -0-. This is done by merely painting in the entire square with horizontal strokes (direction) from top to bottom (travel), thus obtaining constant, even color throughout the square. This will be a "wet into dry" exercise. Do not wet surface with water first. Use wrist and arm movement when flowing on color. When finished flowing on the color, wipe off the excess paint from the brush and, working from top to bottom, cover the entire surface again to cover any "holidays," or gaps, in the paint. This must be done immediately, before the paint is allowed to set and start to dry. There must be a slight sheen to the surface or it is too dry, and your brush will tend to pick up color rather than flow it out.

In square #2, grade the wash from lighter (color −1) at the top to darker (color +2) at the bottom. Just above center will be the base color -0-.

Along with the ¾-in and ½-in flat-tipped brushes, select a third brush (a 5/16-in flat-tipped lettering brush). Because of the longer bristles, brush strokes can more easily be eliminated with its use.

First, wet the square with water using the ¾-in brush. When the shine is almost gone from the surface, flow onto the still-moist area some white; not too much, but enough to slightly tint the surface so that it is apparent that some paint has been applied. This will tend to soften the acceptance of the colored pigment to be applied next. If too much white is initially applied to the area, it will tend to dilute the color as it is applied.

Now that this has been done, dip into the base color -0- with the ½-in brush and paint the center of the square still moist from the water and white pigment. Cover about one-third of the area or more, working across from left to right, or right to left, or both. Work rapidly, but do not scrub the surface.

Now, using the ½-in brush, start at the upper wet portion of the -0- color and rapidly flow to the top of the square color −1. Clean the brush and flow on color +1 starting at the bottom of the wet -0- color, and work downward to the edge. (See Figure 12-8.)

You now have three definite tonal values of blue (hopefully still moist). Use your butcher's tray and add intermediate tones by first blending on the tray. At this time, clean the brush again and dip back into the -0- color and a bit of water. Again cover the area of -0- color and work both ways, into color −1 and into +1, blending the colors together where they overlap to get a good, continuous, even-graded tone. Finally, while this is still slightly moist, take a clean, moist 5/16-in brush and dip into color −1. Blot the brush on a towel and work very lightly over the entire square, applying horizontal strokes to the surface. These must start at the lightest color and work through all variations and end up at the bottom of the square at the bottom edge of the +2 color.

If you were to work from dark to light instead, you would find that the darker pigment tends to pollute the colors in both the -0- and −1 tones too much. It is best working from light to dark. As you work from the lightest to the darkest, the pigments tend to blend themselves in the brush as you proceed, thus minimizing the effort.

One should have a satisfactory graded wash at this point. This technique will hold true for all colors, either when intermixing tones of one color, or when mixing a number of colors together.

Remove tape or masking paper carefully. Note the clean, color edge definition. Look for edge thickness of paint. If a noticeable height difference between painted and unpainted surfaces can be observed, the paint had too much body. Also as this paper is being pulled off one should examine the surface of the water-color paper that was left unpainted under the masking paper. If the surface is marred in any way, a hair dryer should be used to first warm the masking paper before continuing to remove it.

PRACTICE SOLID SHAPES
In order to define shapes with color, one must know the basic fundamentals of shapes: light reflection, shade, and shadow. Refer to Chapter 5, "Perspective Theory and Practical Office Layout," Chapter 6, "Value Study of Shade and Shadows," and Chapter 10, "Pencil Rendering," showing solid shapes and how they are treated using tonal values. Solid

objects will be treated in much the same manner here. The only real difference is that paint will be used instead of pencil strokes.

The basic fear of paint-and-brush technique should, by now, be dispelled. Having done the step-by-step graded wash exercises, the feel of the brush and paint should not be so new and mysterious. Practice will help to overcome these fears.

To begin our new exercise, either draw and transfer to water-color board, or draw directly on the board these simple solid objects: (See Figure 12-10.)

1. Cube

2. Pyramid

3. Cone

4. Sphere

(Note: Conventional light will be used for these practice exercises.)

Place each shape on a piece of water-color board and surround each with drafting tape or masking paper. Review the section on graded washes and flat, one-tone washes. Again, we will use the blue values −1 through +3.

Examine the light falling on the cube. This will be the first exercise. Remember, if light is falling on this object at a 45° angle from front to back

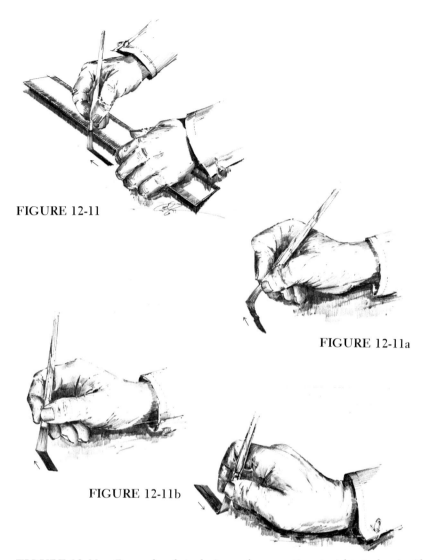

FIGURE 12-11

FIGURE 12-11a

FIGURE 12-11b

FIGURE 12-11: Proper brush technique when creating straight strokes is aided by the use of a straightedge which, when elevated slightly, forms a guide for the brush ferrule.

FIGURE 12-11a: This illustration shows the wrong way to hold a brush if proper strokes are to be made. Direction of flow is important for a smooth wash. Therefore, stroke direction and sequence must be preplanned.

FIGURE 12-11b: The correct ways to form brush strokes when using a flat-tipped lettering brush. Note the square edge at the start of the stroke—an advantage of using a flat-tipped brush.

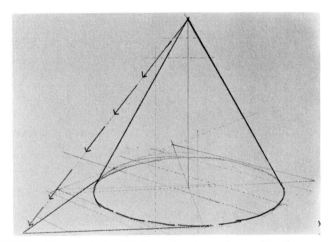

Figure 12-10: The conical solid shown has been drawn directly on medium-surface water-color board. For instructional purposes, lines of construction and light-direction designation are shown.

and from right to left, the top will be the lightest color tone (−1), the right side will be color tone -0- (the base color), and the left side will be +1. Of course, shadows should also be drawn in at this time and will be color tone +2. Color +3 will be used for accent shadows at the base of the cube to tie it to the floor.

The outer margins have now been taped, making confinement of pigment much easier. For interior color separations, something new will be added to your technical skill. You must learn both in graded washes and in plain washes how to confine the paint within a given area by using a brush and straightedge. This technique is very easy but requires practice to obtain proficiency. This is one of the most used of any individual skill you may master. Not only is it used for edge borders, but your control of any straight line situation is assured when the skill is learned. One thing to remember about the interior color separating that must be done is that it is much easier to paint a darker color over a lighter color.

VALUE STUDY

Before actual painting is begun, lay a piece of tracing paper over the previously drawn cube and rough out a value study with a graphite stick. You will find that this will be a very helpful full-size reference as you are painting.

PAINTING A CUBE

Begin painting the cube with the lightest color first. Be certain that the interior plane intersection lines have been pressed sufficiently into the paper surface so they will still read when painted over. This will be explained and practiced more fully later, but it is good to follow the procedure even on items as simple as our three-dimensional cube.

Flow clear water onto the area of the entire cube. Let dry until shine disappears and flow on just a bit of white. This will soften the surface as described earlier. Now, let the board almost dry (until shine is gone).

Flow onto the top surface of the cube −1 color-tone, keeping the value constant and even. Do not be concerned as yet about painting onto the other adjacent surfaces. Let dry thoroughly.

Using a straightedge, a ⅛-in flat tipped brush, and -0- color, form the edge between colors −1 and -0-. Color -0- is darker than color −1 and should cover very readily, forming a nice, crisp, straight line where the two tones meet. Follow indented pencil line in surface while that new color is still wet. Continue flowing on color -0-, with a ½-in flat tipped brush creating a flat wash. Do not be concerned about painting onto +1 surface at this time. Let dry.

FIGURE 12-12: The cube is shown completely rendered. Note the sharpness of line between planes of different values. This "line," or "hard edge," was formed with the aid of a straightedge as shown in Figure 12-11. Notice the masking paper that has not been removed at this stage.

Now, with a clean #4 brush and color +1, form edging between this surface and −1 and -0- colors. You should now have crisp edges along all internal color separation of the cube. (See Figure 12-12.)

Continue washing in the balance of +1 color while edges are still wet. Do not let these edges dry during the painting process. Here again, do not be concerned with painting into the shadow area. This will be covered with the +2 color as the later shadow is painted. Let dry.

Remove the masking paper. If removal is difficult, warm the paper slightly with the hair dryer and remove slowly.

CONFINEMENT OF COLOR

To paint the shadow, use the tape or pressure-sensitive masking paper as a confinement agent. Use only your #4 brush. If the area to be covered were larger, a larger brush would be used. It is imperative to keep these areas moist while you are painting within them. You may find that wetting the area with water first will help you to keep up with drying time. Let the water be absorbed, as was stated before, until the shine is almost gone.

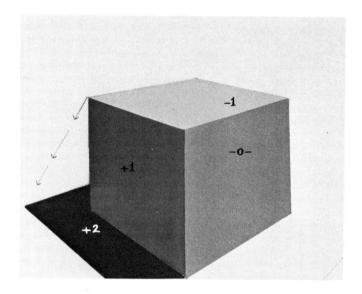

FIGURE 12-13: Here the masking paper noted in Figure 12-12 has been removed from around the cube. Masking paper was also used to confine the pigment while painting in the shadow area. Notice how the clean break between the pigment and bare water-color paper has been formed using a sharp blade when cutting through the masking paper. Observe how "dead" the shadow appears without a strong +3 value at the base of the cube to tie it to the shadow area.

FIGURE 12-14: After the sphere has been painted and the masking paper removed, the shadow area may be delineated using a 5/16-flat-tipped lettering brush. One may choose to mask this shadow area as was done for the sphere, or it may be painted directly without the aid of masking paper.

This wetting process is particularly helpful when dealing with very large areas that must be confined.

After the balance of this flat wash forming the shadow has been finished, remove the tape very carefully as before and check for any "bleeding" of color under the tape. If this has happened, use a bit of white on your #4 brush, along with the straightedge, and clean up these edges. (See Figure 12-13.)

One will notice that hard-line accent shadow value +3 has not been added in this figure. This resulting shadow is "dead" and does not tie the cube to its shadow. Accent shadows are always necessary and one must be aware of them.

PAINTING A SPHERE

The balance of the shapes can now be painted using essentially the same process with only slight variation. The only exception to the whole procedure is the masking portion of the sphere. Masking or drafting tape has a

tendency to not want to bend around corners, and if you perhaps succeed in accomplishing this, you will probably find the bleed factor very high. Masking paper will be used to cover our sphere area, after which the outline of the sphere will be cut out of the masking paper with a small, sharp, cutting blade attached with tape to a compass. The sphere area of the masking paper will then be removed and the painting process can continue.

A sphere, unlike any of the other four solid shapes, is probably the most difficult to master. (See Figure 12-14.) The problem here is that all motions of painting are circular and the entire sphere or circle on the paper must remain moist during painting. There cannot be any touch-up, so it must be correct before the board dries.

First, one must examine very closely what makes a sphere read as a sphere. Notice the reflected light that makes it appear round; the hot spot of light at the point where the highest concentration of light strikes the surface; and the way the color or tone is graded to gradually get darker and then grades back to a lighter tone at the edge. All of these principles must be incorporated into the painting of this familiar shape.

Refer again to Chapter 6, "Value Study of Shade and Shadows," and review the technique used to designate the ball in the excercise shown. (See illustration Figures 6-8 and 6-9.) It was much easier in pencil to control the grading of tone because nothing was drying and one had plenty of time to work. Not so with this medium. It is imperative to not only master technique, but also speed. Speed in this case is an integral part of technique.

To begin painting (using the same values of blue as in previous exercises), flood the water-color board with water and flow onto the surface a bit of white. Let board dry until the shine has almost gone. Now dip a ½-in brush into the lightest color (−1), and in a circular motion, paint the entire sphere with the exception of the hot spot. Use a clean ½-in brush with the water blotted from the bristles, and blend in the white hot spot with the −1 color.

Now dip a ½-in brush into the -0- base color and darken the center section of the sphere. Work this darker color more to the lower left of the sphere than on exact center. Remember, the top and top right are the lightest areas, and the lower left from the center will be the darkest. Blend in the −1 color with the -0- color gradually, at the same time removing most of the paint from the brush by blotting on a towel. Work only from light to dark.

Using a third brush, add +1 color, blending into -0- color. Finally, with a ⅛-in brush, blend in a small amount of +2 color in the lower center left.

Clean a ⁵⁄₁₆-in flat tipped brush. Dip into white and blot almost all of the water and paint from the bristles. Start from the hot spot and, with a circular motion, cover the entire sphere for a final blending process, ending at the dark area at lower left. You will notice that as the brush moves to the darker area it gradually absorbs and blends into this darker color. Again, work only from light to dark. You should now have a good representation of one of the three-dimensional shapes common to your everyday life. Let thoroughly dry.

Remove the masking paper. If for any reason the masking tends to lift the nap of the board, warm it slightly with a hair dryer and remove carefully. If there has been any bleeding, touch this up with white. Be careful when the masking paper is first placed. To reduce the bleeding, seal the edges by pressing down on them with any smooth, rounded instrument that will not discolor the illustration surface. Do not depend on white touch-up.

Let the board dry thoroughly, and again lay the masking paper over your

illustration. You will be able to see the pencil lines of the shadow boundary through this paper masking agent. Cut lightly with a small sharp blade and remove area to be painted.

Paint this shadow. Refer again to Figure 12-14. Because of the smallness of the area, use the "wet-into-dry" (using a brush wet with paint onto a dry surface) technique with a +3 color. When the shine has almost gone, blend into this some +4 color in the area where the shadow touches the bottom of the ball. In reality, this part of the shadow is darkest because it gets less reflected light than the portions further away from this intersection. Remove the masking paper and you have a finished exercise.

PAINTING A CONE AND PYRAMID
Now that you are familiar with the painting techniques discussed for the previous exercises, continue painting the other remaining shapes and their respective shadows. These exercises may seem dull and perhaps boring to you, but their importance cannot be overemphasized. (Refer to Figures 12-15, 12-15a and 12-16.)

FIGURE 12-15 The straightedge is used as a guide for all straight-line painting. Here the shadow area is finished using a ⅛-in flat lettering brush.

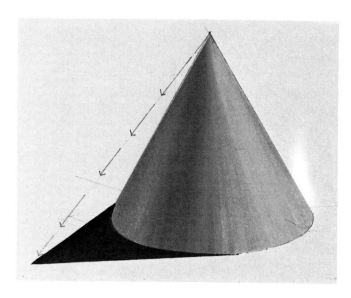

FIGURE 12-15a Pencil lines denoting shape and light direction may be erased after painting is complete. Note that some edges need to be cleaned up.

FIGURE 12-16 *Above:* Shown here is a typical practice board. Exercises such as these must be mastered before the student can go on to more complex projects.

As was stated in Chapter 6, "Perspective Theory and Practical Office Layout," almost everything you will draw or render can be broken down and simplified into any of the five basic geometrical solids; i.e., cube, cone, pyramid, cylinder, and sphere. The principles are exactly the same for the painting of a pyramid-shaped building (TransAmerica Building, San Francisco, for example) as for our example above. The only difference is in the scale relationship of the shape to its surroundings; and it is the scale that differentiates between objects that we see. A pyramid or any other basic form is constant whether it is a toy, an Egyptian tomb, or a building.

PAINTING BRICK WALLS AND FLOORING
Colors to be used are tones of umber, burnt sienna, and rust. These techniques work as well for acrylic colors, designer's colors, and transparent water color as for bottled opaque pigments; however, no white is used with transparent water color.

Before any painting is to be done, brick designation must be pencilled in so perspective of individual bricks will be easy to follow. Remember to press into the surface sufficiently so that lines are easy to read even when painted over with color. (See Figure 12-17.)

For this exercise we will be mixing the value designations as before, but this time a red-brown brick color will be the base color -0-.

First give the area to be painted a light wash of white mixed with rust

(orange and brown). Vary the tone and also the chroma or color. Note the preliminary diagonal shade lines. This will help you to determine how dark or intense to make each brick as you progress. To do this, brush water onto the surface to be rendered, with a bit of white for softness. When surface water has disappeared, flow -0- base color onto the brick surface. While the board is still moist, dip brush you were painting with into +2 color and add soft, blended shadow lines in a diagonal manner as shown. These will form the basis for the wall color as well as brick character.

Using all colors mentioned and a ½-in to 5/16-in flat lettering brush (depending on the size of individual bricks to be painted), randomly paint individual bricks using at least 3 values of brick color. Do not paint too many and do not get too wild with color contrast. Refer to the pen-and-marker illustration in Chapter 14, Figure 14-9d, to observe brick placement, positive and negative space, and coloration of the three basic values of brick color. Follow predetermined shade and shadow areas. Remember, it is the total look that we are after; only a suggestion of painted individual bricks is important. Do not get involved too much with detail. Get used to knowing when to stop. You will have to use two or more brush sizes because bricks get smaller in perspective. (See Figures 12-18a through c.)

Notice the advantage here of using the flat-tipped lettering brush. One stroke for each brick is sufficient. It is important not to overwork this

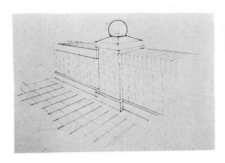

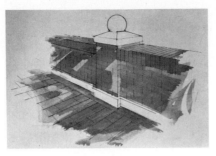

FIGURE 12-17   FIGURE 12-18a

FIGURE12-18b   FIGURE 12-18c

FIGURE 12-17: Bricks must be studied before they can be drawn. Joint position, size and type of brick, pattern, and method of construction must be observed and remembered. This illustration was done on a light sepia mat board. In the initial stages of illustrating bricks, accurate layout must be made so that brush strokes are not placed at random.

FIGURE 12-18a through c: Observe the progression of these various stages of the same illustration. Notice how the first wash, even though it will be glazed over later, has its own character. If transparent acrylic colors are used, the character of the first wash is reflected in the subsequent glazes, using an almost dry brush painting onto a dry board.

exercise. Note the shadows under bricks. They form the visual designation that distinguishes one brick from the other. Here again, do not get too busy, and do not overwork.

Refer to the finished restaurant illustration, Figure 12-19, showing a brick floor. Note particularly how the individual bricks are darker in shadow areas, and how important and well defined each brick is in the foreground. A suggestion of a brick floor is made in the back area, but definition is purposely left a bit vague.

PAINTING PLAIN WALL SURFACES

Wall surfaces usually take up a very large area in most renderings. An interior designer, when commissioning a rendering, is concerned with a total look, unless he is selling a specific product. Wall areas should form only a background to enhance the more important items in a room. The decorator may be demonstrating to a client a new rug design whereby the floor would play the important role in the illustration. However, in any case, each part of the rendering is very important and must be treated as an integral part of the whole atmosphere—one that every designer hopes will sell the job.

Walls have a much different character than do floors and ceilings. They are vertical surfaces, but not necessarily flat surfaces. They bend, curve,

intersect, reflect, and contain pictures, wall coverings, fabrics, ornaments, windows, and doors.

Light source has much to do with the value placed on walls depending on their placement with relation to the light source in the room. As was explained in Chapter 6, "Value Study of Shade and Shadows," the conventional theory of light tells us to conform to the self-imposed axiom that light falls at a 45° angle from both the vertical and the front horizontal, unless the illustrator decides on a different light source. (Refer to Figure 12-23, p. 144.) In this illustration, the chandelier comprises the single light source within the room. This illustration will be used to demonstrate techniques for walls, carpet, ceiling, mirrors, and frames, and should be examined and copied by the student as the discussion proceeds.

In order to clarify in our minds which walls are to be the darkest, lightest, and medium in tone, we must make a value study. Notice the word "tone" is used here instead of color. Color is important; however, the tone, or value, is what we must first concern ourselves with. Of course, colors will vary, but most important is the value or tone. Squint at your value study. Each plane must read; it must be distinguished from its adjacent or intersecting plane. If it does not do this, change your value study.

At this time, take notice of the value study and see if there is an

FIGURE 12-19

advantage in varying the value of color or tone within each wall in order to achieve interest. A water-color teacher once gave this writer a bit of good sound advice. He said, in essence, that in a good water color, the artist should not paint more than one or two square inches of painting surface without something happening to the surface. He meant that there should be a change in value, color, or intensity; all this being for one purpose, and that is to interest the viewer.

This, too, is partly true for an illustration. You, as the illustrator, do not have all the freedom afforded the water-colorist who paints nature. You have a client to please, and this is only done by being as realistic as possible in portraying his design idea while giving the illustration a feeling of inviting the viewer in for a closer look. You are not learning here only how to paint pretty pictures; you are primarily learning how to create a visual selling aid.

Once you have decided if there should be slight changes in values within the wall surfaces, you are now really ready to paint. It is assumed that before any painting is begun, required colors have been mixed, water-color board has been washed, a value study has been done, and the illustration has been transferred to illustration board.

Refer to Figure 12-20, studying the walls first. Flood the proposed lightest wall (if applicable) with water, let soak for a minute or two, and flood again, this time washing a small amount of white into the surface. (If wood panelling is used, no white is used.)

Next, while the paint is wet enough to still have a shine, brush into the entire wall surface the lightest of the wall colors you have mixed, this being yellow ochre and chrome yellow light. Again, while this is still wet, but this time just as the surface is losing its sheen but not yet drying out, blend into the lightest color, the medium color of the wall. In the corners and in the shadow areas only, add a bit of the dark wall color. Using this technique, you have been painting wet into wet. For picture shadows and hard shadows of plants, chairs, mirrors, sconces, and other furnishings, you will use the wet-into-dry technique. When painting hard shadows, it is sometimes a good idea to first give the suggestion of object shadows (during the wet-into-wet process) with the medium color, and then, right next to the

object casting the shadow, add a crisp brush stroke of the darkest of the color values using the wet-into-dry process. A successful illustration has both softness and crispness. Refer again to Figure 12-20 to see how these principles apply.

To give further interest, a few 45°-angle diagonal brush strokes should be painted into the surface while the surface is still capable of accepting paint and producing a soft line. This must be done with the utmost restraint and taste. Learning methods of creating atmosphere will take much practice and determination on the part of the student, but it can be very rewarding.

The balance of the wall surfaces are handled as in the preceding manner, keeping in mind the total, over-all values of the illustration. After all the walls are complete, stand back and squint at the drawing. You should be able to see clearly the values within the walls. At this time you will know if they each read. If they do read true to the value study, your efforts have been successful to this point.

Do not try to paint the final hard shadows in until the balance of the rendering has been done and all objects such as pictures and mirrors are finished.

PAINTING CARPET FLOOR COVERING

For the purpose of this illustration (Figure 12-23), let us examine the procedure used to illustrate the carpeted floor (Figure 12-21). Other surfaces can be handled similarly. Notice the progression of walls, ceiling, and drapery shown in the illustration. These items are painted in sequence and, although we are discussing walls and floor-covering techniques, the student should examine all aspects of each portion of this step-by-step example.

For this example, a base of Hooker's green and yellow oxide is used for the carpet. As was stated, when light is reflected from a surface, some of the parts of this light are absorbed, some are reflected. This, as we now know, is the reason we see colors as we do.

Light is also blocked out when an object comes between the light source, or sources, and the surface upon which that light is falling, thus creating shade and shadows. It is this constant play of light, shade, and shadow that we will use to give our carpeted floor interest.

With the board in front of you, slightly inclined but not too much, select the 1-in flat brush. Dip the brush into plain water and cover the area of the floor you are going to render. Let the board dry slightly, or until most of the shine is gone. This will take a little experimenting to get the timing just right because of the larger area to be covered. Note that no masking is used in this exercise. Dip the brush into the white borrow cup and flow a small

FIGURE 12-19 *Opposite:* Bricks, tile, wood flooring or any material that is highly patterned must be drawn to be in scale with the illustration. One must be especially aware of clarity of pattern in the foreground. This clarity need only be suggested as the pattern recedes into the background.
Designer: John Dickinson; Illustrator: The Author; Project: Dining Room—Mills Hyatt House, Charleston, SC.

quantity of white onto the moist board, giving softness to the work. This is especially important when illustrating carpet. Now clean the brush, working rapidly. Do not let the board dry during this wet-into-wet operation.

Next, dip the brush into the lightest −1 color and flow onto the still-moist board where most of the strongest light would strike the carpet. While this is still moist, dip into the base color -0- and cover the balance of the floor. Keep in mind that the front edges of the floor are very important and should be vignetted as shown. Do not be concerned about carpet pattern at this time. Do not create too many strokes when vignetting. This must be done with much restraint and taste. Too many vignetting lines and strokes tend to stop the viewer's eye instead of inviting his vision into the illustration. The chairs in the foreground will aid in this vignetting process.

After this base color has settled but is still moist, flow into this color some +1 color and +2 color, in areas where the floor would naturally be in shadow. The +4 color would be the areas in greatest shadow, such as under tables, chairs, and sofas, but is not put in at this time. Do not make these preliminary shadows too defined at this time. The time for final definition will be later.

After the wet-into-wet technique has been carried out as shown in the example, let the board dry completely. Again, use +2 and +3 color to further define shadows in crisp strokes with flat-tipped brushes. The area to be covered will determine the brush size to be used. For this process, do not wet the board before painting, but paint in definite strokes, being free and loose. Be careful not to get the surface too busy and overworked.

Remember, the reason for not using the one-step direct painting method for the whole floor surface was to ensure a contrast between the softness of the wet-into-wet areas and definition of the wet-into-dry areas. The carpet now has interest in both value and color variations, and in texture as well. Refer again to Figure 12-21 and compare your work with the illustration.

PAINTING CARPET PATTERN

At this time, if the carpet has a definite pattern it should be painted in. Again, each color within the pattern will require different tones and values. The lightest and more definitive colors will be in the light area, and the darkest, more nondescript will be in the shadow areas. Be aware of what actually happens in reality. Study color photography; it is a great help in determining the amount of pattern to use. Notice how the pattern becomes much smaller as it recedes in the perspective. Also be aware of how much of the pattern is eaten up within deep shadow areas and how, or if, the base color has changed in these shadows. (Refer to Figure 12-22.)

The +3 and +4 color is usually not put into the floor to create the hard-

line shadows until after all furniture has been finished in the illustration. This was also true, as you remember, when painting wall surfaces with pictures and accessories. The crisp, dark shadows are those distinguishing marks that tie furniture to the floor, pictures to walls, etc.

PAINTING A CEILING

Refer again to Figures 12-21 and 12-22. The student should follow all of the steps stated for the painting of wall surfaces when painting the ceiling. Paint the ceiling using raw umber mixed with white to obtain the various color tones required. Note the darkness in corners and at the perimeter with the center left light simulating the halo around the chandelier.

PAINTING MIRRORS

Mirrors are highly reflective surfaces. They are so reflective that they reflect everything as it appears in actuality. If one were to treat mirrors this way in renderings, it would be found that not only does one have to do double work by painting the exact reflection of everything that would appear in the mirror, but the rendering would become static, uninteresting, and confusing.

A mirror must, above all, appear to sparkle and reflect. The following technique will give you a basis upon which you can create mirrors that will truly enhance your renderings. This technique will not work for all styles of rendering, but complements very well the technique being taught here. It will be up to the individual to practice and transform what he is learning into his own way of illustrating.

Begin by taping the outline of the mirrored surface. The technique of painting a mirror is messy and speed is important. You should not have to be concerned about keeping within a given area, but should concentrate more on the look of the mirror you are creating. With masking paper you can leave a wide border outside the painted area. Cut carefully and peel off the paper that covers the intended mirrored surface. Refer to the finished mirror in Figure 12-23 and the close-up photo of a mirror in Figure 12-24.

You will need three flat-tipped brushes (one ½-in and two #8 lettering brushes) plus one ⅛-in flat tipped brush and one #4 pointed brush. The colors should be mixed directly on a butcher's tray; since the quantity is very small, it is not worth mixing this small amount of color in an egg tray. Colors needed are white, cool gray (white and black), and cobalt blue.

Wash surface with water and wait for shine to recede until almost dry. Dip the ½-in brush into the white and blot it on a towel. Glaze into the right edge of the mirror one or two vertical strokes. These will tend to dissipate into the moist surface.

Now dip the brush into the previously mixed gray tones (it does not

FIGURE 12-20 *Above Left:* Working from lightest to darkest, first wall and ceiling areas are painted, complete with shadows. Be especially aware of light direction. The darkest of shadow areas are not to be painted in until paintings, mirrors, etc. are finished.

FIGURE 12-21 *Above Right:* Carpet and drapery areas, all within the same color range, are added next. Note that the pattern within the carpeted area has not been painted at this time. But primary shadows have been established.

FIGURE 12-22 *Left:* Patterns within carpet and drapery areas are added next. Shadow within this pattern is as important as in areas having no pattern. Any transferred lines within the rendering that have been lost during the painting process must be reestablished before the painting of objects such as chairs, tables, and the chandelier may be accomplished.

FIGURE 12-23 *Above:* The last steps include the placement of the darkest shadows to help objects relate to their resting places. Plants, flowers and other accessories are then added to make the space inviting and inhabited. Scale figures are not needed in a rendering such as this, as the self-contained atmosphere has been created to form a strong enough statement without them and the furniture given a scale relationship to the rendering.
Interior Designer: Anthony Hail; Illustrator/Design Consultant: The Author; Project: Lounge—Mills Hyatt House, Charleston, SC.

FIGURE 12-24: *Left:* This close-up detail of a typical mirror shows suggested reflection only. Accurately defined reflections are not rendered in this painting technique. When painting, the number of obvious strokes, both vertical and diagonal, should be kept to a minimum.

FIGURE 15-25: *Right:* Representation of mirrored surfaces may be suggested through the use of color where accurate reflection of objects is not required.

matter which tone) and blend some vertical strokes adjacent to the white. Continue this across the face, skipping uneven amounts of the surface. Use the straightedge for these strokes.

Dip the #8 brush into the gray and into the blue (not too much blue) and interject, with vertical strokes, a few darker blue-gray blended areas. Work the darkest areas into the opposite corners of the mirror while the surface is still moist. Add a bit of black to the blue and blend this color into the far reaches of the corners and edges to simulate frame reflection. Also, with this dark, blue-black color, begin to indicate reflections of nondescript objects (only an indication of shapes, not complete objects).

Now, with a clean #8 brush, glaze into the still-moist surface three or four diagonal 45°-angle lines. These will blend into the surface and appear soft. Do not use too much white. Let it dry.

With a ⅛-in brush dipped into black and blotted almost dry, add a few crisp vertical strokes on the edges, in the corners, and in the center; again, this is to further emphasize the reflected shapes. Do not make these strokes continuous; they should be broken and should fade into the balance of the surface. Let this dry.

At this time, if desired, use a #8 flat-tipped brush and glaze one or two vertical white lines as a finish reflection. Clean up the edges with a thin black line at the outer edge. Do not make the line continuous; it should be broken.

When you have mastered the technique as shown, you should be confident enough to try anything. This is probably one of the most easily overworked exercises you will do. If the proper strokes are painted in the proper sequence, the results should be satisfactory, but this does require much practice.

Painting the Frame around the Mirror. Remove the tape around the mirror surface. You are now ready to put a frame around this mirror. For our example we will use a carved, gilded frame, as seen in Figure 12-23 and Figure 12-24.

The colors used will be Hooker's green, yellow ochre, Vandyke brown, yellow-orange and cadmium yellow light. Here, again, you will mix directly on the butcher's tray, the amounts of paint being very small.

Draw the outline of the frame, leaving most of the carving out at this time. An indication can be put in, but do not get too descriptive. When painting a frame like this or any highly carved surface, one must remember a very important aspect: *do not be concerned as much with the carving as with the shadows cast by the carving*. It is this factor that will make the difference between success and failure.

A value study done in pencil or tracing paper is very helpful at this time. Study intently the frame you are going to reproduce. Note how the light only strikes and reflects from the high spots, and all the definition of the shape of these high spots is determined by the dark shadow areas behind them.

Mix a color made up of yellow ochre and a touch of Vandyke brown. Wash wet into dry the complete area of the frame with this color and let it dry.

Now, using your value study as a guide, begin painting in the shadows with a color mixed half Vandyke brown and half Hooker's green. If this gets too highly contrasted, add a bit of white. Continue to do this until all carving has been represented. Further accent the deepest shadows with Hooker's green and black; not too heavy, just enough for good definition.

For the high areas, mix yellow ochre and cadmium yellow light together to give a nice, mellow, medium gold, and sketch in the high areas of the

FIGURE 12-26: *Above:* This pencil sketch was used for preliminary idea acceptance between the client and the designer. It was then used as an under-drawing for the illustration shown in Figure 12-27.

FIGURE 12-27: *Right: Examine wood grain in the mahogany panelling.* All shade and shadow was predetermined on a value study before painting was begun. Note how absence of color within the stair area suggests a highly polished, reflective surface.

Design Consultant: Anthony Hail; Designer/ Illustrator: The Author; Project: The Big Four Restaurant, San Francisco, CA.

moldings all around the frame. Do not hit every one. Remember, what you leave out is important too.

Squint at the result as you go along and see how things are progressing. You are now ready to give the final touch to your mirror frame. Using yellow-orange straight from the bottle, dip a #4 pointed brush into this mixture and highlight only those tips of molding that would catch the light. Use the traditional 45°-angle light source now familiar to you from previous exercises.

Remember to emphasize opposite corners, if applicable. Place some dark shadows behind this mirror frame to tie it to the wall and to give dimension to its distance from the wall.

You should now have a beautiful representation of a carved, gilt-framed mirror. Refer to Figure 12-25 to observe how another illustrator using opaque colors has created an illusion of mirror through the use of color to represent reflections.

PAINTING WOOD
Wood, as was previously stated, is unique in that no white is used when mixing the colors. At most, four color tones, depending on the species depicted, are used wet into wet. The fourth and fifth are used as wood grain, hard-line shadow under paintings, moldings, etc.

The fact that wood has a definite characteristic (grain) which painted surfaces do not have, creates individual problems for the illustrator. The procedure is rather involved; and, again, not only requires practice in the execution, but study as to wood types, each having its own color, grain pattern, texture, and characteristics that must be captured.

Look closely at wood. Draw grain character. Notice the flecks in the surface. Notice how grainy oak is when compared to birch or maple; how rich in grain walnut and mahogany are, each with a different color characteristic. These are things you cannot fake. You must know how woods look before you can reproduce them.

Mahogany is the wood pictured in Figure 12-27. In this rendering, a preliminary presentation of a hotel lobby, the wood exemplifying Victorian craftsmanship was all important. This sketch will be used as the example from which a study should be made by the student as he is practicing the painting process. Refer to Figure 12-26, the initial pencil under-drawing for this illustration.

Begin by flooding the surface with water. As soon as the shine has disappeared, wash into the surface a mixture of yellow ochre and burnt sienna. Do not get this too red with the burnt sienna. This should settle into the paper but not dry. You are now working wet into wet. Flow onto

the paper, following a predetermined grain pattern, some Vandyke brown. Brush this into the previous mixture. Do not scrub the surface. Let the brush bristles fan out. By now you may think that the entire surface is becoming too dark and not descriptive enough. You are right.

Therefore, while the colors are still moist, remove some of the color following the grain pattern with a clean, moist, ½-in flat-tipped brush. Blot on paper towel as you work. You may need two or three brushes working all simultaneously taking colors out and adding small amounts of burnt umber, Vandyke brown and black. This is the way grain patterns are formed.

The grain patterns are never worked wet into dry at first. There is little or no control using that method, and this is one operation that definitely requires control. Wet-into-dry grain definition is done only as a final procedure using a brush with the bristles fanned out so each hair makes its own mark.

After the grain pattern has been established, rendered to satisfaction, and the light has been determined, decide where interest is needed.

FIGURE 12-28: Reflections from horizontal surfaces can be created by an absence of color (can be lifted from the surface using a dry brush when paint is still wet) or they can be added later using both dark and light vertical strokes. Too much white in reflections will cause them to predominate and they won't appear convincing to the viewer.
Interior Designer: George Onhauser & Associates; Illustrator: The Author; Project: College Food Service—Kalamazoo College, Kalamazoo, MI.

FIGURE 12-29: The wood tones in this conference room are much darker than those shown in Figure 12-27. (See also Figure 2-4, page 8 for color plate.) The illustrator must be familiar with all wood and grain pattern and color in order to successfully reproduce them.
Interior Designer: Noal Betts Design, Inc.; Illustrator: The Author; Project: Fidelity Bank N.A.—Fidelity Plaza, Oklahoma City, OK. Architect: Ray Binnicker, AIA.

Remember, interest is created by something meaningful happening on a surface. In the example, note that there are pictures and moldings creating some interest. Also, diagonal-light indications are present. These are broad, loose, diagonal-light strokes as would appear in some lighting conditions; strokes that must not be overworked. They must be subtle, definite, and must tell the story. Study the example given in Figure 12-27.

Use a ½-in flat-tipped brush and some +2 value for the preliminary shadows and to further accent the darkness of the flooring at the floor/wall junction and in the receding corners. This technique can be used to illustrate a wood floor or any other horizontal wood surfaces. This will be done almost as a transparent wash, working wet into dry. This process is a glaze, not a solid, heavy, color treatment. Do not leave too much paint on the brush. Use a paper towel to blot as you go. The floor will now begin to take on a dimensional characteristic.

Reflections in wood, such as occur in table tops and floors, are an important part of the atmosphere you are creating. (See Figure 12-28.) Notice where reflections will fall.

Real reflections usually only appear when the floor is wet or waxed, but in our case we are going to build into the floor a partial shine so you will get the experience of this technique.

Taking your ½-in brush, blot it almost dry, but leave a bit of +2 value color on. Blot out onto a paper towel and practice on a piece of scrap board. Use the straightedge as a guide and be certain that the reflection lines are absolutely vertical. Nothing is more disconcerting than reflections that are slanted, thus looking totally unreal. Try to be aware of what would actually be reflected in the floor. Make reflections mean something and tell a story. Do not lay the reflection glaze on too heavily. It should be almost transparent, but there must be enough pigment present in the brush so as to lay a light film on the painting surface. Do not overwork. Sometimes a few strokes of very diluted white may be used to further accent the reflective quality of the floor; however, do not overuse the white.

Now that the reflections in horizontal wood surfaces are illustrated, one must give the floor further dimension by painting in shadow lines between the boards, if applicable. These lines are really only shadows and are consequently not hard, continuous lines. They are broken by the vertical reflections that are seen in the surface. These lines must stop and be interrupted by reflections. If this is not done, not only is the illusion of reality lost, but the lines appear static and uninteresting, instead of divisions in the planks.

If nailheads are to be suggested in the plank floor, as in colonial styling, they should be done at this time. Each nailhead should be dotted in the foreground planks. Use a tone lighter than the plank and give a slight shadow for each. This little shadow gives more dimension to the planks. Remember that definition decreases as the floor recedes; therefore, more definition should appear in the foreground than would appear deeper into the picture.

Parquet floors are handled in much the same manner, keeping in mind plank direction when painting individual boards. Usually more reflection will appear in parquet floors because they are shinier than a rough plank floor.

Refer to Figure 12-29 to examine another example of the importance of wood representation in a rendering. This conference room has walnut paneling, which is rendered in much the same way as mahogany or any other wood species, but colors must be altered.

PAINTING HARD-SURFACE FLOORING

Hard-surface flooring (vinyl tile, marble, ceramic tile, etc.) is treated in a similar manner. For the following example, not only will the flooring be illustrated as a tile floor, but each tile must be separated from each other because of color.

Refer to Chapter 5 for a review of how to lay out a floor grid in

FIGURE 12-30a

FIGURE 12-30a: Tile floors made up of alternate light and dark colors can become a problem for the illustrator if the proper sequence is not followed: *1.* Paint lightest floor color including reflections and shadows, painting over entire floor area to be covered. *2.* Mask entire floor and cut through masking paper along all tile division lines. *3.* Peel masking paper from alternate squares. *4.* Paint darkest-colored tiles complete with shadows and reflections that correspond to those of the lighter color. This is easily accomplished by painting over both unmasked squares as well as masking paper. When the paper is removed the floor should look like the one in this illustration.

FIGURE 12-30b The student should be aware of the following correct sequence of steps:
1. Ceiling. *2.* Floor. *3.* Walls and furniture. *4.* Rug, mirror frame, chandelier. *5.* Plants, final shadows, finishing of any portion not done. *6.* Mat rendering, ready for presentation.

FIGURE 12-30c Finished illustration ready for matting and presentation.
Interior Designer: John Hallock; Illustrator: The Author; Project: Preliminary Presentation for the Metropolitan Club, San Francisco, CA.

FIGURE 12-30b *Above,* **FIGURE 12-30c** *Below.*

FIGURES 12-31, 31a: *Above Left and Right:* Masking paper was used in these two renderings to divide carpet colors in the same manner as was employed for the tile floor shown in Figure 12-30.

Architect: Chatham and Sehulster, AIA; Project Designer: Tom Sehulster; Graphics Designer: Sheri Simmons Sehulster; Illustrators: Umberto Baldini, Sid Delmar Leach; Project: Joseph Magnin Store, San Jose, CA.

perspective. This can then be used as the basis for the tile flooring you are going to illustrate.

Begin by referring to the finished illustration (Figure 12-30c) to observe the total look of this rendering. Notice the clean lines between the tiles. These are formed by using masking paper over an initial white floor complete with shade, shadow, and reflection designations studied previously in this chapter. After the board is dry, a sheet of masking paper is spread over the entire floor and smoothed in place. The grid drawing should be dark enough to read through both the first application of paint and the masking paper. If not, these lines must be darkened with a finely pointed pencil before applying the paper.

Cut along each grid line in both directions using a utility knife, cutting only through the masking paper. Now, carefully lift off every other square leaving the balance intact.

Using three gradations of dark gray to black (add a small amount of burnt umber to black to make it warmer in nature) paint the entire floor

FIGURE 12-32a

150

FIGURES 12-32, 32a: Latticework is not difficult to illustrate if the student becomes very familiar with the pattern of shadows. Notice the variation in background color. This variation forms interest behind the lattice and tends to minimize the busy look in this type of wall treatment.
Interior Designer: George Onhauser; Illustrator: The Author; Project: College Food Service— Kalamazoo College, Kalamazoo, MI.

FIGURE 12-33: Multiple light sources must be minimized to avoid confusion in an illustration. Notice that although there are numerous sources of light within the room, conventional light has been used to determine all shadows behind wall accessories.
Interior Designer: Anthony Hail; Illustrator/Design Consultant: The Author; Project: Best Friend Bar— Mills Hyatt House, Charleston, SC.

area including the masking-paper-covered surface. Follow any shadow lines and reflections previously painted in the white floor below. Grade some tiles individually from light to dark (using the three values of dark gray). The masking paper may then be pulled off leaving a clean back-and-white tile floor, complete with character. Clean up any reflections that do not read and add more if necessary. Refer to Figures 12-30a through c to observe the total progression of this illustration.

PAINTING GEOMETRICAL CARPETING
Masking paper is very helpful when illustrating a geometrical carpet. Using exactly the same techniques as those explained for the previous exercise, a rendering of two or three colors of carpeting may be executed in much the

same manner. In Figures 12-31 and 12-31a, a specialty store was illustrated using acrylic polymer colors. These were used in a very light viscosity so they appear much like transparent water color. Masking paper was used to separate the carpet colors. All shade and shadow areas were first painted in the lighter-color carpet, so that when covered with masking paper, all of these color differences could be seen through paper and followed within the darker color. This creates a feeling of continuity in a floor having a strong geometrical pattern.

PAINTING SPECIAL WALL COVERINGS
Specialty items such as latticework can become a problem for the illustrator. Latticework reads only through a careful use of shade, shadow, and its

background (seen between the boards where intersection occurs). Refer to Figure 12-32 showing the use of a great deal of this busy material.

The red walls behind the latticework were first handled in the manner discussed previously under plain wall surfaces. (See Figure 12-20.) As one may observe, many variations within the red occur. All shade was indicated on this background but all hard shadows were left until the lattice was illustrated.

Red tones in all opaque mediums, with the exception of acrylic colors, tend to bleed through any color (especially white) painted directly over them. If acrylic polymer colors are not used, a spray-workable mat-finish fixative is required to stabilize the red color before painting the white latticework.

Using a straightedge and a flat-tipped lettering brush, paint all lattice boards. Use some gray to dark gray in shade and shadow areas. This a very simple procedure.

Shadows of overlapping white boards should next be indicated at each intersection on one edge only. (See enlarged section in Figure 12-32a.) Remember, light is falling from the left front in this illustration. Next, using dark gray to black, indicate shadows of board thickness being projected onto the red background beyond. Plants and mirrors are an integral part of this rendering and should be examined further.

If striped wall covering is being used, treat the pattern as a value to be darkened or lightened as a unit. This means that every color in a stripe must have at least three values. Stripes are difficult to master, but with practice you will gain confidence and skill.

If acrylic colors are being used to paint striped wall covering, the entire wall can be treated as a plain surface with no shadows; all stripes would be the same value. After all stripes are delineated, the shade and shadow may be worked directly over the previously painted lines. Acrylic colors do not bleed or lift and can be used in a transparent manner when a glaze such as this is desired.

Refer to Chapter 6, Figure 6-12 and to Figure 12-33. Walls with moldings are handled much the same as are walls with pictures. The entire wall is worked wet into wet for colors −1, -0-, +1, and +2. Color +3 is added when the board is almost dry, but not "bone dry." Color +4 is added after surface is dry and all pictures and moldings are finished.

Note the diagonal light pattern and highlights on tops of moldings. It is usually noted in an illustration of an interior that one common light source will cast the principle amount of shading from one 45° direction on wall surfaces. Little emphasis is placed on the importance of lamplight unless it is the only source of light. In this case, it is well to observe an actual

FIGURE 12-34: This rendering of the same subject shown in Figure 12-33 is much more rigid in feeling. This more highly structured approach meets the demands of many clients and is an excellent approach when exactness of detail is required.
Interior Designer: Anthony Hail; Illustrator: Larry Bratton; Project: Mills Hyatt House, Charleston, SC.

example of a similar lighting problem. (Refer to Figure 12-33.) Light is falling, being reflected, and casting shadows, from all different directions. It is, therefore, sometimes necessary (with the use of artistic license) to simplify this light. One can create an effective lighting mood if light direction is simplified, and it is much easier than it if were handled in a literal sense. Here, again, you must know when to stop.

Compare Figures 12-33 and 12-34. Each was treated in the illustrators' individual approach, each are good sales tools, and each appeals to different types of clients.

CAUTIONS

1. *Premature Drying.*
If the board should happen to dry too much before an entire area has been finished (wet into wet), let it dry completely and then very carefully wet the

entire area with clean water (a spray bottle is good for this as it does not disturb the surface) and continue from a point at which you stopped painting. The secret is to not let the board dry until you want it to dry. It should always remain moist in those areas you are working wet into wet. A small portion of glycerin added to the paint will retard drying, but overuse of glycerin will create a disaster.

2. *Overworking.*
Do not overwork your drawing. Not only can it become too busy, but it will become muddy if you are not sure of your strokes. Each stroke must mean something and should never be scrubbed into the board unless a special effect is desired.

3. *Repair.*
You can repair a line drawing rather easily, but to repair an opaque water-color rendering is another problem. This can be done successfully, but only if done very carefully. The painting can become overworked before you are aware that it has happened.

4. *Contrast of Textures.*
The freshness and softness of ceilings, floors, and some wall surfaces are all important to the total look in a rendering. However, these surfaces must form the background for all hard-line shadows, plants, furniture, and accessories that go into the total illustration. These elements are usually quite detailed and descriptive and must be distinguished from their soft backgrounds.

5. *Know When to Stop.*
The importance of knowing when to stop and say "that is enough" is as important as any of the work done to this point. Too many renderings are ruined, or at least their effectiveness is reduced, by overworking.

6. *Under-Drawing.*
You must be certain that all lines representing tables, chairs, light fixtures, or other features that may unavoidably be painted with color while working wet into wet are indented into the paper surface before painting. Otherwise, you will lose these lines. This problem is usually eliminated by the use of sufficient pressure of the stylus during the transfer process. If lines are not indented enough, redrawing with a hard, sharp 4-H pencil may be necessary. The importance of this process will be brought out very strongly when you further define these tables and chairs for shade, shadows, and delineations. Refer to Figure 12-22 and notice the darkened pencil lines that can be seen through the paint, denoting chair legs, coffee table legs, and the chandelier. One way to further alleviate the problem of losing lines is to create register marks at the top of the drawing with push-pin holes at the time of transfer. If lines are lost, it is a simple matter to reposition the original drawing and retransfer onto the painted surface. Be careful not to smudge graphite from the transfer paper onto the painted surface, it is *very* difficult to remove.

It is up to the student to study all of the illustrations in this chapter and practice, practice, practice. The techniques are here for the determined student of illustration. Opaque water-color medium is a very sought-after form of rendering within professional circles, and learning the necessary procedures will aid the student in becoming proficient in this exciting illustration medium.

CHAPTER 13

Transparent Water Color

INTERIOR DESIGN RENDERINGS done entirely in transparent water color are not seen very often in today's interior design market. There are a number of reasons for its lack of popularity among illustrators. First of all, this medium is extremely difficult in which to work. The student must practice long hours to master the particular skills needed to create illusions in this medium, as in any medium; but transparent water color is not a forgiver of error. In other words, mistakes are practically impossible to correct because of the transparent nature of the medium. One does not have that added advantage of opaque color with which to correct errors. Changes and corrections of design given by the designer to the illustrator after completion of the art work are also practically impossible to achieve without there being irreparable damage to the working surface.

Water-color renderings may be done on any number of papers, either mounted or unmounted. Regardless of brand used, the surface of water-color paper is very unstable. This surface will show all correction attempts when subjected to erasure, scrubbing, and overworking.

If one were to list all of the good and bad points about transparent water color when used as a commercial interior design rendering medium, the bad points would certainly win out. On the other hand, transparent water color when used for exterior architectural illustrations is one of the most excellent of mediums. With the latter, one has the loosely painted vastness of sky and landscape to contrast with the hard-line surfaces and forms of the building. Water color offers the illustrator any number of "float" techniques that give great interest and illusion of reality to these vast sky and landscape surfaces. The transparent quality of water color gives depth and softness that cannot be achieved through any other medium (with the exception of acrylic colors when used like water color).

Aside from the correction problems, let us analyze another aspect for a moment. Up to now the student has been exposed to opaque color (color that one could, because of the pigment-vehicle make-up, completely cover areas of prepainted color, rectify a mistake, or implement a design change). With the opaque media, if you will recall the exercises, highlights and

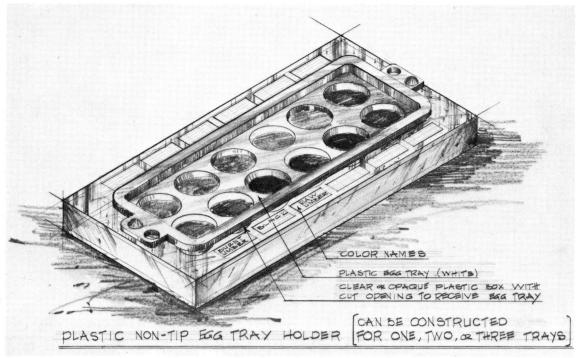

COLOR NAMES

PLASTIC EGG TRAY (WHITE)

CLEAR or OPAQUE PLASTIC BOX WITH
CUT OPENING TO RECEIVE EGG TRAY

PLASTIC NON-TIP EGG TRAY HOLDER [CAN BE CONSTRUCTED
FOR ONE, TWO, or THREE TRAYS]

FIGURE 13-1: In order to keep egg trays from tipping during use, and to identify colors within the cups, a box of the type shown here is needed. This box may be made from wood, plastic, or metal.

lightest areas were usually painted last with white or a derivative of white, gold, or yellow; whatever the color chosen, highlights were painted last. Water-color painting, however, because of its transparent nature, must be handled in a much different manner. Highlights are left without paint being applied to them throughout the painting process. In short, one must *work from lightest to darkest* at all times. This lightest-to-darkest approach was true for most of the opaque and acrylic painting techniques, but one always had assurance that, after all was done, any corrections could be handled quickly and neatly with opaque color, so one did not need to be as careful in painting.

Value studies are always a sound preamble to painting in any medium, but with water color they are a must. Examination of a value study will help the beginner to reverse the thinking process, which is necessary in order that a sound approach be taken. Remember that color cannot be successfully removed once it has been applied.

TUBE OR BOTTLED COLORS

Transparent water color is available in concentrated liquid or cake form. The liquid form comes in either bottles or in tubes, but it is recommended

that the student use the tube colors for all exercises in this chapter. The use of cake water color is discouraged. If one wants to experiment with bottled colors, this is acceptable only after the techniques of mixing tube color are fully understood. Do not confuse these bottled water colors with opaque bottled water color. The type we speak about here is transparent, highly concentrated, and works more like dye. Used straight from the bottle, these colors are potent indeed.

BEFORE PAINTING IS BEGUN

Begin by taking two egg trays (preferably white) and empty into each cup a substantial amount of each color desired. Fill each cup about two-thirds full. This should take about one full tube of the ½-in × 3-in tube. Tap the egg trays on a hard surface until the color settles into the cups and forms a flat surface of color. Be certain to group colors into spectrum (color wheel) relation (blues together next to greens, and so on). Group all earth colors together; i.e., burnt umber, raw umber, Vandyke brown, etc. This will forego hunting for a color.

Proper labeling is an absolute must. After colors have been used for a while, they will not appear as they did upon emerging from the tube.

FIGURE 13-2
Illustration: Sid DelMar Leach; Interior Designer: Lightcap/Blacker and Assoc.; Architect: Lawson-Itaya-Espalin, AIA; Project: Office of California First Bank, Stockton, CA.

FIGURE 13-3 *Above:* This illustration of a building entrance in Sweden was painted in transparent water color using the dry brush technique. Preliminary washes were flowed onto the moist paper surface and left to dry. Subsequent glazes of transparent colors were then applied on a dry surface with flat-tipped lettering brushes.
Illustrator: The Author

FIGURE 13-4 *Right:* Masking paper was used to good advantage when doing this illustration. The medium chosen was transparent water color.
Architect: Hendrick and Mock; Illustrator: Umberto Baldini; Project: Atlas Galleria Hotel.

Another variation will be noted as the color in each cup hardens. Most dark colors will (because of intense chroma) appear very similar to other colors with equally intense chroma; therefore, some form of permanent labeling must be affixed to the trays. Adhesive tape with color designations can be attached to the edges, but this might come off or get in the way when you are working rapidly. The best solution found by this writer is to attach each egg tray to a box made of plexiglass by cutting the proper size and shape hole and then attaching the egg tray to the plexiglass box. (See Figure 13-1.) This plexiglass (white) may be marked in any way as long as the color designations are clear and legible. Another reason for using this box is to keep the egg tray from capsizing while dipping the brush into a cup.

Once the egg cups are filled, tapped for settling, suspended into plastic boxes and labeled, one must wait for the color to set. The color is too soft to work with immediately after it emerges from the tube. When color is this soft, too much color adheres to the brushes and proper control is difficult to maintain.

Unlike other forms of color pigment, water color, when dry, may be made liquid again through the addition of water. Once it is dry in the cups, it will retain its solidity throughout the cup even if the surface is wet. This fact lets the artist transport the egg trays without fear of spilling the color, providing the pigment is set before transporting. One should be cautioned, however: certain colors will remain very sticky in the cups even though dry, while others will crumble and break apart after four to six months time; and if left covered airtight for any length of time without first drying, mold will form on some colors, particularly alizarin crimson.

SOFTENING COLORS
Now that you have egg trays filled and labeled and the colors have settled and dried, it is time to experiment. In order for the brushes to pick up pigment, the surface of each cup should be moist. This is best accomplished by dropping into each cup about four or five drops of clear water; an eye dropper is excellent for this purpose. These drops should just moisten the hardened color, thus softening it enough for easy pickup.

PRACTICE EXERCISE
Place egg trays, brushes, bottle of clear water, water-color board, frisket paper, utility knife, straightedge, natural sponge, and paper towels on a table adjacent to your drawing table. As for all forms of art, the artist should select a space where he will be comfortable, and one that has plenty of light.

WATER-COLOR BOARD PREPARATION
Cut water-color board into four sections of equal size. Be certain to use the same board surface for practice that you would use for a presentation rendering. As in other forms of water-diluted illustrative pigment, water color will absorb at a different rate with each particular board surface. If single-weight board is available, by all means experiment and practice using it. The only difference between the two thicknesses, besides cost, is that the double-ply board will remain flat longer. A point to remember: when water is applied to one side of a flat water-color board and left to dry, the surface receiving the moisture will shrink more than it did when the board was manufactured. As is true with any laminated material, if one surface shrinks and pulls at a different rate than the opposite surface, cupping and bending of the board will result. Single-ply board will, of course, bend and cup easier than double-ply board.

There are two ways to handle the problem of cupping water-color board. One is to wet the back with an equal amount of water so drying and shrinking of the opposite surface is equal. A second method is to staple the entire board to a slightly larger sheet of plywood parallel to the left margin. (This placement will facilitate the use of a T square.)

WASHING THE SURFACE
In order to get rid of its waxy surface, water-color board must be washed for water-color usage, as was the case for opaque colors. It is, however, more important in transparent colors to be absolutely certain that the surface of the water-color paper is not scrubbed. Any directional scrub marks will show when the color is dry. More color will sink into the valleys formed by a wet sponge dragged across the surface, and these valleys, of course, will read darker than surrounding surfaces, thus destroying the uniformity of the surface.

TRANSFERRING
Predrawn shapes (geometrical solids) will be used for practice of graded washes, shade and shadow, and general brush techniques. The solids should be quite large and shadow outlines should be part of your beginning drawing. Using the transfer sheet previously described and a ball-point pen, transfer to the water-color board the outlines of all solids you are going to paint. Use more than one per sheet but do not worry about placement. Do not allow drawings to overlap, but be as frugal with the practice supplies as your budget requires. Drawing surface is expensive and once used it cannot be used again.

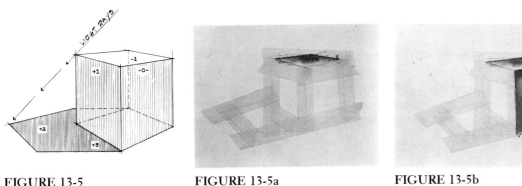

FIGURE 13-5

FIGURE 13-5a

FIGURE 13-5b

FIGURE 13-5c

FIGURE 13-5d

FIGURE 13-5e

FIGURES 13-5a through e: Note that masking tape instead of masking paper has been used here to divide the intersection of planes. Transparent water color was used for this cube illustration. Refer to the text for a review of graded wash procedures. The value study shown in Figure 13-5 is for average values within each plane as each plane graduates in tone from one edge to the other to achieve both plane definition and interest.

VALUE STUDY

Once all solids have been transferred to the respective board sections, a value study for each should be made by using a tracing-paper overlay. Establish conventional light from the upper right as was discussed in Chapter 6, "Value Study of Shade and Shadows."

MASKING AND PAINTING

Mask each board surface with masking paper. Cut through the frisket paper along all lines drawn. Mark frisket over the drawing with value numbers as shown in Figure 13-5. Always think of values within your drawings in terms of numbers; −1 being the lightest, then -0-, +1, +2, to +3, the darkest color.

Think of each plane of the solid as a graded wash. Graded washes in transparent water color achieve the same result as in opaque water color. (Refer to Figure 12-8 in Chapter 12.) Think "light to dark" and "light against dark" and you cannot go wrong. Each darker-value plane should grade in tone from one portion to the opposite. This not only helps establish the value planes, but gives each plane interest within itself.

1. Peel off the frisket paper for the area with −1 value, noting the direction of the grading. (See Figure 13-5a.) Use Payne's gray as the color. Mix with water on the white butcher's tray. You will be able to see the values of the mixed colors against the whiteness of the tray.

Apply clear water (enough to just set the surface) to the board within the uncovered section. As the shine starts to leave the surface, drop into the wet surface, and at the darkest corner, pigment from the previously mixed colors on the butcher's tray. Tilt the board slightly in the direction desired so darkest color will remain more to the darkest corner. The color will bleed naturally into the clear-water surface and form a beautifully graded wash when dry.

2. (Figure 13-5b) Peel off the masking for the area with -0- value. Using a straight piece of frisket, divide the surface −1 value from the surface -0- value. At this time, mix darker tones of Payne's gray. Instead of using clear water to first set the surface, begin by using a tone at least twice as dark as −1 value. Proceed by dropping darker values into the corners and follow Step #1 to the conclusion (figures 13-5c through e). Proceed with each plane as in preceding steps until the final shadow has been laid down.

FIGURE 13-6:
Architect: John Bolles; Interior Designer: Michael Bolton; Illustrator: The Author; Project: Sheraton Harbor Island Hotel, San Diego, CA.

3. Peel off the frisket and examine work from a distance, squinting the eyes to establish true value relationship.

The above procedure is used to confine color within specified areas while painting in transparent water color. During each step it may be desired to add some diagonal light and shadow indications, giving each surface added interest. Do this while the graded surface still has a sheen, or it may be too soon or too late. Either will ruin the desired effect. *Do not use a hair dryer to speed drying of pigment.* The uneven drying will cause rings of darker value around the heated area.

GLAZING

Glazing is the process by which the tone and chroma are built up through a series of almost transparent color washes, one over the other. This technique produces great depth in chroma and intensity.

Glazing used in connection with painting predates the time of the great masters. Their glazing techniques were, of course, done in similar media of either egg tempera or oil colors.

Unlike oil colors, present-day water color dries fast and is stable after it is dry, providing water is not applied to the painted surface and left long enough for the applied pigment to lift. Water-color paper has a fairly rough surface with many hills and valleys. These valleys trap water and, because of this, loosening of previously applied paint happens rather rapidly. If the preceding is true, the student might ask, "how is glazing possible within this medium?" The "dry-brush" method of applying water color is the only

161

FIGURE 13-7a  **FIGURE 13-7b**

FIGURE 13-7c **FIGURE 13-7d**

FIGURE 13-7: In this water color, glazes were used as described in the text. Note that brush direction marks can be seen as the steps progress to the finished cube. If acrylic plastic colors thinned to water-color consistency had been used instead, the lifting and shifting of pigment would not have occurred.

really successful way to accomplish this. Figure 13-3, 13-4 and 13-6 were painted using the dry brush glazing technique. One will find in his experiments in this medium that the brush used to apply pigment to a surface already covered with color will tend to pick up as much existing pigment as it is laying down if there happens to be too much water in the brush, if the stroke is too slow, or if the surface is wet before the glazing application is begun. If one is careful and works quickly, one can cover a previously painted area with brush strokes that do not lift the color already on the surface. The brush for this purpose must have exactly the right amount of water—almost dry. As you will recall, the glazing technique using acrylics is very different because no lifting occurs when paint is applied to a dry, previously painted acrylic surface.

Remember, only if the correct amount of water is used and the strokes are swift enough, can color successfully be glazed over existing water colors

without lifting. Only practice will provide the student with enough experience to enable him to develop a true feeling of the medium.

What will happen if one does make the mistakes of overworking the medium beyond its capacity and tries to correct these errors through the use of opaque color? This question always arises among student artists, and the answer is, unfortunately, not what one wants to hear. Once an illustration being done in transparent water color is overworked, nothing can save it enough to be within acceptable professional standards. One will always see the labored portion in the finished product. Freshness and the spontaneous feeling of the medium are lost in overworked areas and these qualities can never be regained.

GLAZING PROCEDURE
(See Figures 13-7a through d.)

Because this medium is transparent, one can, if very careful, approach the exercise found in figures 13-5a through e in a somewhat different manner. The resulting look of each plane will however be much flatter and less interesting, but this technique does have merit. This glazing process will work only if the size of the total drawing is not too large and the chroma is not too intense.

1. Begin by peeling off shadow area first and flow into it an even +2 value. After this is dry, peel off area where +1 value will go. Refer to Figure 13-5.

2. Flow into both +2 and +1 surfaces the same value as you used on +2 surfaces. Note that +2 is now twice as dark as +1. Be careful of lifting pigment as you proceed. If lifting of pigment is a problem and the chroma too intense, acrylic colors used at water-color consistency should be considered. This lifting will cause uneven and muddy plane intersections and will become more of a problem as you proceed because of pigment buildup. Peel off each successive section of masking medium as you proceed.

3. After the work in Steps #1 and #2 is completely dry, peel off -0- panel and repeat as in Step #2.

4. This step repeats Step #3. Note that as you proceed, you are adding glazes to each preceding surface, doubling their value intensities with each step. When finished, the results should look very similar to the first exercise, except that intersections of planes will not be as clear and sharp, and grading of planes will not be apparent. If grading is desired, this can be done in a loose manner after each preceding step. This must be practiced well before satisfactory results can be obtained, so do not despair. It is

FIGURE 13-8 Student project. This illustration demonstrates a good example of a transparent water color rendering. The rug was painted by dropping color droplets onto a moist surface. All other portions of this illustration were done using a dry brush technique.

difficult. Acrylics diluted to water-color consistency work much better than do water colors when doing this particular exercise. (Refer to Chapter 12.) Diagonal light indications may be successfully added to surfaces by the placement of strokes from an almost dry brush onto the moist, not wet, not dry, but moist surface. Figure 13-2 is a good example of this.

DIAGONAL LIGHT

It is also possible when adding indications of diagonal light lines (refer again to Figure 13-2) to wipe out or lift pigment with a damp (not wet or dry, but damp), clean brush. This must be done just before the shine leaves the surface, or you may be too early (and the effect will not read) or too late (there will be no blending or softness to the strokes). The frequency of use of these diagonal artist's touches is something one must attain a feel for and is not something one can learn from a book. An overabundance of these strokes will be disastrous to the final result, and too few light lines mean nothing. Do not use paper towels or sponges to lift pigment. Each will leave hard edges.

It would be good for the student to practice these techniques on some other familiar solid shapes such as a cone, sphere, or pyramid, to gain more insight into the techniques needed to handle this difficult medium.

These practice techniques, though brief, will acquaint the student with the medium of transparent water color. The preceding examples were painted in transparent water color with the addition of some opaque highlights. They should be examined closely by the student. Transparent water color is best used as a sketching and "free-painting" experience where exacting requirements do not get in the way of free expression of the medium. Painting an interior illustration completely in transparent water color is an experience every student should have at least once. It will, however, make him appreciate more fully the advantages of acrylic colors if the transparent look is desired.

CHAPTER 14

Color Rendering— a Simpler Approach

IT MAY BE THEORIZED THAT COLOR illustrations are easier to identify with than are black-and-white renderings and sketches. Color adds that part of realism not found in a pen or pencil drawing no matter how photographic the technique. Many times a black-and-white sketch will suffice; in cases where decisions as to design criteria are still being made, color is not usually required. If, on the other hand, color is required and time or funds are not available for a water-color or acrylic illustration, a fast but descriptive color method is in order. How does one obtain a full-color rendering without going through all of the procedures previously described in Chapters 12 and 13?

Let us assume that a line drawing has been done in either pen or pencil and has been used not only to study design but also to obtain the client's preliminary reaction to that design. Let us also assume that the client has requested a color study of the project in question but would not, at the preliminary design phase, pay for a full-color acrylic, opaque, or transparent water-color illustration. We now have the problem facing us of how to obtain the required results while spending the least amount of money possible.

Many methods of coloring line drawings are now available to the artist. Technical advancements in quick-drying transparent color have been many, and the artist now has better product choices within a greater range than were available in past years. No longer does the original drawing become a finished piece of art by merely adding color, as in the early forms of architectural presentation popular in the 1920s and 1930s when water-colored original tracings were mounted and used as final presentation art. Wrinkled as they may have been, no other choice was then available. Photoprinting was limited and photoprint papers were only available in the traditional matte or glossy surfaces, not suitable for the addition of color, especially water color. Neither felt-tipped marking pens nor polymer plastic colors had yet been invented.

PRINTING METHODS

Original drawings should never be used for the application of quick color. Before any color can be applied, a print must be obtained. Reproduction methods as well as innovative color systems are the keys to new and fast coloring techniques. Ozalid® printing will give excellent results to the illustrator looking for a fast, inexpensive method of printing in black or brown line on white or sepia paper. Photocopiers offer clear and representative line-drawing reproduction, all done in various sizes on the same machine. Each of the print types processed on these machines can be colored quickly and easily to produce a satisfactory color illustration.

New water-color mural papers have been developed that can be used for photo-reproduction of line drawings. Water color can then be applied directly to this reproduction after dry mounting. (See Figure 14-1.) This illustration was reverse printed before color application; an added advantage to photo printing.

Photo-reproduction on clear positive film may be used for presentation. By applying color to the back of this film positive, one can produce fast color illusion.

Photo-reproduction offers the illustrator the greatest number of surfaces to be used for the application of fast-drying color. The selection of photographic papers on which to print is becoming more plentiful, and new techniques are being developed by inventive and impatient illustrators.

ENLARGEMENTS AND REDUCTIONS OF DRAWINGS FOR COLOR APPLICATION.

Within the photographic process, one has the opportunity to substantially "blow up" or reduce a line drawing to whatever size is best for the presentation. Line width increases or diminishes in direct proportion to the size of finished drawing, and care must be taken so that pencil and pen lines do not become lost or more important than the color to be applied (See Figure 14-2.)

CONTINUOUS-TONE-POSITIVE FILM PRINTS

Great care must be taken in the reproduction of pencil work. Unlike pen drawing, which offers pure black and white for contrast, pencil depends on

FIGURE 14-1: This pen illustration has been photographically printed (reverse image) onto mural paper that will accept water color. Here, transparent water color is being applied using a 5/16-in flat-tipped lettering brush. Transparency of water color allows black photographic line work to read even though it is painted over with color.
Architects: Moulton and Clark, Inc.; Illustrator: Chun Ishimaru; Color Application: The Author; Project: Outdoor Restaurant and Street Scene—Bavarian Village, Twin Canyon, UT.

FIGURE 14-2: Photographic enlargement and reduction offer the illustrator numerous choices as to sizes of prints available to him. He will also find that pen lines reproduce more clearly and are therefore far superior to pencil when a selection of a technique for the finished art is being made.

FIGURE 14-3: When pen drawings are vignetted, as in this illustration, a complete lack of background tone on the photographic print is very important to ensure clarity of color, if color is to be applied to the print. If high-contrast copy film is used in the initial photography, solid black lines with no background tone will be the result.
Architect/Designer: Donald James Clark, AIA; Illustrator: Jerry Taylor; Project: Living Room of Residence–Strawberry Point, Marin County, CA.

tone for its end results. If contrast is too great within the photograph, such as when high-contrast copy film is used instead of a continuous-tone film, most of the beauty of pencil stroke, value, and character is lost. Tone negatives are an absolute must when photo-reproducing pencil work for the application of transparent color. Absence of background is much more difficult to achieve in a tone negative. If the background is left completely blank in some cases, much of the tonal contrast within the pencil drawing will be lost.

HIGH-CONTRAST POSITIVE FILM

Pen, on the other hand, is best handled by the use of a high-contrast copy film. The sharpness of contrast gives pen-drawing reproduction its original character, and a completely white background (or in the case of film negatives, a clear background) will result. The lack of background is very important when the drawing is in the form of a vignette. (See Figure 14-3.)

PHOTOSTATS

Cost of reproduction must be considered at the time of process selection. The above-mentioned film reproduction processes can be very expensive compared to other forms of photo-reproduction. The photostat is a very good and inexpensive method when pen drawings or other line work is involved. The photostat, unlike a true film process, is accomplished through the use of a paper negative. (See Figure 14-4 and Figure 14-4a.) Although made of paper, this is a true negative and is the complete reversal of a positive; i.e., all areas that would normally be read as black on the

167

FIGURE 14-4 *Left:* Photostats are made using a paper negative. All line work that is dark on the original reads as white against a dark background on the negative.

FIGURE 14-4a *Right:* This is a photostat positive print made from the paper negative shown in Figure 14-4. Notations shown are the illustrator's questions to the designer, for whom the rendering was being made.
Designer: Anthony Hail; Design Consultant/Illustrator: The Author; Project: Preliminary Design for a New York Apartment.

original and on the positive would be completely white on the negative, and vice versa.

Costs of photostats of a reasonably large size (20 in × 24 in is normally the largest single-size print available) are much less costly than film negatives and prints of comparable sizes.

Photostats give the artist the advantage of quick reproduction with the added flexibility of enlargement and reduction.

DISADVANTAGES OF PHOTOSTATS
Problems occur when color is to be applied to the surface of a photostat.

FIGURE 14-5: Photostats do not offer the illustrator good results if color application is needed. Neither the glossy nor matte surfaces accept color well. Here, marker color is being applied. The reader should notice how the build-up of pigment at the end of each stroke and absence of color within the stroke create an unacceptable result for anything other than preliminary color studies for use in the design office.

Both matte and glossy paper surfaces are usually available, but neither are very receptive to color overlay. No tooth exists to grab the color and the paper is not very absorbent. (See Figure 14-5.) One will find that continuous-tone washes are almost impossible to achieve with marker, water color, or even acrylic colors. Color buildup at the end of each brush stroke and uneven absorption capabilities are the primary cause. Especially on the glossy surface of a photostat, fingerprints are also a problem. Body oil from fingers is absorbed unusually fast and is impossible to remove; oil will repel pigment.

APPLICATION OF COLOR

It is recommended that the student experiment with many combinations of color-reproduction possibilities. Our discussion here will explain some of the fastest and most successful methods of color application.

DIRECT APPLICATION——WATER COLOR

We will begin with a line drawing as shown in the illustration Figure 14-6. For our example, we will have this line drawing photographically enlarged to twice the size of the original, printed on water-color mural paper, and dry mounted.

Color, upon application, must absorb smoothly and be easily graded to achieve tonal variations. (Refer to Figures 14-7a through d for a step by step color application of the drawing shown in Figure 14-6.) Color must, above all, be transparent. Lines will be lost or grayed if an excessive amount of opaque pigments is in the paint chosen. Transparent water color, acrylics used in water-color consistency, and colored markers are all fully transparent and may be used. In these figures notice how the color is left transparent to retain line. Masking paper has been applied to the surface to mask out any painting over into another area, but, unless the lines below are rigidly followed when cutting this paper, white gaps will appear between the painted surfaces when the paper is pulled off.

After experience has been achieved by the student, he will realize just how much time will be saved using the photo-reproduction principles. No longer will he be made to spend laborious hours transferring a drawing onto water-color board prior to painting. One will, of course, sacrifice some quality in the illustration using this process; however, rendering time is cut by more than one third.

In a total water-color rendering, no dark pen lines are present; only shade, shadow, and color are used to form the illusions. (See Figure 14-8.) In photo-reproduction, one merely fills in the spaces between the lines to achieve satisfactory results with color. This process is not as simple as it may appear—it takes a great deal of practice.

Markers offer many advantages to the designer. Marker color is readily absorbed into a water-color surface, dries almost instantly, will not smudge, is waterproof when dry (unless water-soluble ink has been used), and is completely transparent. Notice in the illustrations, Figures 14-9a through d, how markers were used to apply color directly onto a line photoprint. (See p. 172.)

The illustration Figure 14-9a shows a very complex and successful application of marker color over a mounted, photographically enlarged line drawing. The magnitude of this rendering (size 30 in × 40 in) was a definite problem handled very admirably. The observer should notice how vertical applications of marker were used for carpet suggestion, but that direction of strokes has been changed to suggest shadow (Figure 14-9b). One must be cautioned on the stopping of colored marker strokes when interrupted where objects occur. Unless the applicator is lifted immediately from the paper, a darker spot of color will result which will not completely blend into the balance of the strokes.

Note the steel trusses and the ceiling beyond in Figure 14-9c. The trusses were left light and the darkness of the color behind makes them read well without confusion. This is a very difficult area in which to use colored markers, as all strokes must be interrupted when meeting the suggested truss members. Masking in this case would have been very difficult, as all pen lines were drawn freehand; therefore, any rigidity in cut masking would result in color divisions that would be too perfect for freehand line work.

The bricks were suggested by first washing the surface with an over-all light tone and picking out brickwork with two successively darker colors (Figure 14-9d). The reader should notice the suggestion of the bricks. In order to retain a loose feeling to the drawing and to avoid monotony in the brickwork, many spaces were left with only the application of the first two values of brick color.

Plants were, of course, very much needed to soften the rigid lines of steel, brick, glass, metal ducting, etc. These plants were drawn in the initial pen drawing stage and were illustrated in such a manner that as much color as possible could be applied within leaf areas on the blown-up illustration.

The delicacy of line work and the knowledgeable application of colored markers makes this a very successful illustration.

Sepia prints reproduced by the direct-contact Ozalid® method are easily and successfully colored with marker colors. (See Figure 14-10.) After the print has been run it may be dry mounted and colored directly with no fear of buckling paper, as is the case with water-based color. Water expands the paper fibers causing buckling and uneven absorption; but most markers dry fast enough, and the chemical-base color will not expand the paper fibers. A uniform, flat-color rendering will, therefore, be the result.

Examine closely the use of scale figures in this drawing. Complete absence of color gives these scale figures presence without drawing attention to them.

The tonal background of a sepia print can give an illustrator an opportu-

FIGURE 14-6: This line drawing done in ink has been printed twice the size of the original. The print, made on mural water-color paper, has been dry mounted and is ready for the application of color. See figures 14-7a through d for continuation.
Architect: Donald James Clark, AIA; Interior Designer: Val Arnold and Associates; Illustrator: Robert Sutherland; Color Application: The Author (for the purpose of this book).

FIGURE 14-8 *Right:* The complete absence of pen lines in this water color could not have been achieved using the photographic reproduction methods described for Figure 14-6. One must transfer the drawing to water-color board and illustrate the subject using techniques found both in Chapter 12, "Opaque Water Color," and Chapter 13, "Transparent Water Color."
(Refer to page 157 for color plate.) Architect: Lawson—Itaya—Espalin, AIA; Interior Designer: Lightcap/Blacker and Associates; Project: Office of California First Bank, Stockton, CA.

170

FIGURE 14-7a

FIGURE 14-7b

FIGURE 14-7c

FIGURE 14-7d

FIGURES 14-7a through d Shows the complete progression from beginning to finished illustration using acrylic colors as water color on mural paper that has been dry mounted after development of print. Note the use of masking paper to confine the wall area when applying color. The ceiling in this instance was left until last in order that balance within the rendering could be maintained.

FIGURE 14-9a *Left:* This rendering has been done using marker color on photographic "mural" paper, dry mounted to a double-thick backing board.

FIGURE 14-9b *Below Left:* Strokes created with the colored marker change direction and intensity in shadow areas. Absence of color within scale figures tends to tie the entire rendering together without the distraction of clothing color.

FIGURE 14-9c *Below Center:* Application techniques using marker colors within areas broken up by unpainted areas, such as the steel truss system shown in this rendering, are very difficult to master. It takes a great deal of practice to learn to control the marker's chisel point. To create the shapes desired, one must be able to draw with the entire surface of the point in contact with the surface of the paper, as well as with only portions of the point touching the paper.

FIGURE 14-9d *Below Right:* Here again, the stroke created by the chisel-pointed marker can be used to great advantage when special materials must be suggested. Bricks are easily formed by short individual strokes over a background of lighter marker pigment. Markers may successfully be overlapped without lifting color, as the two overlapping colors will blend together. Because of this, an almost unlimited selection of colors is possible with this medium.

Designer: B. Brukoff Interiors, Inc.; Consultant: Michael Wolfe Siegel; Illustrator: Charles Pigg; Project: Renovation of Old Pavilion—Stanford University, Stanford, CA.

FIGURE 14-10 *Top:* This marker-color rendering was done directly on sepia-printed Ozalid® paper. The over-all sepia tone of the paper complements the lack of color around the perimeter, while the applied color is concentrated within the area that will be important to the client.

FIGURE 14-10a *Bottom:* After printing and dry mounting the print, added pen lines (either in sepia or black, depending on the printing process used) may be needed to add texture or outline. This must be done after the application of marker color, as the marker color will disperse most varieties of quick-drying ink. On most surfaces, however, this does not occur with waterproof ink.

FIGURE 14-11 Because acrylic colors are somewhat transparent when used on the rear surface of clear film-positive prints, i.e., that surface which is not printed with the image and mylar, the pigment must be covered with an over-all opaque coating of acrylic paints of a high viscosity (thicker than whipping cream). This will give the colors body when viewed from the face side. Notice the use of a hair dryer will speed drying.

FIGURE 14-11a: This finished illustration has been painted using polymer plastic colors on a clear film-positive print. This type of paint is very flexible and adheres well to smooth surfaces.
Designer: B. Brukoff Interiors, Inc.; Consultant: Michael Wolfe Siegel; Illustrator: Charles Pigg; Project: E. S. T. Headquarters, San Francisco, CA.

nity to color only that area of the print as he may see fit. Vignetting, through the use of plants, people, and some uncolored furniture, leads the observer's eye into this picture. The pointing finger of the receptionist also

helps the viewer's eyes to spot the central portion of the space.

Marker illustrations, while seemingly simple to execute, require much practice and personal experimentation to achieve satisfactory results.

Shading (graded washes) using two or more color overlays can be a problem area, and must be studied diligently by the beginner. Each stroke reads as a stroke and cannot be faked; therefore, all strokes must be in relationship to the total design of the illustration or they will be no more than colored strokes.

Examine the magnified portion of Figure 14-10 (see Figure 14-10a). Note that pen lines and some texture can be added over the marker color, but this must be accomplished at the proper time so that inks do not intermingle and become incompatible.

COLORING OF FILM POSITIVES

Clear film positives offer the finest of line reproduction when an absolutely transparent background is desired. As was stated, these film positives are expensive. Many times when a clear background is required, the Ozalid® method using mylar sheets can give almost the same results. Printing on a clear sheet of mylar will give somewhat the same look as will a clear film positive; but there will be some loss of clarity because of the frosted tooth on most Ozalid® mylar stock. Thickness of material as well as clarity of background must be considered; but if the budget is low, the mylar print may be completely satisfactory.

Color applied to the back side of mylar prints will produce an adequate preliminary color study suitable for presentation, but the frosted side does dull colors. Because acrylic colors are somewhat transparent when painted onto clear film-positive prints or clear mylar, a solid, opaque coating must be painted over the previously painted illustration to give a uniform opaque look to it. The illustration used is the same as that used in Figure 14-1, except that instead of printing photographically on water-color paper, this drawing has been printed on clear film. (See Figures 14-11 and 14-11a.)

Flat color will result on clear film positives if the proper viscosity of acrylic colors is chosen in which to work. Polymer colors of the consistency

FIGURE 14-12 *Top:* This photograph may look a bit strange at first glance. The illustrator is positioning a clear film-positive print over a light-line Ozalid® print of the same subject that has had color applied to it. The right side of the film print has been registered, i.e., placed directly over line work below, while the left side of the film is being lowered into position. The film positive is absolutely clear and the colored print may be seen beneath; hence, the double image.

FIGURE 14-12a *Bottom:* It is important to properly register the film print over the print below or "flashing," i.e., double images, will result. Caution: Unless the expansion characteristic of the Ozalid® paper is kept to a minimum, flashing over most of the finished illustration will result.

FIGURE 14-13: In this pastel drawing, the illustrator has very successfully captured the feeling of this room using a loose technique that is definitive but not exacting. Care in preparation of a pastel drawing includes absolute cleanliness, i.e., the illustrator rests nothing on the surface that may smudge the pastel. Spraying with a fixative is a must to ensure stability of the medium after all drawing has been accomplished.

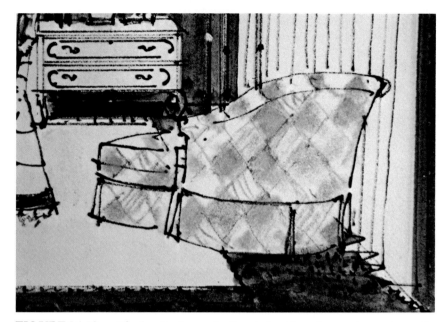

FIGURE 14-13a: Blocks of color are further defined by using a soft pastel pencil and a strong outline which, when combined, form a chair that gives the viewer a suggestion of shape without the use of shade and shadow techniques.
Interior Designer: Merline Leaming, ASID—Clark Leaming Co.; Illustrator: Gary Collins; Project: Residence, Salt Lake City, UT.

of thick cream are best to use for this purpose. These colors are flexible, adhere well, and will resist cracking even though the clear film is very flexible. Poster color would chip off under the same conditions, and water color would not adhere to the film evenly. Notice the street scene sketch Figure 14-11a that has been colored in this method. Because of the order of application, the last color applied is not the first color seen. One must prepaint any additional shadows onto the film before the main body of color is added. When viewing through the clear surface one views the first application of color first.

LINE OVERLAY
An additional application of mylar prints and clear positive film (this may be referred to as a film positive) is used as a line-drawing overlay. With this system, one can make line prints on clear film and use this overlay to clarify a rough, color under-paintng.

The illustrator must first obtain a black-line Ozalid® paper print on which to apply color. Lines are purposely left *very* light, hardly readable. Color in almost any form may be applied after dry mounting and care need not be paid to exact boundaries of color blocks. Clarity is achieved when the overlay is superimposed over the color block study. The lines which have been imprinted on the surface of the film positive when placed with proper register over the light lines of the color block study done on the Ozalid® paper print provide the clarity. A technique of this type is sometimes used when two or more color schemes for the same project are under consideration. This can be very advantageous to the cost-conscious designer. (See Figure 14-12.)

Caution: If lines of the print beneath are left too strong and the clear film positive is not properly registered, *flashing*, or double images will result. (See Figure 14-12a.) Uneven expansion characteristics of mylar and paper-superimposed prints may also create this undesirable effect.

FIGURE 14-14a: Here the illustrator has combined marker colors with pastel and charcoal pencil. Of course the marker colors of necessity are applied first, then pastel over and line work with a soft charcoal pencil last.

Interior Designer: Merline Leaming, ASID—Clark Leaming Co.; Illustrator: Gary Collins; Project: A State Government Office, UT.

PASTEL

Pastel drawings (Figure 14-13) are not often used for design presentation. One reason for this is that they are extremely messy to produce. Pastel alone cannot successfully be used to do architectural rendering without some form of line surrounding all objects. However, charcoal pencil used in conjunction with the soft pastel helps to define shapes after the pastel is used as a color value study. As you will see in the illustration Figure 14-13, line determination is primary, and value and color clarity are secondary in

importance. If one were to observe the drawing without line structure, one would see only an insipid grouping of smudges. Notice particularly the chair (Figure 14-13a). Line, here, determines the chair shape, and pattern is only suggested.

This undefined quality is removed with the addition of blackness of line in pastel work. Charcoal pencil is the only type of line-forming device that can be applied over a surface as greasy and unstable as pastel without first fixing the surface. By necessity, pastel drawings are seldom more than 18 in × 24 in.

FIGURE 14-14b: Basic wood tones for this cabinet were applied to the tracing paper. Pastel was then used very sparingly to indicate highlights. Charcoal pencil is combined with felt-tipped pen to form grain pattern in the wood, as well as create the lines used for designation of architectural features. If charcoal pencil is used for line work, it is laid down on the surface after the pastel is in place. If pen is used for line work it must be applied before pastel in order not to become polluted with the pastel color.

FIGURE 14-14c: Pastel was used for highlights suggesting light reflection on the mirror shown in this illustration. It was the last medium used following colored markers and charcoal pencil.
Note: Be certain that the fixative used to prevent smudging of the pastel will not dissolve the marker color and dissipate the color onto the adjacent surface area.

Pastels can be used in combination with colored markers if the correct sequence of steps is observed. Pastel, being an oily, compressed substance will not accept other forms of painting media without first fixing the pastel with some sort of fixative. A fixative coats the surface with a clear matte film that protects the work and forms a tooth that will accept charcoal and other drawing media. Thus, in order to combine pastel and marker media, the marker must be applied first.

Refer to Figures 14-14a through c, a pastel and marker rendering of a government office. Here, the flexibility of two media combined gives the reader a good idea of how many ways there are to illustrate an idea. A feature that has been added to this illustration is the introduction of felt-tipped-pen ink lines in areas when added lineal "punch" was needed. Felt-tipped-pen ink will "take" over pastel only after it has been fixed. The softer lines that can be observed in the marble floor and wall divisions were done with a dry felt pen and charcoal pencil. Clearprint® tracing paper is the surface chosen for the pastel renderings shown here. This quality paper accepts both pastel and marker well; and, being somewhat transparent, it eliminates the necessity of a drawing being transferred before a final illustration is begun. The process used for the above pastel and colored-marker rendering would be as follows:

1. Draw the complete under-drawing using soft pencils to create dark lines. They must be readily seen when viewed through tracing paper.

2. Place Clearprint® tracing paper on the under-drawing and tape it in place.

3. Using stick pastel and an additional piece of architectural sketch paper, create a rough value study.

4. Lay in all wood tones using colored markers of a wood-tone variety. (See Figure 14-14b.)

5. Referring to the value study and fabric, carpet, furniture, and wall coverings start to lay in the colors using stick pastel. Try not to blend too many colors as they will tend to gray. The richer-looking colors are obtained by laying down the purest of each color and blending as little as possible. Start with light and work to dark colors. Notice particularly the light-ray patterns on walls and ceiling. These are used to give life to otherwise plain surfaces.

6. Add fixative to the surface only slightly and in very thin applications; not enough to create a shine when dry, but enough to stop the smudging characteristic of the pastel medium.

7. Add any additional pastel, such as white for reflections in a dark wood

table, and diagonal white light streaks across the mirror. (See Figure 14-14c.)

8. Again, apply one light coat of fixative.

9. Next, draw accent lines with felt-tipped pen or a very soft charcoal pencil. (In this case, both were used.) This is accomplished with the aid of the T square and triangle; but in each case, the supporting surface may not be the pastel drawing. These instruments must be supported slightly above the drawing surface. Cardboard taped along the T square will support one end of the triangle, and a similar strip of cardboard will support the opposite end. One may find one's own method of supporting these items, as methods do vary from one person to another.

10. Fix the entire drawing with two coats of fixative.

11. Wrap the entire paper around a sheet of white mat board or mounting board. Secure it at the rear with masking tape. Note that if this tracing paper is left short of the mounting-board edge, black photographic tape may be used to secure it and create a strong design element.

12. Wrap the rendering with .005 acetate and secure this on the rear.

13. Cover the tape and raw edges on the back side of the drawing with a clean white sheet of paper and cement in place.

When working with fast coloring techniques, there are a great many media combinations possible within a rendering that will give a variety of results; some good and some not so good. It is felt that the student should learn the most widely accepted methods of rapid coloring techniques as shown in this chapter, and to make himself aware of other possibilities within this area of illustration. Speedy and economical execution aided by photographic reproduction methods are, of course, the backbone of the fast coloring techniques. Therefore, if time and financial reasons dictate a more economical color rendering approach, the methods discussed in this chapter can be employed to create satisfactory and professional design sales tools.

CHAPTER 15

Color Boards— Their Use and Construction

COLOR BOARDS (more accurately one would call them "sample and color boards") are presentation aids that, along with sketches and renderings, show the client the actual samples or photographs of surfaces, drapery, carpet, paint, plastic laminate, wood, wood color, pictures of furniture, file cabinets, chandeliers, plants—all those items that will go into the make-up of a design that the client may be buying.

All designers, whether making a presentation of an interior, graphic, industrial, or architectural design, must have sales aids in addition to renderings. Renderings can only show so much. Actual samples of materials, paints, hardware,carpet, drapery, and other decorator and architectural accessories are always needed to bridge the gap between rendering and reality. So is the use of color boards.

These boards are not "boards," but are made up of presentation board, illustration board, or mat board, and upon these boards are mounted samples and pictures. Samples of items such as fabric, carpet, tile, and drapery are usually affixed directly to the mat board or are behind windows cut in an overlay mat board. The actual construction of these types of boards will be covered later in this chapter.

Renderings in color are rather easy for the average client to understand. Looking at a good rendering is like looking at a color photograph, but with that additional touch of fantasy that makes it special and different from a purely photographic representation. An "artist's concept" is a term we are all familiar with. Within the artist's concept are many things that may still be in question by the client. If all items and materials that need to be shown for an accurate description of the project are not indicated clearly enough in the rendering, the client may not be able to relate to them. Remember, renderings show an over-all concept, and the specifics shown depend on the artist, the medium used, angle of view, and size of the illustration. By using color boards, the client can more easily relate the illustration to the proposed reality.

All areas within a project probably will not be shown to the client in the form of renderings. This would, on a large project, be much too expensive. Architectural features that are important and give an over-all impression of the subject matter are usually the only areas shown in renderings. All other areas must be indicated to the client in such a way as to maintain interest and answer any questions he may have. Color and sample presentation boards tend to fill in any gaps between the fantasy of renderings and the reality of the project, making up a total color concept.

Problems always arise when showing a client black-and-white renderings. Whether these renderings are line drawings or completely rendered value-related delineations, relationship to reality is very difficult. If the drawings are representative enough, and adequate color and sample boards are presented along with the black-and-white drawings, relationship to reality within the client's realm of imagination may not be too difficult. Of course, there are always those clients who claim to have absolutely no imagination and, indeed, one finds they do not.

"Touch and feel" are two terms that are directly related to color boards. Clients may feel textures; ponder over surface treatments; examine fabrics, woods, metals, and so on. For them, experiencing a feel for new environmental spaces is a very tactile experience. For example, within a rendering, deep-pile carpeting can merely be indicated; whereas, giving a client the opportunity to touch and feel this deep-pile carpet makes the selling job of the design much easier. The designer should not be too upset in cases where the client does not like samples of items shown. By process of elimination one will find out what the client does want, thereby saving time and money.

All of the above-mentioned practical theory has but one aim: *to communicate with the client in such a way as to make the client completely aware of what he is buying and, thereby, sell the design*. A client, purchasing something as intangible as design, does not like surprises. When the intangible finally turns into a new environmental space and it is not what the client expected, the designer may be held at fault.

WHEN SHOULD COLOR BOARDS BE USED?
Many jobs do not warrant the time and effort to create boards. If one determines that these aids will be needed, factors such as scope of work, the complexity of materials used, and the number of clients involved help to determine if, how many, and what type of boards are to be used. Because renderings and boards do rely on each other in a presentation,

similar requirements must be used to establish complexity, size, budget allotment for all presentation material, etc. At this time, one must establish whether or not the boards are to be used in audio-visual presentation. Because this is also a determining factor, anything to be photographed for slide presentation need not be of a large size. One can, of course, blow up the photographs of presentation aids to whatever size one wants, limited only by size of screen used. This can be an area where preparation time can be saved.

RESIDENTIAL PRESENTATION
Residential design is generally open to a more informal presentation approach. Sketches instead of renderings usually suffice for pictorial representation, and large-sized "on loan" samples of fabric, carpet, drapery, and other furnishings may be used instead of hard-line, structured color boards. Display of sample fabrics in close relationship to carpet, wood, and other materials will satisfy most residential design presentation criteria. One must also remember that the designer is rarely making a presentation to more than two individuals when selling residential design.

One must be certain of the client-designer relationship and what image the designer-decorator is trying to project. The wrong presentation in terms of image can spell success or failure of a project in the initial stages. Self-image is very important to many designers. A hard-line, structured presentation would not complement certain flamboyant decorator personalities. This type of decorator presentation would probably require a very loose and impressionistic rendering; the more left to the imagination, the better.

CORPORATE PRESENTATION
A corporate presentation is likely to be more highly structured than a residential design presentation. The number of persons present, the time allotted for presentation, personalities of the executives involved, and other such factors determine to a great extent how color boards are created and used to sell design.

Assume that your firm is to present design drawings and renderings for the refurbishing of corporate office space and public areas. The renderings have been made in full color; floor plans, elevations, and alternate design suggestions have been prepared; and it is established that color and sample boards are needed, as the budget allotment is adequate for top-quality visual aids. The designer must then establish the look of the over-all presentation package and determine how to proceed with this last phase of preparation.

Color boards must follow the guidelines listed below.

1. The size must be equal to that of the renderings used.

2. Mat color should be constant throughout the presentation.

3. Title blocks determining the project, design phase, and client and designer information, must remain constant and must be easily identifiable, while at the same time not dominating the board.

4. All items for presentation should be of consistent size, not too big for ease of handling during presentation and transportation.

5. Each board should be constructed to stand by itself without the use of an easel or wall shelf. (See Figure 15-1.) If easels are available, by all means use them; however, one must prepare for unforeseen conditions that may be out of the designer's control.

6. All lettering and borders must be constant throughout. Client and project name, logo if required, etc. must be highly visual but must not distract from the product being sold. Remember, you, the designer, are not selling these corporate executives renderings and color boards; you are selling the product these visual aids represent.

7. Mat color must not distract from the samples, reorient point of interest, nor be stronger than the mood designated by the renderings. Mat color, if inappropriate, can change the entire look of an illustration. One must keep all matting either within the color range (palette) of the design being presented or use a neutral, warm, gray-beige color. The warm tones of gray-beige are most universally flattering and can be that one mat board color to complement all colors. Of course, there are always exceptions to every theory, but this author has found the preceding to be true in most instances.

COLOR-BOARD CONSTRUCTION

There are two basic methods of color sample-board construction to be covered here.

1. Window Method (See Figure 15-2.)

2. Plant-On Method (See Figure 15-3.)

"Window" matting is exactly as the name implies; that process where windows are cut through a top sheet placed over a backing sheet so that each window frames a sample or picture. This type of board is, of course, more difficult to execute, but is also more professional looking.

Direct "plant-on" means that fabrics, tile, wood, carpet, pictures, and

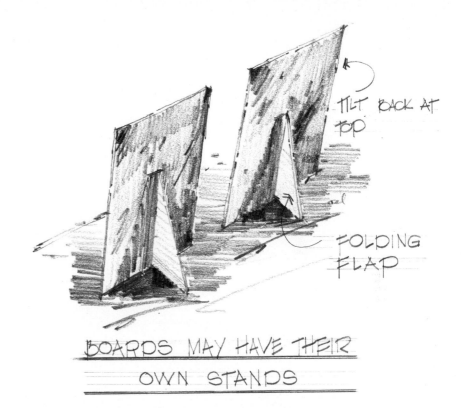

FIGURE 15-1: This rough sketch shows a cardboard support that can be quickly made and fastened to the back of each color board with contact cement. The supports enable the designer to stand each color board by itself and each support folds flat for ease of storage and transportation.

other samples are affixed to the surface of a mat board in such a way that color, harmony, balance, and texture (all elements of design) are used to create a pleasing presentation. This type of board is usually more unstable because of its single-thickness construction. Depending on the weight of samples mounted to this board, an extra sheet of backing board may be required to keep the surface from collapsing.

MATERIALS REQUIRED

1. Mat knife (a hardware store utility knife is best)

2. Mat cutter for bevelled-edge cutting (optional)

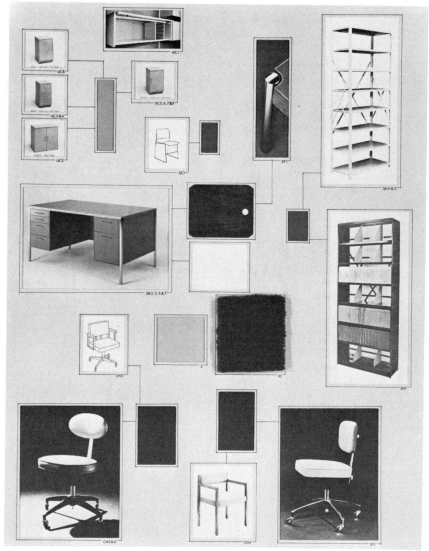

FIGURE 15-2: This is a good example of a window type of color board, i.e., individual openings are cut from a mat board to form "windows" through which are seen color chips, fabrics, tile, wallcovering, etc. Note lines around windows.
Architect: Lawson—Itaya—Espalian, AIA; Designer/Illustrator: Lightcap/Blacker and Associates; Project: Office of California First Bank, Stockton, CA.

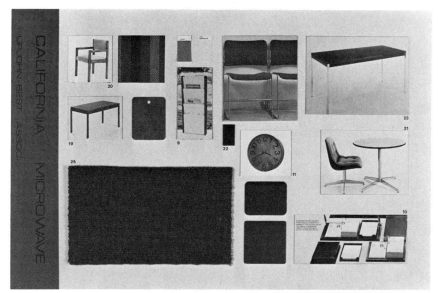

FIGURE 15-3: This example of a plant-on color board gives the viewer an alternate and much simpler approach to a sometimes tedious project. Material samples are colored cemented directly onto a mat board to form a pleasing visual presentation.
Interior Designers/Illustrators: Upjohn-Best; Project: California Microwave, Sunnyvale, CA.

3. Mat-board sheets

4. Contact cement (industrial type) (Caution: this cement is extremely flammable)

5. T square and large (14-in) 45° triangle

6. Pen or ruling pen with waterproof ink

7. Tracing paper (18-in roll of white, thin, architectural sketch paper)

8. Masking tape

9. Transfer letters (rub-on type)

10. Rubber cement

11. Rubber cement eraser

12. Backing board (mounting board)

PROCEDURE FOR WINDOW METHOD

1. The student should begin by determining the size of the face sheet. Remember, this must also correspond with the size of the renderings being used and should be the same color as mats used on renderings. Once size is determined, cut backing or mounting board of a size slightly larger than the face piece.

2. Lay out all samples required and position these on the mounting board in a pleasing manner, following principles of design; i.e., balance with regard to size, color, and texture. Colors must be positioned so positive and negative space are in good relation to each other. One must maintain a border that is in proportion to the size of mat used. A good rule is that the top and each side border be equal and that the bottom border (not including the title block) should be at least ¾ in to 1 in larger. The purpose of treating a title block as a separate unit is that there are as many title-block sizes as there are design firms.

3. Tape corners of samples in place. Those thick, hard samples, such as carpet, plastic laminate, tile, and wood, should be placed and marked with a surrounding line, but not placed permanently. (See Figure 15-4.)

4. Position the architectural sketch paper over the surface of the secured samples, wrapping this around edges of backing board and securing with tape temporarily. (See Figure 15-5.)

5. Now, with your T square and triangle and felt-tipped pen, mark accurate window patterns on the tracing paper. (See Figure 15-6.) This type of pen will mark clearly without having to use so much pressure that it will tear through the fragile paper. Mark areas to be used for border and title-block placement to lessen confusion; be certain to crease the paper around all edges so accurate placement onto the face sheet can be accomplished.

6. Remove tracing paper only after first stepping away and viewing the total graphic design of each window placement. Turn board upside down and view it with the same design criteria in mind that you used for the sample placement. The resulting design should be as pleasing as it was right side up. If not, maybe you should reconsider certain areas.

7. Place the tracing sheet over the previously cut (but blank) face sheet of mat board. Wrap this around the back as you did earlier, and secure lightly with tape. Follow creased paper edges and line these up with edges of the mat board. Take into consideration the allowance of over-sized backing board referred to in Step #1.

8. Using an extra thickness of scrap board underneath, cut through both tracing paper and mat board to create a window effect. (See Figure 15-7.) Use a straightedge and utility knife for this process. Be certain to make all one-directional cuts first, then turn the board to accomplish cuts in the other direction. Do not cut past corners. Cut only to the corner and trim corners with a blade later. Fine sanding with a sanding block may be required in order to remove frayed or uneven edges after cutting. Mark pressure dots (made with hard twisting motion of the pencil) at line intersections for the border and title block so these can be located easily after the paper has been removed. Dots indented into the surface can be re-located and used to register the original under-drawing again if another transfer of any portion is required.

9. Remove the paper and trim-cut the corners. Make all cuts sharp and crisp with no fraying or uneven lines. If, for some reason, the knife strayed or the straightedge wandered during cutting, this problem can be masked over in the next step.

10. Using the straightedge and either a sharp felt-tipped pen or ruling pen, outline each window with a strong but fine line. (See Figure 15-8.) Add border lines, title block, and transfer lettering. Keep in mind all of the elements you have learned to date. Border lines should be firm and dark, but not overpowering. The same applies to the title block. Some design firms get so carried away with their own ego and self-image that title blocks become the main point of interest. Remember, you are not selling title blocks; you are selling design.

11. The next step is to secure the two sheets (face and sample backing sheet) together. Some designers prefer to use rubber cement for this purpose; some like to use double-faced tape. One advantage of rubber cement is that samples can be changed at a later date without ruining the window cover. The disadvantage of using rubber cement is that heat creates a reaction between rubber cement and the boards and releasing is very common. Release of the rubber cement happens also with age of the boards. Never use white glue. It takes forever to dry. Spray-on contact cement is so unpredictably messy that spraying too much can ruin samples.

This author prefers to use contact cement for the bonding process. *Contact cement is extremely flammable and the fumes are toxic.* Therefore, care must be maintained at all times during its use. This product is available both clear and colored and is found in most any hardware or paint store. It is the product used in industry to secure plastic laminate to cabinet work. Bonding is extremely permanent and additional care must be exercised in order not to allow bonding until both front and back sheets are in

FIGURE 15-4: First, place samples, including carpet, tile and other thick samples on a backing board. Then, tape all fabric and flat samples in place and mark around all the thick samples. Permanent placement of these thicker samples will be shown in Figure 15-10.

FIGURE 15-5: Place a sheet of architectural sketch paper over the samples and secure to the back of the board.

FIGURE 15-8: After removal of paper, clean up any ragged window openings and draw an ink line around each opening to further define it.

FIGURE 15-9: Apply contact cement to both the back of the windowed mat and to the backing board around each sample. Be careful not to get contact cement on the samples because it is very difficult to remove. Let both surfaces coated with contact cement dry, but for no longer than recommended by the manufacturer. Adhere the surfaces to each other, being careful to register the samples to the windowed mat.

FIGURE 15-6: Mark around all areas that will be removed to create windows.

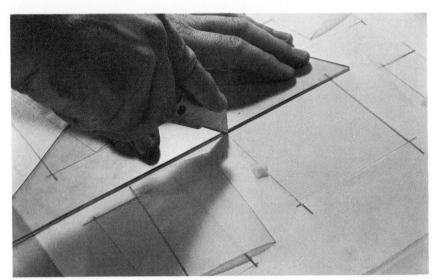

FIGURE 15-7: Cut through both paper and mat after affixing the paper to a clean mat board.

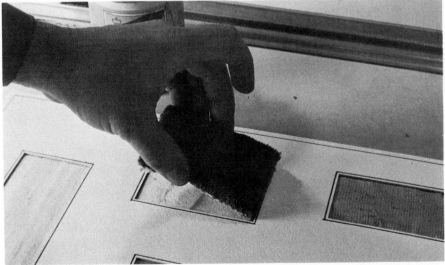

FIGURE 15-10: Lay in all thick samples after coating the back of each with cement and letting the cement dry. Finish the color board by adding borders, support stand, logo, tape, around the edges if desired etc., thus creating a fine presentation aid.

line with each other. Contact cement was properly named, as it does bond on contact. After applying sparingly to the back of the window sheet, apply cement to areas between taped samples on the backing board. (See Figure 15-9.) Let the cement dry, but not longer than one-half hour, since the bonding ability wanes after this time.

Once each surface is coated and dry, place a sheet of brown wrapping paper between the backing and face boards, allowing only the top edges of the two boards to touch together after proper alignment. Press along this top edge and pull out the sheet of paper, slowly pressing glue-coated sheets together as you progress. The glue will not stick to the pull sheet (if it does, the contact cement is not dry enough).

12. Finally, you are ready to drop those hard-edged samples into the areas previously outlined in ink. (See Figure 15-10.) This is also accomplished with use of contact cement. Note: even if rubber cement is used to bond the front and back sheets together, contact cement should be used to secure heavy samples; otherwise, these samples may fall to the floor during presentation. This becomes very embarassing and can be avoided simply by using the proper cement.

13. Taping the edges with colored or black cloth tape is becoming more popular probably because more specialized art-related materials are availa-

ble with which to accomplish these specific tasks. Tape around the perimeter can do three things: first, it protects the edges; second, it provides a band of color or tone at the perimeter; and third, hinges can be made using this tape. When cloth tape is used to attach boards to each other, these boards need to be grouped together in proper presentation sequence. However, do not bind more than three boards together with tape hinges. Tape is not very strong and it has a tendency to pull away from the surface if subjected to heat, or if the samples add too much weight and each board becomes too heavy.

PROCEDURE FOR PLANT-ON METHOD

1. Begin by again laying out all samples to be used as was done in Step #1 of the previously discussed procedure. One added element must be observed here. Because samples are not covered by a mat, each must be trimmed square. All fabric must have the edges folded or stitched so ravelling will not be a problem.

2. Place a sheet of architectural sketch paper directly over the face of the samples and tape paper to back of the board. (See Step #2 of "Window Procedure.")

3. Using a straightedge and triangle, mark around the perimeter of each sample onto the sketch paper.

4. Now mark the corners of each square onto the face sheet with the sharp end of a push-pin. Samples should be placed squarely below pin lines on paper.

5. Remove tracing paper and samples. Lightly pencil lines between pin holes forming square areas within which to apply cement.

6. Coat each square with cement to edges shown with pencil lines, as well as the back of each sample. Let dry.

7. Position each sample over its corresponding space and press into place.

8. Drawing ink lines around samples highlights the area occupied by each. These pen lines will achieve almost the same effect as does a mat.

9. Apply borders and title block as was stated in Step #10 of the previous procedure. Proceed to Step #13 if taping and hinging are desired.

It is an excellent practice to place brown wrapping-paper flaps over the face of each board (easily removed) both to heighten suspense for the client at presentation time, and also to protect the surface of both board and samples.

Your efforts should by now have been rewarded with sample boards of a highly professional nature. One can experiment and try new ways to approach the same subject, and it is hoped that this will be the case. If, in the meantime, practice is continued in a professional manner, your presentations using the above described methods will be professionally acceptable and will be a valuable aid to the selling of design.

CHAPTER **16**

Audio-Visual Communication

THE ACTUAL PRESENTATION OF A DESIGN may often be the difference between its selling or not; and considerable thought must be given to how the presentation is made, to whom it is being presented, and to what is to be included. Is the presentation being made to a Board of Directors, a committee of a local church, a chapter of ASID or AIA, or to another type of group? Each audience will have its own special interests and each will bring with it a special background. The designer should have at least a general idea of the viewpoint from which the audience will perceive the proposed presentation in order to aid in its preparation.

When the prospective group's background, prejudices, and interests have been determined as accurately as possible, an over-all approach can be formulated based on what it is one is trying to sell and how this product will be coordinated within the presentation. For example, if one is showing the layout, furniture, and colors for an entire office building floor, a decision must be made as to what the important elements are, whether it will be the over-all plan, the furniture design, or some other detail.

Audio-visual presentations offer a relatively easy method of putting information before an audience while, at the same time, offering the designer certain advantages of time, simplicity, and professional showmanship.

Going back to the previous example, suppose one desired to show an entire floor plan to a large group. With standard prints or boards, sizes are limited to about 3 ft × 4 ft and to a small number of boards. With a slide projector and screen, one can increase this to 8 ft × 10 ft or even larger using any number of previously photographed displays. With the addition of a second projector, one might leave the over-all plan on one-half the screen, while showing, on a larger scale, some other individual areas of importance. Similarly, two projectors would allow the program director to superimpose images showing comparisons of schemes or furniture selections.

Other techniques which might be utilized include close-up photography of fabrics, fixtures, and other details to emphasize why certain selections have been made. Graphics, charts, and written information can be easily added to the presentation with a minimum of expense and inconvenience. One or two trial presentations, even for the office staff or friends, will make one realize the potential and need for even more professional presentation techniques. With the use of various audio-visual aids, the techniques of design presentation are almost unlimited.

EQUIPMENT REQUIRED

Selection of equipment and hardware is most important. During the period when the designer is experimenting with presentation techniques, it is probably most economical to rent equipment as needed. However, after one has made a commitment to the use of audio-visual aids as a permanent part of presentation, the design office will most likely want to own its own equipment.

PROJECTORS

Slide projectors are the basic workhorse of the system and one should be prepared to buy a projector which most closely fits an individual's particular requirements. Prices can, depending on needed features, range from under $100 to well over $1,000. Simple projectors with low light-output lamps can be purchased from any number of photo supply dealers; specialized projectors and lenses, on the other hand, must usually be purchased from audio-visual suppliers. In any case, one should determine what type of physical environment (small conference rooms, auditoriums, living rooms, or some other space) will be most often encountered when making presentations. If, for example, it is determined that most presentations will be held in a corporate conference room of perhaps 15 ft × 20 ft, a photo supply dealer can help in the selection of the best lens for that use. (In this instance, the 4-in to 6-in zoom lens would be most flexible.) Image-reversing lenses should be used in rear-projection situations, and your local audio-visual dealer will be glad to assist you in making the correct selection. Mirrors, if used in the above situation, will project two images—one from the glass surface and one from the silvering on the rear. If you project an image onto a mirror, a reverse image will be projected from the mirror to the screen unless an image-reversing lens is employed.

The projector itself should have a fan which runs after the lamp has been turned off, thus increasing the useful life of the lamp by cooling it off. In addition, one should select a projector which has a remote-control system to facilitate changing slides from a location away from the machine. If there is the possibility of using slide-synchronized presentations, one

FIGURE 16-1 *Above:* Sophisticated audio-visual communication systems like the one pictured above are usually planned during the initial design phase of a building. Adding space such as this within an existing building is difficult, if not impossible. Three hundred seat auditorium with three-image rear projection screen. Screen is 18-ft wide and 6-ft high. Lectern contains remote controls for all audio-visual equipment and lighting.
Audio-Visual Consultant: Robert M. Morris, AIA Jr.

should look for a projector which will accept direct wire hookups from the synchronizer. Presentation programming equipment will be discussed in more detail later in this chapter.

If requirements reach beyond systems designed for rooms smaller than 30 ft long, a projector emitting more light will be required, as standard lamps are too weak to properly illuminate the screen from a long distance. Actually, as the distance from the screen to the projector is doubled, the light falling on the screen is cut to one-fourth. Therefore, if the projector is providing sufficient light on the screen at approximately 20 ft, only 25% of the same light intensity will reach a screen that has been moved back to 40 ft. Obviously, if the audience cannot see a well-illuminated image, they are not going to be impressed by what is shown to them.

Similarly, if a 16 mm movie projector is required, one should have some idea of the size of the room in which it will be used. As with the slide projectors, room size will determine what lenses are needed and whether

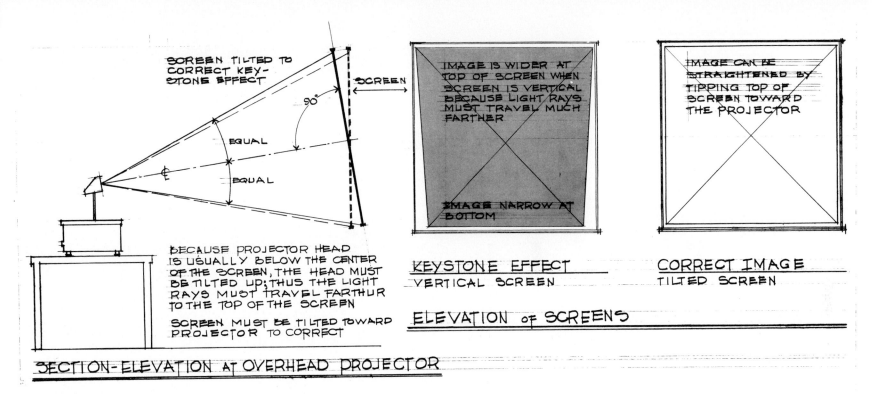

SCREEN TILTED TO CORRECT KEY-STONE EFFECT

90°

SCREEN

EQUAL

EQUAL

BECAUSE PROJECTOR HEAD IS USUALLY BELOW THE CENTER OF THE SCREEN, THE HEAD MUST BE TILTED UP; THUS THE LIGHT RAYS MUST TRAVEL FARTHUR TO THE TOP OF THE SCREEN

SCREEN MUST BE TILTED TOWARD PROJECTOR TO CORRECT

SECTION-ELEVATION AT OVERHEAD PROJECTOR

IMAGE IS WIDER AT TOP OF SCREEN WHEN SCREEN IS VERTICAL BECAUSE LIGHT RAYS MUST TRAVEL MUCH FARTHER

IMAGE NARROW AT BOTTOM

KEYSTONE EFFECT
VERTICAL SCREEN

IMAGE CAN BE STRAIGHTENED BY TIPPING TOP OF SCREEN TOWARD THE PROJECTOR

CORRECT IMAGE
TILTED SCREEN

ELEVATION OF SCREENS

FIGURE 16-2

or not there is a need for a high light-output projector. Movie projectors are not normally available with zoom lenses as standard equipment.

Overhead projectors are used quite regularly in industry and corporate presentations. Utilizing a transparent acetate film, these projectors allow the operator to write or draw directly on the transparency while discussing it with the audience. These transparencies can be produced in some office copy machines and are relatively inexpensive. The projected image possible with this type of machine is quite large within a relatively short distance away from the projector; however, one should be aware of the "keystoning" effect often present if the screen is not perpendicular to the projector's lens. Keystoning is caused by the light at the top of the image traveling farther from the projector to the screen than that at the bottom of the image, resulting in an image with a trapezoidal, or keystone, shape. (See Figure 16-2.) By tipping the screen out at the top, one can eliminate most of this problem. Overhead projectors are fairly cumbersome to handle,

however, and are not as professional appearing as are slide projectors.

SCREENS

Projection screens will also affect how an audience perceives a program. Front projection is the most common method because it is the most economical. Projection surfaces are numerous and they vary from the use of a white wall, to specialized screens designed specifically for lighted rooms. Actually, white walls are not a bad surface for most informal projected presentations, as this white surface is not too unlike the matte-white screen surface one can purchase. It gives fairly even distribution of the reflected light over a reasonably wide angle, and the amount of light reflected is within the bounds of acceptability for most circumstances.

Glass-beaded screens are the most common type sold and are excellent in the majority of circumstances. This type of screen will give added reflectance, but will cut down somewhat on the angle of that reflection.

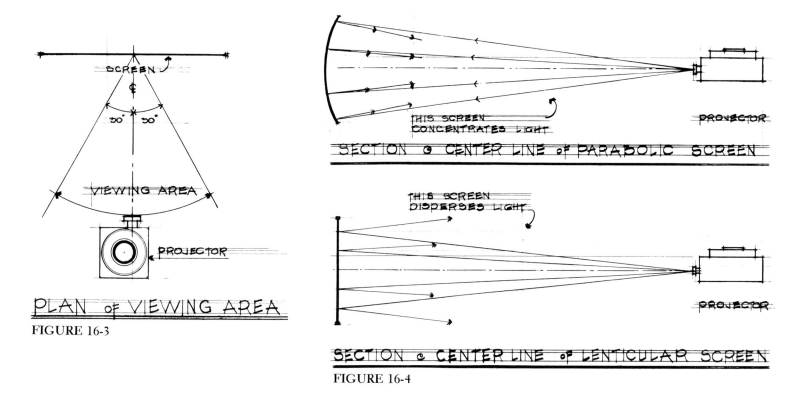

PLAN of VIEWING AREA

FIGURE 16-3

SECTION @ CENTER LINE of PARABOLIC SCREEN

FIGURE 16-4

SECTION @ CENTER LINE of LENTICULAR SCREEN

Glass-beaded screens do, in fact, have a "multiplier" effect; i.e., the light incident on the screen is boosted and concentrated toward the viewer who is in a direct line between the projector and the screen. As a direct result of this, a certain amount of light is lost to the viewer sitting at a wider angle to the center line; however, this type of screen has good reflectance within about a 30° angle on each side of the screen center line. (See Figure 16-3.)

Lenticular screens are formed of small, reflective surfaces which concentrate the reflected light from the projector into a wider area in front of the screen. These screens are a fairly good solution in rooms which have some unavoidable room light from partially shaded windows or other sources, and coverage is good within about 45° of each side of the screen center line. Matte, glass-beaded, and lenticular screens are available in roll-up formats, both manual and electrically controlled.

Special screens are also made which can be used in fully lighted rooms by use of parabola-shaped, reflective surfaces. (See Figure 16-4.) The entire screen surface is shaped into a parabolic-type reflector which can concentrate reflected light back into a fairly tight pattern. This screen is excellent in lighted rooms, and may also be used where close examination of slide color fidelity and detail is of utmost importance. Once one moves about 20° off the screen-to-projector center line, however, no image is visible.

Rear-projection screens are available in a number of configurations. These screens are made by the application of chemical substances to a surface of either glass or plastic. By intelligent selection, these screens can be used for audience areas from long, narrow auditoriums to short and wide board rooms. Rear-projection screens are normally employed as either small portable display units or are attached to the wall in permanent installations, such as training rooms, board rooms, and the like. (See Figure 16-5a.) They are somewhat fragile and are subject to damage if abused, so care should be used in their mounting and maintenance.

Self-contained rear-projection screen systems included in some attaché-case "theaters" are useful for small groups of perhaps six to eight people. (See Figure 16-6.) They contain a projector (slide, 8 mm, or filmstrip), a

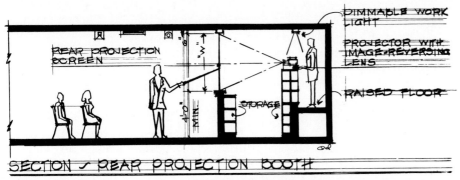

FIGURE 16-5

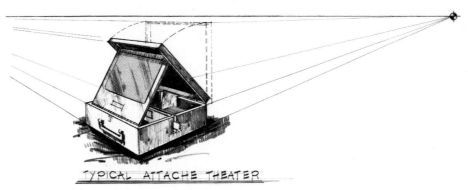

TYPICAL ATTACHE THEATER

FIGURE 16-6

FIGURE 16-5a Inside of a typical rear projection room showing slide projector and audio rack. Audio recording studio can be seen through the control window. *Audio-visual consultant: Robert M. Morris, Jr. AIA.*

small rear-projection screen and, in some equipment, sound and synchronization capabilities are available. Units such as these are especially effective in a one-on-one situation where a preprogrammed message can be played and followed, perhaps, by a series of selected slides accompanied by live narrative. Larger photo equipment dealers usually can supply these machines, and they are relatively inexpensive items.

AUDIO EQUIPMENT

The addition of a sound track to a pictorial presentation can bring an entirely new dimension to selling design. Care should be taken, of course, in the selection of sound-track material. Rock music does not necessarily belong as part of a Victorian restoration presentation; nor does Mozart seem the best choice for a disco design. Music should be used to create a mood and a background for the visual presentation, and a careful selection of music can be integrated into the presentation in a number of ways. Background music can be recorded on cassette tape and either played throughout the program or be cued at appropriate times by remote control by you or your assistants.

Sound equipment can be as simple as a pocket-sized cassette recorder or as sophisticated and expensive as one's budget will allow. A purchaser should consider the different types of sound recording equipment, speakers, and input devices, all in direct relationship to his budget; and, for other than the permanent installation, a cassette sound recorder will be more than adequate.

A number of additional aspects should be considered, however, before making the final purchase. One must decide between battery or alternating current (household current of 110 volts) models. If power supply is a problem, a unit with either battery only or both battery and alternating current should be selected.

Fidelity is also a big consideration. Inexpensive recorders will not reproduce sound that feels right to the audience. For synchronized sound and visuals, a stereo recorder will be required. Reel-to-reel is preferred. Some expensive professional cassette units have sound tape with synchronization capacity. The machine selected should have the capability of being able to record and play back; not all machines do both.

Ideally, one should have a four-track reel-to-reel tape recorder for the best sound reproduction. Tracks one and two can be used for music, track three for narrative, and track four for slide-synchronizing pulses. However, the high cost of a four-track recorder may necessitate the use of a two-track, or stereo, machine. By the use of a mixer, one should be able to combine all the necessary background music and narrative onto one of the tracks with the slide pulses on the other.

As a rule, cassette recording machines are less expensive and easier to use than reel-to-reel units; however, the larger reel-to-reel recorders should not be ruled out. The tape is easier to edit and these machines are usually equipped with a number of features not always available in cassette units.

Also consider whether the machine has the capability whereby other devices can be plugged into it so sound can be fed directly by connecting cords; i.e., one may want to record background music from a record, and to avoid recording extraneous noises that would be picked up by a microphone. One should select a machine with an "aux in" (auxiliary in) connector to plug in other audio devices such as tape recorders and hi-fi equipment. Similarly, a "line out" connector to plug into another tape unit or built-in speaker system may be desired. A line-out connector is similar to the aux in, but is used to send the signal out to other recorders, speakers, or other devices.

A microphone is required to record narrative, and as with most equipment, they vary in size, use, and cost. Many of the new cassette units have built-in microphones that are acceptable for use in recording meetings, but are not of sufficient quality for use when recording music or special programming. Separate microphones are available which are easy to use and give higher quality to the recorded voice. A microphone on a stand placed on a table in front of the narrator will gather the sound better and be of greater convenience than the microphone built into the cassette unit. Microphones with variable pick-up patterns give further flexibility when more than one person is recording. Most audio-visual dealers are glad to assist in making the proper selection of all equipment and in filling particular requests.

Placement of speakers is most important in projecting sound. The best speaker location is at the front of the room in order to give the sound "presence"; as if it were coming from the same area as the picture. To accomplish this, however, the audio signal must be brought to the speakers from the projector/tape-recorder location. If the room does not have a built-in speaker system, duct tape should be used to secure the power and speaker cords to the floor to reduce hazards.

CAMERAS

Good camera work is as important as the slide projector in the preparation of audio-visual presentations, but one does not need to be a professional photographer to achieve satisfactory results. With good equipment, study, and some practice, fine quality photographs can be achieved by almost anyone. Slides can be made with any number of cameras, from simple pocket models to expensive 35 mm or 2¼-in × 2¼-in motor-driven models.

The most versatile camera is probably the 35 mm single-lens reflex. Employing a through-the-lens light meter, this camera allows one to see exactly what image will be recorded on the film before shooting a subject. The built-in light meter eliminates having to carry a separate piece of equipment and is sufficiently accurate for most work. Accessories for 35-mm cameras are numerous and available at most camera outlets. Some of the more common accessories one may wish to investigate include tripods, flash units, wide-angle and telephoto lenses, and various filters. A copy stand is a good investment if drawings are to be photographed.

While the camera, projector, and their accessories are expensive, the investment in good equipment will repay itself many times over in terms of both quality products and pride of workmanship.

Film can be processed at home or it can be done commercially. The costs of purchasing and maintaining one's own darkroom equipment may be excessive if plans include the processing of color slides; and for the majority of circumstances, commercial color processing is of adequate quality. For special work, most large cities have custom film processors listed in the yellow pages, and these firms will handle slides on an individual basis as well as work with the designer to come up with special color work or other individual processing requirements. However, if normal quality is sufficient, general film processors can handle most needs.

Let us assume color slide transparencies to be the major audio-visual medium. These transparencies can be made with the use of common camera formats. One should be aware that the use of different types of color films will result in slightly different transparency coloration. Some films will have a slightly green or blue cast, while others emphasize the red end of the spectrum; each type of film has its use.

Other factors that determine film type and usage are color fidelity and possible graininess of the finished transparency. Lighting used in areas to be photographed plays a role also in the determination of film types selected. Incandescent, fluorescent, natural daylight, and photoflood all create different lighting situations that help to determine proper film selection. Photo supply dealers are very helpful in handling individual problems and should be consulted when in doubt, as the average camera store has an apparently overwhelming array of equipment.

Once photographic efforts have been concluded and the designer is ready to begin putting a program together, all materials must be edited. The initial editing of slides can be done by laying them out on a light table and selecting those slides which have the best composition, color, and subject matter. In order to avoid later confusion, unwanted slides should be removed immediately. They only add to what will become an already difficult final editing process. Number, in pencil, the slides remaining so they can be kept in order. These numbers will probably change later, but at least one has a beginning point. A small hand-held slide viewer or slide-projector stack loader is convenient for close inspection and for reviewing large numbers of slides quickly. After the final editing, all slides should be stored in numerical order in slide sorting containers.

Movie film is both more difficult to take and to edit, as editing requires a viewer with dispensing and take-up reels and a lighted screen. Cutting and splicing film is not complicated, but does require some experience. It is best to leave the more difficult procedures of movie-film execution to professionals.

AUTOMATIC PROGRAMMING DEVICES

If automatic slide changing is desired, selection of a projector with a built-in timing device should be considered; or remote, automatic timers may be installed if a more elaborate system is needed. This automation may also be combined with a sound tape by the introduction of nonaudible signals in the recording stage of production. With this system, signals are fed into the projector so that slide changes are timed perfectly with the sound track.

In order to accomplish these timed changes, a slide synchronizer is needed. These machines are available for rent in most large cities at an audio-visual dealer or camera store. With a synchronizer, one can prepare an entire program with slide changes that can be cued to the precise moment when the music hits a particular note, or when the designer has finished a certain word in his narrative.

The use of this type of presentation calls for careful thought, and patience is required during both the planning of the story board and the recording of narrative and music. A written script is mandatory, both for editing and coordination with the slides and music. This script is marked at those precise times the slides are to be changed or the music is to fade or be increased in volume. This basic synchronization of sound and picture results in a very professional presentation if all preparation and production have been performed in an exacting manner.

The combined use of two or more projectors at one time requires additional equipment. Fade-dissolve units are available that will control projectors in various combinations. Principally, these devices turn off the lamp on one projector as they turn on the lamp of another allowing one to change screen images without blank screen intervals between slides. By combining a number of these units, one can put together a program which actually appears closer to 16 mm movies than slides. Multiple projectors can be controlled by computer-type programmers, but costs for these controllers vary from under $75 for machines which put a single pulse on audio tapes, to several thousand dollars for multi-media-system computer-programming devices.

Remote-control devices are equally versatile, as well as being equally varied in price. Simple remote controls for forward-reverse, on-off, and focus are included in the purchase price of some 35 mm slide projectors. On the other hand, 16 mm movie projectors may require some additional electrical remote controls which must be provided by you. These are costly and sophisticated to install unless the audio-visual installation is permanent. Here, all controls for most of the room's systems can be built-in, either wireless or hard wired. For the portable systems, minimum remote controls are needed beyond those available with the projectors; and because of the cost and the bulk required for sophisticated systems, these systems are best left for the permanent installation.

Programmers are almost a necessity if one plans to deliver multi-media or multi-projector presentations. The simplest system involves a 35 mm slide projector(s), cassette audiotape (where pulses have been recorded on the tape to change slides at preselected intervals during the narrative or music), and a screen. Beyond a simple system such as this, multi-projector controllers, fade-dissolve units, and other devices are needed. Punched paper tape, multi-track audiotape, or other types of control devices are available. For advanced programming, the best equipment at this time is the computer-type programmer. This device will allow the operator to control numerous projectors, including 35 mm slide and 16 mm movie, sound, room lights, and curtains. Most design offices do not require this advanced type of programming equipment and a very professional and effective presentation can be made using a smaller, less expensive unit.

PREPARATION OF AUDIO-VISUAL PRESENTATION

In order to create a program, the designer must first define what is to be accomplished and for whom. Perhaps the easiest and most organized way to begin is by formulation of a *story board*, a graphic representation of the entire presentation. It outlines general narration, graphic materials, and all other elements of the presentation: music, slide-change cues, and so forth.

The story board itself can be a series of 8½-in × 11-in sheets of paper divided into columns, each captioned for a portion of the presentation: narrative, slide number, music, cues, and so on. Obviously, if more than one slide projector is used, a column is required for each screen image.

Story boards are not meant to be finished works of art, and should be altered and revised as subject matter and format changes are made. The design of the audio-visual program is not unlike the design of any product; the first study, as often as not, is not the best solution.

Once the story-board outline has been completed, one should begin assembling the raw materials of the presentation. The script should be written in detail; all graphic materials assembled; records purchased or recorded; all hardware (projectors, synchronizers, tape recorders, etc.) assembled; and a schedule for putting the program together should be organized.

When organizing the office for production of an audio-visual program, a fairly large area should be set aside. Be certain to include more space than is thought to be necessary because initial concepts of required area may be deceiving. This space should be off limits to other office work. Similarly, time should be set aside for this one activity only, as much concentrated effort is required for professional results.

A question will certainly arise during the initial stages as to sequence of procedures such as, should photos be taken before writing a script or vice versa. There are always obvious photos that will be needed, and these should be obtained before script writing. Drawings, certainly, need to be copied; a number of fabric and furniture samples can be photographed; and possibly model photographs taken. When this has been done, further ideas for both photos and script will naturally fall into place. Each requirement and solution will feed the next, not too unlike the design process itself.

While it is not the intent of this book to teach writing skills, certain elements of script writing for audio-visual presentations must be covered. For whom is the script being written? What is the character and background of the audience? Each member will bring certain prejudices with him to the presentation. Many obviously basic questions should be given some thought and answered in the initial phases of the presentation. What is the program selling, buying, explaining, or suggesting to the audience? Intent should be clear and obvious by the end of the program. Where is the proposed work going to be done? Will tenant relocation be needed during construction? How are proposed objectives to be met? Why is the whole project important to your client and in what way will environmental changes affect his business procedures and employee esprit de corps? These basic who, what, when, where, how, and why questions should all

be covered in the script in detail so that by the completion of presentation an attempt has been made to answer the most obvious questions likely to be asked by the audience.

When the script is completed, read it into the tape recorder or to a friend. Input from an additional person in the office with a basic knowledge of the client and project goals will give added insight into making clear statements that say what is needed.

After a near-final script draft has been reviewed, it will probably be found that there are additional photographs desired to emphasize certain points made in the narrative. Some shots, perhaps of the designer's logo, or the title block from in-office drawings will help to personalize your firm to the audience.

At this point, the package is nearing completion. Almost all of the photos are back from the processor, the script is complete except, perhaps, for some final editing. Background music has been selected, records purchased for recording, and the necessary projectors, recorders, and synchronizers have been assembled. In order to put all this material together one must complete the story board and begin the actual programming.

Before rehearsal, the narrator should assemble the recorder, programmer-synchronizer, and script. The projector should be loaded with slides, taking care to keep them right side up and in numerical order. The actual rehearsal should begin with a musical run-through while reading the script aloud. This will give a good feeling for the timing between the narrative and the music, and it may be found that more or less of one or the other is needed in order to end both at the same time. A few rehearsals with added or deleted sections will finally create a comfortable relationship between the two.

During the recording sessions, particular care should be paid to some items which will have an effect on the final tape. For instance, if a microphone is being used, one should be aware, before recording, of all other noises in the area, such as street traffic, air-conditioning noise, and people walking down an adjacent corridor. Your ear will discriminate and block these out, but they will be picked up by a microphone and may ruin the final tape. Be sure the recording machine is accepting as much tape saturation as it will handle without distortion. When several tracks are overdubbed, a weak signal will often be almost overridden by the hiss of tape noise. Be sure records and tape heads are clean, as dust and grit will cause distortions and noise on the tape. Similarly, recording heads of the tape machine must be demagnetized before starting the final recording. These precautions will give the best possible sound any machine is capable of delivering.

By playing back this first rehearsal, the designer should have a good idea of the over-all effect of the program. It is now time to go to the second phase which consists of final editing and assembling of the total package. Review the story board with its additions and deletions and get all the missing elements together. It is most helpful to have someone not previously connected with the actual production give a critique. His objectivity will point out areas where the presentation is not as strong as expected, as well as aid in the examination of over-all continuity. Is there a strong theme running through the entire program? Are the various individual elements connected in a logical sequence? Does the presentation have a sense of totality and a thematic progression? This review is probably the most difficult part of the entire preparation, and an objective critique will aid in examining the over-all effect the presentation will transmit.

After the audio portion of the program is on tape and it is reviewed for its content, length, and general interest, it is time to put this together with the visual portion. Generally speaking, a prerecorded program should not run more than about ten minutes to prevent the audience from losing interest. Verify again that all slides are loaded in the projector(s) in proper order. With the programming machine attached to the tape recorder and the slide projectors, set the audiotape into the recorder and begin to cue the slides. Turn on the recorder and the cuing device. As narration and/or music hit specific spots, cue the slide(s) to change, a very easy operation. During the first of probably several run-throughs, the script and story board should be marked at points of each slide change. This will give a reference for the following run-through exercises. It will take a little practice, but eventually the slide image will appear on the screen exactly as the music hits an individual note or when the narration refers to a particular scene.

The end result of all these exercises should be a presentation which adequately tells a story and sells a product. The timing of slides and music will be exact, the narration will emphasize just what was intended and the over-all effect will be very professional in all aspects.

It will be of particular interest to the designer to reexamine the original story board. Chances are, but for a few minor changes, content and intent are probably within the limits of acceptability when compared to the end product.

Many times the intended presentation must be made at a site not under the direct control of the designer. One should examine at length the room in which the program will be shown; the size, shape, and any lighting in the room that could cause a problem. Look for electrical outlets, window shades (or lack of shades), chandeliers hanging down too low between the projectors and the screen, and similar physical limitations of the space.

If transportation of audio-visual equipment is required, some early thought should be given to packaging materials for ease of transport. Even if the site is in the near vicinity, efficient packaging of this equipment will make the transportation easier. When one considers that at least one projector, a tape recorder, possibly a screen, connector cords, slide trays, and other miscellaneous gear must be transported, it is easy to recognize the necessity of preplanned packaging. Remember: *proper prior planning prevents poor performance.*

At the presentation site, seating must be considered. Chairs should be arranged so that the heads of the audience will not block part of the projected image. A center aisle should alleviate this problem. Ideally, the seating arrangements should provide for an audience area which is longer from front to back than it is wide. The closest seat to the screen should be about two times the width of the projected image, with the farthest seat being no more than about six times the width of the image. All the seats should be within about 30° to 40° off each side of the axis from the projector to the screen. (Refer again to Figure 16-3.)

The room's lighting system should be controllable from the location where the designer is standing, or someone from the designer's staff should be appointed, before the presentation begins, to be in charge of the lights. If the room has dimmable lights, they should be dimmed down to a level just bright enough for someone to take notes.

Be especially aware of time required for complete set up. Very few things will make an audience less receptive to a presentation than having to wait for the design team to arrive and set up. If possible, have someone at the client's office assist in getting equipment set up well before presentation time. Assistance in getting clearance from building security can prove invaluable as well as assistance in finding extra extension cords, etc., problems that can be overcome early if proper planning is carried out.

AUDIO-VISUAL PRESENTATION PROCEDURE

The director should introduce himself and relate his purpose for being there, setting the stage for the audio-visual presentation. While this may be an important moment in the design selling process, it may be just another meeting for some of the audience. If using a prerecorded program, a brief introduction will suffice, as the program should carry itself. If the program is live, the transition between bright and dimmed lights used for slide presentation must be handled with some care. Once you are into the narration, the program should flow smoothly.

There are advantages to both the prerecorded and the live presentation. With the prerecorded version, the director can introduce the program and

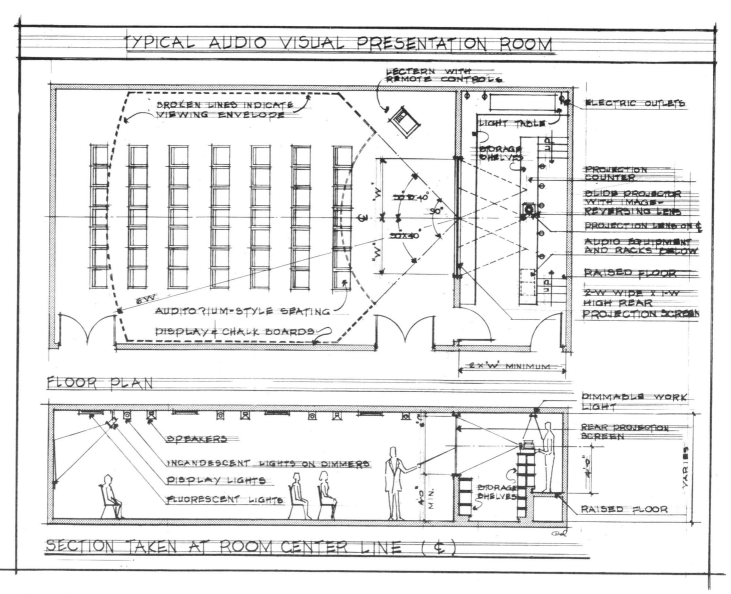

TYPICAL AUDIO VISUAL PRESENTATION ROOM

LECTERN WITH REMOTE CONTROLS

BROKEN LINES INDICATE VIEWING ENVELOPE

ELECTRIC OUTLETS

LIGHT TABLE

STORAGE SHELVES

PROJECTION COUNTER

SLIDE PROJECTOR WITH IMAGE-REVERSING LENS

PROJECTION LENS ON ₵

AUDIO EQUIPMENT AND RACKS BELOW

RAISED FLOOR

2'-W' WIDE X 1'-W' HIGH REAR PROJECTION SCREEN

AUDITORIUM-STYLE SEATING

DISPLAY & CHALK BOARDS

2 X 'W' MINIMUM

FLOOR PLAN

DIMMABLE WORK LIGHT

REAR PROJECTION SCREEN

SPEAKERS

INCANDESCENT LIGHTS ON DIMMERS

DISPLAY LIGHTS

FLUORESCENT LIGHTS

STORAGE SHELVES

VARIES

RAISED FLOOR

SECTION TAKEN AT ROOM CENTER LINE (₵)

FIGURE 16-7

sit back until it is over. Your audience should recognize the nature of the presentation and not try to interrupt with questions. This is both good and bad. Hopefully the presentation will have answered most of their questions by the time it is over. On the other hand, there might be areas where expanding on some point raised by the client may be in order.

The live program will, on the other hand, give an audience the opportunity to interrupt a number of times before the preplanned answers can be shown. When interrupted, the director must eventually get back to the program. If the director is making a formal presentation with a script, he must keep track of where the interruption was made in order to facilitate

198

easy return. In a less formal situation, it should be easier to ad lib back into the subject matter. Experience will be the best teacher and both techniques should be tried to see which gains the better results.

Upon conclusion of the presentation, someone may want to see a particular slide again. With the script marked with slide change cues, going backward or forward to a particular slide should be relatively easy. When ad libbing a presentation, it will probably be somewhat more difficult to find a certain slide; but, again, practice is the only cure for this problem. Also, by keeping programs relatively short, audience interest will be maintained.

AUDIO-VISUAL SPACE DESIGN

(See Figure 16-7.) The design firm dealing primarily with high-budget projects often makes the decision to install an audio-visual presentation space within the office if space can be allotted for this purpose and the expense of such a project can be justified. In preparation for the addition of these sophisticated new facilities, one must consider the parameters within which audio-visual design criteria are determined.

Almost all design parameters are based primarily on the space available; and because the installation is a permanent addition to the design office, additional space is most often required either within the office confines or in close proximity to it. Space cannot be physically enlarged without great expense and is many times impossible even with a large capital investment. Therefore, those in the design office will often find themselves working within space restrictions over which they have no control, the primary of which is usually slab-to-slab distance (the distance of usable height from concrete floor to under-side of concrete slab above) which, of course, determines maximum screen height.

Seating is again based on the "2 × W and 6 × W" formula used previously to set up a traveling presentation. For our discussion here, "W" will be equal to the width of a projected image of a single slide. If, of course, both vertical and horizontal slides are being shown, the space required for image projection must be considered square, or, height equals width.

In today's office buildings a ceiling height of 9 ft is not too unusual and it is this dimension that will be referred to in the following discussion.

For maximum viewing comfort when the floor must remain level, the bottom of the screen must be at least 4 ft from the floor. This will allow those sitting in the rear to view over or between the heads of those seated in front.

For example, if 9 ft is the ceiling height and 4 ft (distance from floor to bottom of screen) has been subtracted, 5 ft remains for image height. At

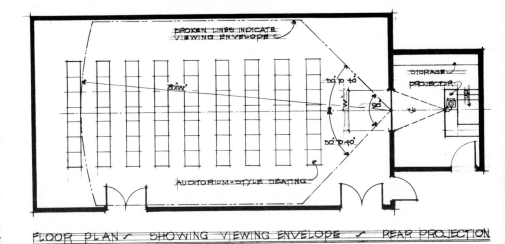

FLOOR PLAN — SHOWING VIEWING ENVELOPE — REAR PROJECTION

FIGURE 16-8

least 6 in should be left between the projected image and the ceiling (for trim), leaving 4 ft 6 in for the height of the projected image.

Assuming one may want to use 35 mm "superslides," or both vertical and horizontal slides for projection, a square area of the screen would be needed for projection; therefore, H = W. If H = 4 ft 6 in, then W = 4 ft 6 in. Thus, the first seat should be no closer than 9 ft (2 × W) away from the screen, and the last row of seats not more than 27 ft (6 × W) away from the screen. Of course, these dimensions may vary some in instances where space just will not meet demands. They are to be used as a guideline only, as individual situations will demand equally individual solutions.

A viewing envelope (that area within a 30° to 40° angle of view on either side of the room center line where clarity of image is best) may allow moving the last row of seats 8 × W away from a screen if a rear-projection screen is employed (see Figure 16-8).

Folding tables and stacking chairs offer the greatest flexibility of seating arrangements. One may wish to set up auditorium-style seating in the morning and seminar-style after lunch. The more flexibility that can be provided in the selection of furniture, the easier will be these rearrangements. A lectern may also be provided for the group leader; and the lectern should contain, if budget will permit, a reading light, clock, microphone, remote controls for slide and movie projectors, and the sound and lighting systems.

The projection room should be deep enough for a projection counter and movie projector (which, with large reels, may be about 36 in. from front to rear), a circulation space and a rear counter for layout and storage. A minimum projection room depth for rear projection should be equal to approximately the diagonal distance of the basic "W" image, plus about two feet (see Figure 16-8). For rear projection, the booth should be set up so one can operate the projectors from behind to avoid interfering with the projected light rays. The room should be painted a dull, non-reflective color, and should be treated acoustically to absorb as much projector machinery noise as possible.

An electrical and mechanical engineer should be consulted as soon as possible, as their work will have a significant bearing on the success of the projection booth. Each 600-watt standard slide projector will generate 3.4 BTU's per watt, or about 2,040 BTU's, and will require about 50 cu ft per minute of circulating air. This type of projector will also draw about 5½ amps of electrical load. A slide projector with a Marc 300-type lamp will draw about 13½ amps, as will a standard 16 mm movie projector. Minimum electrical service in the projection room should include at least three 15-amp circuits and one or two 20-amp circuits.

The electrical engineer should carefully review all the lighting systems in the facility. In the projection area, the design should provide for both an over-all working light as well as dimmable, small-wattage work lights located over the projection counter. The audience area may require several types of lighting: over-all illumination when the room is being used as a conference facility, dimmable lighting for note taking during projection, spotlighting for displays or accent, and other special systems for special requirements.

Similarly, the mechanical engineer should review the audience area to be certain enough air conditioning or ventilation is provided to evacuate smoke and help keep your audience awake and alert.

Acoustics in the audience area should be examined as to how the room will be used and what its relationship is to adjacent spaces. An acoustical consultant may be a very good investment if outside noises become a problem.

While the cost of a permanent audio-visual area is not small, the possibility of monetary gain as a direct result of this type of installation is great, and the sophistication implied by this type of selling aid will be reflected in client satisfaction.

CHAPTER 17

A Realistic Approach to Selling Design

A PROMINENT NEW YORK DECORATOR once said to a design class attended by the author, "The only way to really know your client is to stay in his house and observe everything for at least two weeks." Of course, this is not possible in most cases, especially those relating to commercial design. The art of training oneself to know and be sensitive to the client's needs, likes, and dislikes takes patience, understanding, openness to the client's ideas and the ability to graphically communicate with him.

In most situations involving the selling of something (in this case, design), salesmanship and the techniques of selling vary only slightly, if at all. One must, in all cases, make the contact, prepare for the presentation, make the presentation, and ask for the order. In very simple terms, this is what selling consists of in almost any market.

The professional designer depends on selling ideas and products to maintain financial stability; therefore, a sense of business principles and selling techniques is very necessary to create a successful practice. If the design office is large enough, initial contact is usually made by sales people who then turn the client over to a design team. It is then up to the head of the design team, working very closely with both client and suppliers, to create a product compatible with the needs and desires of the client and be within prescribed budget requirements. In the smaller office a designer may assume multiple roles of salesman, artist or illustrator, designer, estimator, and director of the presentation.

Once the product has been created and proper sales aids (graphic illustrations of the product, samples, product information, budget breakdown, and scheduling) have been prepared, preparation for presentation must be completed, and many factors should be considered before this all-important phase of design sales can be initiated.

Communication with the client may be either formal or informal, and it is to the benefit of every designer to learn the advantages, disadvantages, justifications, and requirements for each situation encountered. Before one considers the presentation as a whole, there are certain criteria that

must be established in order to determine the scope, need, type, and method of presentation. These are:

1. Size of the project
2. Money allotted for presentation/sales
3. Number of clients
4. Choice between a formal or informal presentation
5. Location of presentation
6. Quantity and type of visual aids required

If the reader will notice, all six of the above considerations are dependent on each other, yet any one stands by itself in importance. Size and importance of project determine the money allotted for the meeting. The number of clients involved determines where the presentation is to be held, how formal it will be, and the number and type of visual aids needed.

Before approaching any selling job, remember the six P's of sales presentation: *Proper Prior Planning Prevents Poor Performance*. Regardless of the solutions, planning is required. Also, under any circumstances, one must have the tools with which to do the best job. Whether requirements call for a simple sketch explaining an important idea to an individual client, or a full-color illustration for use during a very formal presentation to many clients, the designer must have the knowledge and skills to produce these tools. It is usually not practical to have a full-time artist at one's disposal; therefore, explanation of ideas in graphic form still depends on the skills of the designer.

COMMUNICATION ON A ONE-TO-ONE BASIS
The most common form of communication between designer and client is on a one-to-one basis where most idea transfer and acceptance take place in the form of informal conversation. In these conversations, lack of understanding on the part of the client is often found if the designer does not incorporate sketching as an integral part. The designer should, after examination of the project in question, absorb as much information as necessary from the client, sketching his interpretations of the client's ideas as the discussion proceeds. Then, and only then, can both designer and client examine the sketches and either agree or disagree on the designer's approach. Regardless of a positive or negative response on the part of the client, a starting point has been established in the communication process. Tracing paper can then be used as an overlay to further develop ideas.

When the client and designer have agreed on a design direction, further development of ideas is possible with the aid of additional sketches, floor plans, elevations, and final design illustrations. It is this visual bond between the ideas of the designer and the understanding of the client that is so necessary before complete client/designer communication can be achieved.

A FORMAL PRESENTATION
The problems relating to idea transfer to more than one individual increase on a ratio in direct proportion to the number of persons involved. For example, in preparation for a presentation involving 20 members of a board of directors, much more consideration must be given to the formality of presentation. The designer must ask all of the questions previously mentioned and decide what approach will best suit the situation.

Location of the presentation is of prime importance. Twenty executives is a large number of people to assemble, make comfortable, and maintain at full attention. If the designer has at his disposal conference facilities to handle this number of people then, by all means, he should consider keeping the most control possible by using this space. If not, space should be acquired that will afford the design team the opportunity to create client comfort, adequate lighting, and sound control. Only in the most extreme circumstances should a presentation be done on the home ground of the client. The psychological benefits of performing a presentation in a space under the direct control of the designer and his staff are many. Pre-presentation preparation, mood setting, sound and lighting control, and audio-visual aids may be set up so as to offer the captive audience the best flow of information in the shortest amount of time. The executive's time is very valuable and maximum use of presentation time is of supreme importance.

Graphic aids should be of the utmost clarity and must be large enough so they are seen clearly by the person sitting farthest away. Renderings, graphic aids, color boards, etc. must be of a large size (at least 30 in × 40 in) for a presentation of this scope. It is not unreasonable when working on a large project to consider photographic transfer of all material to slide form so it can be projected as large as possible.

FIGURE 17-1 *Opposite:* The presentation room in this photograph shows an entire presentation ready for final rehearsal. Before the actual presentation begins, individual areas within the over-all presentation will be covered. As the presentation progresses, each area will be exposed to the viewer to further augment the discussion pertinent to the particular area being uncovered.
Designer/The Burdick Group; Photograph: The Burdick Staff.

In Chapter 16, "Audio-Visual Communication," one found that sound/film synchronization of this type of presentation allows the designer the opportunity to preview, erase, and add to the presentation so as to make it flawless. An additional advantage to this type of approach gives the design team complete freedom during presentation to concentrate on client comfort, mood setting, and refreshments, all contributing to final acceptance of the project. Before clients arrive, your staff should make arrangements for coffee, tea, ice water, ash trays, etc. Clients love to be pampered and their well-being is imperative.

Professionalism in all phases of sales presentation is mandatory. Excellent visual aids presented poorly can add little to client acceptance. You as the designer, and your staff, will be appealing to executives who are professionals, and they in turn expect you to be professional. Nothing can appear as unprofessional as a slide projector out of focus, sound tape not properly synchronized with projected pictures, or light switches that are not under direct control of the design team (never ask a client to switch off a light or draw a blind to darken the room).

Formation of presentation structure has its roots back in the beginning of the design phase. As design ideas develop, the designer may find that many approaches are considered, discarded, and revised.

Accurate notes, drawings, and preliminary work sketches of these rejected ideas should be kept. Because they have been considered by you, they have probably been considered by your client at one time or another, and reasons for rejection should be noted for future reference. These notes will be invaluable during the question-and-answer portion of the presentation, as will be discussed later in this chapter.

Some clients will want to be the designer and will try to insist on having everything their own way. Care must be taken, while still maintaining professional control, to make these individuals feel involved during the presentation in order not to alienate them from the issues and solutions. Involvement builds interest and tends to make clients think many of the solutions achieved are really their own ideas.

If you are dealing with a corporation, you must know your clients and their status within the corporate structure. There are those whose positions weigh much more heavily than others when decisions are made. One should gain as much information as to likes and dislikes of the most important executives present. *Know to whom you must appeal, and gear your presentation toward those individuals.*

Acute awareness of client's mood must be realized; any joking should be within the immediate limitations of client acceptance. Presentation is a time for serious business, but it should not become boring. The designer should always be sensitive to the ever-changing mood of the client, and gear his presentation accordingly.

Regardless of how an approach is carried through, however, clients are only concerned about results. The design must:

1. answer all criteria given by the client and/or circumstances involved,

2. be aesthetically pleasing,

3. be possible within the given budget,

4. please the clients,

5. be constructed on time, and

6. satisfy the designer's ego as well as that of his client.

FORMAL PRESENTATION PROCEDURE

In order for any formal presentation to proceed properly, the designer in charge should first welcome the guests, introduce himself and his associates, and then proceed in the following manner:

1. Explain the given requirements of the project and what the end result will encompass. Generally, it is best to keep all graphic aids covered at this time. Each should have a plain, brown cover constructed for easy removal as required. If all graphic aids are left in view, keeping the client's attention on the immediate discussion may be difficult.

2. Lead your clients through the design thought process using notes taken as designs were being formulated and then selected or rejected. Clients love to see how a problem was approached and solutions were achieved. However, one should not include more information than is pertinent, thereby burdening the client with unnecessary information.

3. Make the client aware of any special considerations required by national and local building codes, conditional-use approval, etc. that may require effort on the part of the client, such as appearing at hearings. These proceedings, when required, are usually attended by the designer or architect as part of his fee requirements, but many times the owner is required to be present for discussion, and usually it is in his own best interest to do so.

4. Keep suspense at a high peak by enthusiastically praising the end result of the design. By this time the group of executives should be very curious to see what the designer is describing.

5. Uncover drawings, plans, and color boards of areas as they pertain to the immediate discussion. Here one should create as much surprise and

suspense as possible. (If an audio-visual presentation is being made, refer to Chapter 16, "Audio-Visual Communication.") Additional boards and illustrations should be uncovered as the presentation proceeds, explaining in detail aspects of the design important to the listener. Construction difficulties and structural changes should be included in the explanation, but should not be belabored. The presentor must not become too wordy.

6. After sufficient time has been given for thorough understanding of problems and solutions, budget allocations and projections should be covered. Apart from the aesthetic value of the project, the greatest concern of your client will be the budget. If a specific budget has been given and indications are that the project will come in under the budgeted amount, you will have a happy client. However, if a larger budget is necessary, one must be prepared to defend these indications.

7. Open the remainder of the presentation session to questions and answers. Closer observation of materials, fabrics, drawings, and other samples may be required at this time. Your notes collected during the design phase will be invaluable. You will find that most questions asked will be covered in your notes, providing both client and product have been thoroughly researched.

The remainder of the presentation time may be used for closer examination by the client of materials, drawings, and renderings. If it is appropriate to do so at this time, all remaining phases of the design agreement should be discussed. Copies of this preliminary agreement should be distributed to each board member so as to lessen confusion if questions arise. It is usual procedure for members of any committee to meet and discuss the project, budget requirements, and agreements at a later date. If the presentation has been a success and only a small number of revisions are necessary, the signing of a final contract usually follows in a short period of time.

A *presentation of high quality will sell good design*. Poor presentation of a good design may or may not sell. It is up to the designer, design team, and associates to assemble the best possible presentation in any situation in order to ensure success of a project.

This book, if followed diligently, has given the reader an opportunity to learn those skills necessary to produce almost any design-aid selling tool he might need, and to properly present these tools. The reader may say, "I do not need to know how to draw or create a full-color rendering or make a presentation. All I must know how to do is to find those skilled persons that already know how to do this." This is true only to a point. The more graphically skilled and conscious of good presentation techniques is the designer, the greater are his opportunities to communicate with his clients, thus ensuring success.

INDEX